# MIRACLE DRUGS

## Frank Minirth, M.D.
## P
## S

Published in Nashville, Tennessee, by Thomas Nelson, Inc., Publishers, and distributed in Canada by Word Communications, Ltd., Richmond, British Columbia.

The Bible version used in this publication is THE NEW KING JAMES VERSION. Copyright © 1979, 1980, 1982 Thomas Nelson, Inc., Publishers.

Library of Congress Cataloging-in-Publication Data

Minirth, Frank B.
    Miracle drugs : how they work and what you should know about them / Frank Minirth, Paul Meier, Stephen Arterburn.
        p.    cm.
    Includes bibliographical references and index.
    ISBN 0-7852-7865-6
    1. Mental illness—Chemotherapy—Popular works.   2. Psychotropic drugs—Popular works.   I. Meier, Paul D.   II. Arterburn, Stephen, 1953–   .   III. Title.
RC483.M565  1995
616.89′18—dc20                                            95–35177
                                                              CIP
Printed in the United States of America.

1 2 3 4 5 6 — 00 99 98 97 96 95

# CONTENTS

# Authors' Note

This book is not intended to be used as specific medical instructions for individuals. The information is nonspecific—that is, for very general reading to gain information and, we trust, enjoyment. Specific drug reactions and side effects vary widely from individual to individual and at times vary within a single individual as that person's age, health, and metabolism change.

For any specific medical information, we refer you to your doctor—not this book.

May we recommend also the *Physician's Desk Reference*, an excellent and comprehensive work with specific data. The *PDR* is compiled from manufacturers' information and disclosure sheets, and is updated regularly.

This book contains our personal impressions. With it we hope to allay unsubstantiated fears which persons may have and provide some guidance regarding precautions they ought to consider. We repeat: It is in no way intended as a medical guide for any specific individual.

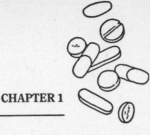

## CHAPTER 1

*In no other area of life have
I ever seen where a friend
and a foe coexist together as
I have seen in psychiatric
medicine.*

DR. FRANK MINIRTH

# FRIENDS AND FOES

EXPERIENCE THE GRAND CANYON! THE GREATEST NATURAL WONDER IN THE WORLD! That's how the travel brochures described it. But as Elisa Stuart looked out over the canyon all she saw was a big empty hole in the rock.

She stood on the canyon rim at Moran Point, her ribs pressed against the solid iron pipe rail, and tried to enjoy the scene. She really did try. But not much happened. Okay, the colors were nice and the patterns were interesting. The weather was clear. But to Elisa the Grand Canyon looked like a million postcards she had seen.

Maybe appreciation took too much effort. Elisa didn't do anything these days that required much effort. One of the reasons her family was touring the Grand Canyon now was to lift Elisa's spirits. The trip was her husband Ben's idea.

A warm breeze began to rise from the inner canyon. She

never felt a wind come from below her before, but the novelty didn't hold her interest for long. Nothing did anymore; not fun activities, not travel, not even marital relations. The world was one big blah.

Elisa left Ben and the kids to unfold their map in the wind and point out features to each other. John, age ten, and Tammy, age eight, sapped her strength instantly with their needs and demands, their constant yelling—"Look, Mom!"—and their nonstop movement. Why couldn't they be more sedate?

She climbed back up the chiseled stone steps that led to the parking lot. The brief uphill climb didn't leave her out of breath, but it wearied her nonetheless. Everything wearied her. She could sleep twelve hours straight, if the kids would let her, and still she'd feel weary.

She sat down to rest on a wooden park bench. A brass plaque on the back of the bench read, *In memory of Katherine, who fell to her death 18 February 1974.* Elisa leaned back against the plaque.

*Fell to her death. Was Katherine a laughing teenager who slipped and tumbled while climbing?* Elisa wondered. *Or was she an older woman who stepped back off the cliffs while trying to take a photograph? Or was she a sad and lonely woman, like me, who jumped to her death?*

Like a gorilla charging out of the bushes, the unbidden thought leaped into Elisa's mind and terrified her. *Did Katherine jump?* A tumble from the high cliffs would be easy. So many problems and so much dreariness would end, just like that. Climb to the other side of the pipe barricade, raise your arms, take a deep breath, and push off with one foot. That's all it would take.

Elisa smiled grimly. As much weight as she had put on this year, she'd drop like a plumb bob.

She tensed, electrified and frightened by the thoughts in her head. Then she relaxed. She, Elisa, would never commit suicide like that, leaping into the Greatest Natural Wonder in the World.

It would take too much effort.

# The Limitations of the Mind

If you are in the same state of mind as Elisa Stuart, you probably have heard all sorts of advice:

"Cheer up. Think positive thoughts. You're feeling blue because you let yourself feel blue."

"You need to speak to your pastor. He'll give you a few Bible verses that will set you straight in no time."

"You don't have faith; that's your problem. If you depended on Jesus, you wouldn't feel like this. You'd be joy-filled."

"It's your fault you feel this way."

Once in a while, counsel like that works. But very often even the finest counsel does nothing to alter a person's mood, and that person may feel guilty because he or she cannot make the advice work. That guilt almost always comes when counsel alone fails to produce a happy outcome. And that is sad, because when counsel doesn't "take," it is very often because it cannot.

Consider this analogy. There's a bush in your front yard that annoys you and other people. Its branches are scraggly and unattractive, and it can be dangerous should some child eat its poisonous berries. Suppose someone tells you to rip that bush out of the ground with your bare hands. "It's rooted too deeply," you say. "I'm not strong enough to do it bare-handed. I need a shovel to dig it out."

Exactly! Elisa was not strong enough to rip out the deep roots of her depression bare-handed. She could listen to all the counsel in the world, but it would do little good. It might loosen the bush somewhat, but there would be no real success. The miracle drugs are the shovel with which to dig out the bush of depression.

You see, the brain essentially functions chemically. The act of thinking involves an elaborate, amazingly swift series of chemical alterations and fabrications, as tiny electrical impulses dart from here to there, carried on nerve threads momentarily united by a molecule or two of temporary matter.

The same applies to emotions. When you laugh, a chemical called dopamine connects neurons in one area of the brain. When you are under stress, another chemical appears in quantity, manufactured by nerve tips. Normal behavior and feelings depend on the right chemicals being in the right places in the right quantities.

Emotional jolts and changes, sudden shocks, old age, and medical problems can alter the brain chemistry. Sometimes the alteration is temporary. At those times, counsel can rearrange thoughts and provide healing help. But at other times, the chemistry, once off balance, remains off balance. In fact, left untreated the balance can get farther and farther out of kilter. The ugly, poisonous bush is now rooted so deeply that the person has nowhere near the strength to rip it out. That bush is there to stay . . . unless the person uses a shovel.

Psychotropic drugs—mood-altering, mind-changing chemicals—can tip the chemical balance in the brain back toward what is necessary for normal behavior and feelings. Look on it as fighting fire with fire: treating chemical imbalance with chemicals. Once the person has the normal chemistry with which to think and feel—the ordinary chemistry he or she used to have—that person can work on problems through counsel and see success.

There are some situations when no shovel will dig out the problems, such as a case of psychosis that has been left untreated for years and now is rooted very deeply. It's sort of like kudzu—once you've got it, it's yours forever. In cases like this, a maintenance drug regimen is needed to keep the balance and allow the person to continue functioning normally.

Elisa's depression was such that she could not turn it around by thinking cheery thoughts, exercising faith, or refusing to be depressed, however hard she might try. Her brain chemistry had been altered to the extent that it could not right itself without help.

Help. That's the role of psychotropic drugs.

# A New Road to Treatment

The field of psychiatric medicine is relatively new. The drugs we use currently arrived with a bang in the 1950s. The story goes like this.

Throughout most of history, when someone descended into psychosis, a loss of touch with reality, there was no way to pull that person back up. Spontaneous cures were rare. Patients were usually hospitalized for the rest of their lives, locked up for their protection and the protection of others. This was tragic because three people in one hundred become psychotic, and about half of the people in the mental hospitals were psychotics. Doctors were startled when they observed that a drug called Thorazine, which was being tested as a possible anesthetic, brought psychotics back to their right minds.

Talk about miracles! Suddenly, people by the thousands were pouring out of our mental institutions and going home for good to lead stable and productive lives.

But although Thorazine helped multitudes of people in mental hospitals, in some cases it caused horrible side effects. We were about to learn that psychotropic drugs can be friends to some people, but vicious foes to others.

That foe aspect is frightening. It may frighten you if you or someone you care about is receiving counsel and the counselor wants to prescribe a drug. You may have heard from others, including sects and organizations devoted to antidrug campaigns, that all drugs are dangerous, that people of faith should never use them, that strong people should never need them, or that mind-altering drugs will turn people into robots.

Although these people may mean well, they are not relying on facts or admitting that not everyone can solve emotional problems with counseling alone.

We the authors, Frank Minirth, Paul Meier, and Stephen Arterburn, have walked both sides of the street, counseling without drugs and recommending medications. Frank has a special interest in psychotropic drugs. Want to know the latest about a drug? Ask Frank. Frank and Paul have many years' experience in both hospital and outpatient psychiatric counsel. Steve is a nationally known advisor and counselor. Among us, we deal with the full spectrum of problems—those that respond to caring counsel and those that respond only to a slam hit with powerful drugs.

Who, or what, deserves a slam hit?

## Questions to Ask

*Frank tells this story:*

A friend convinced a fellow named James Henry to come see me about his nightmares. He awoke every night screaming hysterically, drenched in a cold sweat. He was too frightened to go to sleep anymore, so he forced himself to stay awake for days until he collapsed.

When James Henry entered my office he was dressed immaculately in a black suit, a white cotton shirt, and a black tie. He was young, tall, and overweight. His collar bound his throat so tightly that the fleshy thickness of his neck bulged over the brim of it. He had a scab on his chin, which, I subsequently learned, he got when he tried to stop a barroom brawl a week before.

As he shook my hand in greeting, he flashed me a wide, toothy smile. He seemed too warm and open, like a salesman giving me a winning pitch on an old junk car without an engine. I offered him a seat on the sofa. He dropped his large body down into the deep cushions and gave them a little bounce.

"I'm happy to meet you at last, James. Where are you from? Texas?" I asked as I sat in the chair across from him.

"I'm president of Richland Seminary, and I'm here to save your soul from the devil!" He shook his finger at me.

This gave me good reason to be glad I was sitting down. He held out his hands and turned his palms toward the ceiling. "These hands possess divine powers to heal and save!"

he rejoiced. His chest heaved as though he couldn't quite catch his breath. He leaned his head back on the cushions, closed his eyes, and murmured over and over, "Save o'save. Save o'save."

"I'm really glad you're here and that you want to save my soul, James. I appreciate your sincerity and concern for me. But I want to help you, too. If I'm not mistaken, I understand you're having trouble sleeping—"

He interrupted with, "Yeah! Satan haunts my life constantly!" His eyes shot open and he stared at me walleyed. "He wants to steal my body and make me do these bad things I've never done before." James's face twisted into a pained grimace. "He makes me do awful things in my sleep! He's trying to drag me down into hell with him!" He batted his eyelids and a tear rolled down his cheek. "Oh, God! I can't stand to think about the nightmares anymore, they're so awful!"

I leaned forward and rested my elbows on my knees. "Now listen to me, James. You don't have to be scared of those nightmares anymore. I can make them go away, but you'll have to stay in my hospital for a little while." I begged compassionately, "Please, James, will you let me do this for you?"

"Really?" He sniffed. "You can make them go away and leave me alone?"

"I know you're tired right now. Exhausted. But I believe I can make the nightmares go away."

He wiped his tear-soaked cheeks with the palm of his hand. He nodded and whispered, pain reflecting in his eyes, "Okay."

Now I had had the pleasure of meeting James Henry earlier that summer during a charity benefit and lecture he gave at his church. It was true he was the president of Richland Seminary. But the James Henry I remembered was in his fifties, and was short and slim. This young man was not James Henry. I soon learned he was one of James Henry's students.

For psychotic persons like pseudo-James Henry, reality is

extremely painful and must be avoided. I immediately started him on an antipsychotic drug, which brought him back to reality and his true identity. As his therapy and counseling began, he showed promising progress toward accepting his true self. He slept now free of nightmares, though he believed a divine angel was being sent to heal him.

We have an open-door policy in our hospital. If the patients aren't violent, they may receive visitors. During one such visit, pseudo–James Henry's family pastor convinced him that the medication he was receiving was an anathema—something to be shunned at all costs. Pseudo–James's religion forbade medication and his pastor became his guardian angel, keeping him from wrongdoing. He immediately checked out of the hospital and left with his pastor.

A few years ago, when I went to our hospital to check in a new patient, an odd-looking character was waiting to see me. He was dressed like a military officer, and he introduced himself as Ollie North. He explained how he could command all our patients to invade Washington and run the alcoholic politicians out of town. He tried to make me an offer I couldn't refuse and asked for my assistance with his plans. If I would help him control the patients, he would make me the next president of the United States.

I recognized this man. He was the same "James Henry" I lost track of a decade before. Over the years, he had lost his faith and abandoned his religion.

I admitted him to the hospital and isolated him from the rest of the patients, lest he march them to Washington. This time he stayed for the duration of his comprehensive treatment. Today he is living in his own identity with a beautiful wife and two children. He returned to college and now leads a successful business in marketing.

Were the powerful medicines we gave this patient necessary? Did they help or hinder him? Were they friend to "James Henry," or foe?

Pseudo–James Henry will tell you they are a miracle.

Miracle drugs can be a foe if they are misprescribed. For

instance, a drug that would help Elisa's depression could send James Henry into a howling rage.

Imagine you are buying a saw at the hardware store. You don't ask the clerk for just any saw. There are too many kinds on the market. What do you want to use the saw for? Pruning your apple trees? Or sawing limbs for a campfire? Using the wrong saw can make the easiest job impossible.

Similarly, we have many kinds of drugs to meet precise needs. "Yes," you may say. "But I've read that drugs like Prozac transform a person's character. Do medications merely correct medical problems? Or do they go too far and reshape a person's God-given personality?"

Persons considering a drug regimen to ease psychological and emotional problems and disorders should ask these types of questions. By understanding what the drugs do, they can best work the friendly aspects of the drugs to their advantage and avoid the foe aspects.

A major objective of this book is to give you a balanced perspective on the psychotropic drugs so that you can find clear answers and make informed decisions. We cannot emphasize too much that it is important for the patient to take as much personal responsibility as possible through the course of treatment and cure.

Some general questions come up over and over in our practices. Before discussing disorders and the drugs used for them, let's touch on these questions.

## Are Drugs Really Necessary?

Sometimes, yes. Sometimes, no. One must consider the time and cost factor. We can cite numerous instances, literally thousands of people, who are so depressed, panic-ridden, and anxious that they cannot function. If we use counseling alone, in nine months or so we can usually bring some people up to a comfortable level where they can go about their daily business. If we combine counseling with medication, they can be back to work in three weeks. Why waste time? Why not use both?

## Are Psychotropic Drugs Addictive?

Some drugs used for pain, seizures, and acute anxiety, such as Valium, can be dependency producing. We minimize the chance of dependency by monitoring a patient's use of the drugs. We adjust dosage to achieve desired results with the least amount of drug in the patient's system.

Some drugs (for example, many antipsychotics), require long-term or lifetime use in order to maintain normalcy. We're not talking about addictive dependency here. Most others, such as some antidepressants, return brain functions to normal only while the drugs are being used. The brain may return to its prior state if medication is ended. While using the drug, some patients will need to undergo counseling to uncover the root causes of the depression or other emotional disorder. Sound therapy is the key here.

## Why Do Physicians Change Dosage Levels?

Medicine may be adjusted often early in treatment to attune it to a patient's unique biochemical needs. Later on, it might be adjusted again to a simpler regimen that can be maintained effectively.

Illnesses also alter a patient's responses. A person with a preexisting disease, and particularly a person taking medication for that disease, will use and metabolize drugs differently from a person in normal health. Close monitoring is essential in these cases.

Also, people's physiology changes as they age. The elderly require dosage adjustments frequently, often from year to year. As children grow, any medication they receive should be monitored closely. They're changing rapidly. Which brings up:

## Are These Drugs Dangerous to Children and the Elderly?

If your child has an ear infection, you administer an antibiotic designed to fight the infection. If the child has a vision problem, you buy glasses. If the child is depressed or unable to listen and learn, one way or another you take care of it. One way might include administering drugs.

And older adults? Same thing, only more so. *Parade* magazine reported that 15 percent of people age 65 and older suffer severe chronic depression.[1] To deny them relief would be cruel.

An acquaintance tells this story. "We had to put my father in a nursing home. He complained of pain each day when I visited him, so I talked to the doctor. The doctor said it was just Dad's way of playing on our sympathies so we'd take him out of the home. Unlike many older people, though, Dad realized the advantages of being there and didn't resist it, and I told the doctor so. 'What about some heavy-hitting stuff for the pain? Narcotics.' The doctor refused for fear my dad would become addicted.

"I blew up! 'He's seventy-nine years old, wheelchair-bound, and hurting! Since when is addiction an issue?!' Then I found a doctor who could make him comfortable."

A caveat here. Every medical person can tell horror stories about patients who insisted the doctors were wrong and went from physician to physician until they got the (false!) answers they demanded. There is a balance to strike, and it's not an easy one, between accepting a doctor's opinion and questioning it. Common sense is your best guide.

We the counselors and doctors can explain, educate, and advise. The final decisions always rest with the patient or legal guardian.

In our daily practice we see hundreds of people for whom the psychotropic drugs have been both friend and foe. In the chapters that follow we will share what we've learned with you. We'll also shed more light on the history of some of these drugs.

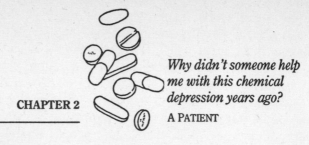

CHAPTER 2

*Why didn't someone help me with this chemical depression years ago?*

A PATIENT

# THE ANTIDEPRESSANTS

## Identifying Depression

In early 1987, Jack Caldwell became a pastor like his forefathers. He made a good one, too. He had grown up in Louisiana in a happy, nurturing home. Jack had a sense of humor. He could deliver a joke and pull a prank with the best of them. He brought to his ministry an upbeat attitude and a powerful desire to help others.

For a while, his life ran smoothly. He married a delightful woman, they had wonderful children, he loved his work, and his church membership grew.

Jack seemed to live the perfect life . . . on the surface.

Hidden in the dark corners of his heart, worries were eating him alive. What would he do if death robbed him of a loved one? What would he do if he lost his home, his job, his ministry? What would his flock think if they found out that deep down inside, Jack harbored doubts and questioned his faith?

Like monsters, his fear and worry drained him of his zest for life, enthusiasm for ministry, and interest in things of the world and things of God. He didn't dare confide in any of the people around him, not even his wife.

Another monster invaded Jack—guilt. He believed things had come too easily for him. He had suffered no privation, no self-sacrifice. Instead of rejoicing in his blessings, he felt guilty that they had been heaped upon him so richly when others worthier than he had to struggle.

In time, he lost his first parish assignment. He was forced out of a second. His monsters had become his reality. Eventually he found another ministry position but no renewed happiness.

I, Frank Minirth, knew Jack casually. He made an appointment to begin counseling with me, but he never got around to coming in to the clinic. He didn't give excuses when he missed his appointments. My secretary finally reached him by phone and convinced him to commence therapy.

When Jack entered my office, I almost didn't recognize him. In the past, he always dressed neatly. When he came to see me that day he was wearing tattered shorts, a stained T-shirt, and sneakers that looked like they had been through a hay baler. He used to wear his jet-black hair combed back off his face. Now it hung in tangled strands around his high forehead. Day-old stubble shadowed his face.

I smiled and offered a hand. "Glad to see you, Jack!" I was distressed to see him looking so despondent.

He declined the handshake and flopped down on the couch. "The only reason I'm here is to get away from Lisa awhile."

I sat down in the chair beside him. "Why do you have to get away from Lisa?"

"You don't understand." His grim countenance made a public executioner look like Pollyanna. "Nobody does. Especially not Lisa." He stared at the ceiling. "This morning she was prying into that phone call from your secretary. So I took a big chance and spilled my guts. The monsters. The doubts. Everything. Guess what she did?"

He didn't give me time to guess. He continued, "She fell to pieces. Crying, screaming like a banshee, like it was the end of the world. I couldn't stand to listen to her crying anymore, so I've been driving around with no place to go. That's why I'm here early. Hope you don't mind."

"No, not at all. I'm just glad you came."

"Maybe she's right," Jack said. "Maybe it is the end of the world."

Silence is often a pervasive goad to get a person talking. I kept silent.

Within moments he began again. "I'm about to lose this latest assignment, Frank. They said, quote: 'You're always late, sometimes you never show up at all, your sermons are lame and meaningless.' Unquote. They're giving me thirty days' probation, so to speak. If I don't shape up, I'm out." He began to fidget in his seat. "You want to know what's really bad this time?"

Again, he didn't give me time to respond. "I tried so hard with this one! I really tried! My whole life, I've been trying to live right. Lisa's been the best wife a man could hope to have. And the kids . . ." He took a deep, shuddering breath. "This morning Joey got to me, and I walloped him. Just hauled off and walloped him. Joey didn't mean to upset me. He's only five years old, for pity's sake! Why do I have to be this way? It hurts so bad I can't stand it. And I tried so hard! So hard." He began to sob, and I let him.

With a sigh that rattled the linings of his shoes, he pulled himself back together. I grabbed a box of tissues off the end table and held it out to him.

A sudden sly grin, a faint spark of the old, irascible Jack, flitted across his face as he waved the tissues off. "I don't need those dainty little paper hankies." He grabbed a fistful of his stained T-shirt. I managed to stuff a tissue into his hand just in time. He accepted the dainty paper hankie and blew his nose. "What's the matter, Doc? Think you're seeing a candidate for the funny farm?"

I realized I was smiling—not at Jack's display, but at the happy insight that the old Jack had not been destroyed completely. "No funny farms in Texas anymore. Hospitals, for those who need them. You don't need them."

"So I'm not sick? I'm just making all this up?" His voice dripped with sarcasm.

"Oh, no. You're not making this up. Millions of people suffer the same kind of pain you're feeling right now. You're not alone. Depending on which study you read, a significant percent of Americans experience a major depression at some time. I'll wager, though, that you feel as if you're the only one with doubts and problems this severe."

"Doubts and problems. You hit it right on."

"I want to ask you something very personal. It's important that you be completely honest with me. Will you?"

Jack watched me suspiciously for a moment, then said, "Okay."

"When the pain gets bad, do you ever entertain thoughts of suicide?"

He thought about my question for a while, then furrowed his brow and responded, "I don't . . . I don't think so. To me, suicide is making a life-or-death decision that's God's alone. It's playing God. Suicide is an unforgivable sin. No, I'd rather die than burn in hell for that." He froze. "Wait! I didn't mean I want to die . . . I meant—"

I was smiling again. "I think I understand. Hear what I mean, not what I say, right?" I leaned forward and looked him in the eyes. "Your present state may be caused by a chemical imbalance, an organic problem. You see, several things can alter brain chemistry." I took a calculated shot in the dark. "Stress. Undue concern. Worry. If worries go unresolved, they become reality and mess up the chemistry even more. Unfortunately the chemicals that are depleted are ones that control emotion."

I explained to him what we know about the chemistry of

emotion and thought patterns, and outlined several drugs that can supplement therapy to effect a cure fairly quickly.

"These drugs, they're not addictive, are they?" Jack asked.

"Not addictive. They're not a cure, either. They get your chemistry straightened out so you can work on the root problems that got you into this state. You can't do that well the way you are now. Once we resolve your worries—"

"And answer the questions that plague me," Jack interjected.

"No promises that we can *answer* the questions, Jack. We can certainly reassure you that everyone has them, though, including me. You don't have to solve all your problems in order to break out of this cycle of increasing depression. All we have to do is make a good start at resolving them, so you can see that they're solvable."

Jack asked a lot of questions and agreed to try the treatment. But he didn't have any confidence that he would find relief. That was natural; he didn't have any confidence in himself at all at that point.

After careful evaluation, I started Jack on Prozac. (We will discuss the basis for this decision later.)

Two weeks later, the old Jack Caldwell breezed into my office. The snappy step was back, and he was groomed and dressed neatly. Best of all, the twinkle in his eyes had returned.

His congregation claimed he was a transformed man. He went from being pitiful, ineffectual, and hesitant to being vibrant and decisive, and they loved his sermons. But they had not known Jack years earlier. He wasn't transformed into a new person at all. He had reverted to his former self, the person he was before the debilitation of depression drained him.

Now depression has a number of causes—medical, psychological, and spiritual. In some people, whatever caused the depression to take root and stay can be resolved. In others, it cannot. Too, a lot depends upon how severe the depression is and how long it has been working on the patient. Common sense dictates a comprehensive approach to find what can be changed and what cannot. Also, people have been treating depression for some years now; we can examine the long-range effects of various methods of therapy, learning what works and what doesn't. Many factors, you see, go into the choice of treatment.

By nature Jack is argumentative, and it took almost half a year of intensive therapy to resolve the root causes of depression working in his particular case. A more pliant person might have reached the same level of understanding in three months. But that, you see, was Jack. It was good to have him back!

## The Symptoms of Depression

It is curious that even in the depths of his frustration and despair, Jack didn't feel blue in the sense we popularly associate with depression. Not everyone who is depressed feels sad, although sadness is often a hallmark of the problem. There are many symptoms of depression.

A small, compact wire- or plastic-bound reference book, the *Diagnostic and Statistical Review Manual—Fourth Edition (DSM—IV)*, gives a careful accounting of exactly what signs and symptoms medical personnel look for when evaluating depression and other problems. It uses technical language, but it is understandable language. We suggest that if you are curious or concerned about possible signs and symptoms of depression in yourself or someone close to you, ask to see *DSM-IV* at your local library or medical clinic.

Popularized and summarized, the symptoms are these:

### Feelings of Sadness or Emptiness

Is the local rhythm and blues radio station *always* playing your song? Prolonged, unshakable feelings of sadness and emptiness can be a sign of depression.

### Decreased Motivation

Often, depressed persons are not motivated to accomplish tasks or make decisions. Doing is no longer a priority. Even simple decisions, like choosing a restaurant, take too much effort. This lack of motivation mars relationships and comes across as a lack of caring, which it is.

## Low Self-Esteem

A person with low self-esteem, a poor self-image, sees everyone else as being smarter, prettier, luckier, stronger, or more desirable. You feel like you're at the bottom of the pecking order. When depression strikes, self-esteem plummets.

## Physical Symptoms

Chronic sleep disturbance—waking up in the night, having trouble falling asleep, sleeping excessively—is a symptom of depression.

Other physical symptoms include overeating or lack of appetite (and the accompanying weight gain or loss), low energy, diminished sex drive, and chronic headaches.

## Pessimistic Attitude

A person with a pessimistic attitude could find a sack of gold and complain because it's tarnished. The pessimist sees the worst in people, situations, and circumstances and fails to notice the good.

## Feelings of Helplessness or Hopelessness

Three-fourths of people suffering a medical depression have the firm conviction that they're stuck in their situation forever and they'll never feel good again. People who are overwhelmed by feelings of helplessness and hopelessness may have thoughts of suicide.

## Thoughts of Suicide

Suicidal tendencies appear more frequently in some types of people than in others. Writers, artists, and musicians, for example, have a far higher suicide rate than do other people in the general population. So do retired police officers. But that doesn't make those tendencies common.

Thoughts of ending it all, of wishing you were dead or commenting to that effect out loud, are a big red flag.

## Anhedonia

Anhedonia is a failure to take pleasure in pleasant things. Once enjoyable activities—going on picnics, watching corny movies, playing Uno—no longer hold any interest. Sex is no longer enjoyable, and favorite foods no longer taste good. This failure to take pleasure in once-pleasurable activities may signal depression.

## Diminished Social Life

People who are depressed often do not enjoy the company of other people. They decline invitations and may eventually stop receiving them. Relationships go on the skids, and their love life becomes a shambles.

## Chronic Fatigue

Chronic fatigue is another symptom of depression. Some people can't get to sleep or their sleep is interrupted many times during the night. Others can sleep for twelve hours and still feel tired when they awake.

## Persistent Feelings of Guilt

Guilt is a natural human emotion that lets us know when we have violated our values. But when guilt persists and can't be resolved it's a red flag. Depressed persons often don't want to resolve their guilt because they are convinced they deserve to feel guilty. They ruminate constantly on the past and can't move into the future.

## Decreased Concentration and Productivity

Concentration and productivity are two different things, but they are closely linked. When concentration sags, things don't get done. The lawn doesn't get mowed. The house doesn't get cleaned. The person falls behind on projects at work. Everyone's concentration lags from time to time. But a persistent inability to concentrate and produce may signal depression.

## Irritability

Everyone has an off day now and then. But when a person is irritable and dissatisfied day in and day out, this can be a sign of depression.

These symptoms are the most common ones exhibited by adults experiencing depression. But bear in mind that children, too, can become depressed, and their symptoms may differ from those of adults.

# Depression in Children

We often overlook depression in children because we look for the usual signs and symptoms. In children, depression may reveal itself through hostile and irritable behavior and through acting out. Children "act out" by being argumentative, resisting authority and discipline, and perhaps engaging in sexual promiscuity. They often find themselves studying the school principal's wallpaper a lot more than they ought and experience other problems with school, such as truancy. Substance abuse in kids is a sign of depression.

Just as there are various symptoms of depression in both adults and children, there are various types of depression.

# Major Depression

The *DSM-IV* reference lists the above and some other symptoms for juvenile and adult depression. We generally define "major depression" as the presence of five or more of the symptoms listed, including the observation that the person's ability to function normally is impaired for several weeks or longer.

Before counselors can make a diagnosis of major depression, however, they must rule out that the symptoms are not caused by the effects of alcohol, prescription or nonprescription drugs, disease, or a catastrophic event in the patient's life, such as the death of a spouse. In the latter case, the individual would experience grief. However, if the grief persisted for two years, that would signal depression. Any strong grief that impairs a person for more than six months or produces severe symptoms, such as suicidal thoughts, is a major problem.

## Dysthymic Disorder

This is what laypeople call a low-grade depression. It comes and goes over a span of at least two years (one year in children and adolescents), but it comes more often than it goes. Some of the signs and symptoms are:

Weight and appetite go haywire. You eat too much or not enough, gain or lose weight, all without an obvious reason.

Sleep problems occur—too much, not enough, broken sleep, inability to fall asleep.

Energy is depleted. Everything takes too much effort.

Self-esteem bottoms out.

Ability to concentrate or make decisions is chronically impaired.

Feelings of hopelessness recur. (To qualify clinically, these feelings don't stay away for more than two months.)

Again, we're assuming that the signs and symptoms are not caused by alcohol, drugs, disease, or sunlight levels (some people get depressed in the far North during the winter when the days are short). For example, if you have an illness like mononucleosis, it's logical you'll feel some of the signs and symptoms of depression.

## Other Depressive Disorders

A lot of women experience premenstrual dysphoric disorder (*dysphoria* is the opposite of *euphoria*). Depression is often a part of premenstrual syndrome (PMS). Women may suffer from irritability, mood swings, anxiety, and other problems. Although premenstrual dysphoric disorder may not happen before every menses, when it does happen it can interfere with work and home life.

Some people experience depressions that are quite temporary. They rank as a depression if they last at least two weeks, but they display fewer than five of the symptoms of major depression.

## Bipolar Disorders

We bring up bipolar disorders here for an important reason. If we prescribe the wrong antidepressant (Prozac, for example) when bipolarity is present, the patient possibly can go off the deep end with a frightening manic bout. Injury or hospitalization or both can result. Instantly, the medicine would become a terrible foe.

In lay terms, *bipolar* means manic-depressive. The person feels depressed at times and euphoric at other times. The effects can be pronounced, with deep, deep lows and wild, wild highs. Other times the effects are subtle. And often the depressive condition prevails with only occasional mild manic episodes, which the person may not even recognize.

Doctors must be extremely careful about identifying possible bipolarity. Children under age eighteen who suffer depression often become bipolar later in life. It's one of the indicators we use.

When we have ruled out bipolar disorder and have made a clear diagnosis of depression, we can begin the many-pronged effort to correct the problem.

## Treating Depression

What exactly went on inside Jack Caldwell's head, and how was his cure effected? We think we know, but as we discuss the chemistry of the brain here, keep in mind that we aren't sure. Some researcher may well come along one day and tell us we're either correct or completely off base. Science does that a lot.

It would be nice to make a tidy map of how brain chemistry functions, then create appropriate drugs to correct malfunctions. In fact, we have been able to do that once in a while. Most of the time, however, we stumble upon a drug that does something positive, then work backward to try to figure out what it did and how it did it. This knowledge then can lead us to design other drugs to do the same thing, but perhaps in different ways.

If you understand how drugs work, you can make better informed decisions about prospective treatment. Understanding what a drug does inside you takes away some of the mystique and makes you a more practical, balanced observer of your own treatment, expecting neither failure nor miracles.

## The Biochemical Picture

When we speak of emotions as feelings or affairs of the heart, we are speaking figuratively. We commonly associate the head with intellect and the heart with emotion, but actually emotional feelings are centered in the head. What the brain does strongly affects emotions, and when the least little thing malfunctions in brain chemistry, emotions can be profoundly altered. In short, it doesn't take much at all to plunge a person like Jack Caldwell into a temporary funk or a near-permanent clinical depression.

The brain is a hard-wire unit of unimaginable complexity. Look inside a telephone and you'll see many colored wires. Pretty simple. Look at the panels in a telephone company substation and you'll see several square yards of connections and myriad hookups. Not quite as simple. The brain is thousands of times more complex than that, with billions more hookups.

The hard wires of the brain are neurons, nerve cells with lots of extending strands, like a spider or an octopus. The tips of the different neurons' strands may lie very close to each other, but they do not touch. The spaces between them are called synapses.

Now consider this: your brain is made up of 100 *billion* cells, and each cell possesses maybe ten thousand synapses. The number of connections in your brain exceeds the number of stars in the heavens. As such, the brain holds unbelievable power as friend or foe.

How do the cells connect? Recall from high school general science how a simple switch works. Usually it's nothing more than a metal bar in a hinge. When you close the hinge two wire tips connect to generate an electric current, and when you open it you break the connection. In your brain, the switches that connect all those tips, the neurotransmitters, are not metal but tiny droplets of fluid. There are a number of kinds. Three such molecules of interest to us here are serotonin (SE), norepinephrine (NE), or dopamine (DA).

At rapid speed, the neuron tip either forms or employs a bit of the chemical neurotransmitter, which allows a tiny electrical impulse to pass across the synapse to a nearby neuron. A thought link or emotional impulse has been completed. The tip may then take the neurotransmitter up again to be remanufactured and used later. All this is done by means of enzymes. Enzymes are chemicals that make a reaction happen but do not themselves take part in the reaction. Think of a foreman walking along a road construction site. He passes workmen. They were working slowly before he came; they work earnestly as he passes; they work slowly when he's gone. He was an enzyme, a catalyst to greatly increase output, though he did no work himself.

The various transmitters are fairly well regulated in most people. If the transmitters and the brain's neuron tips are poorly regulated or faulty in some way, the person may experience depression or mania—or both. Think of regulating an old style windup clock. If it runs too fast or too slowly, you have to either move the pendulum bob up and down or push that little lever in back toward the F or S.

The three common neurotransmitters apparently are not interchangeable, though perhaps some jobs can overlap. Each has assigned tasks. Serotonin does certain things, norepinephrine certain others, and dopamine still others. The key to balanced brain function, we believe, lies with the neurotransmitters and synapses. And it is there, we think, that most antidepressants do their thing.

## How the Drugs Work

If we could pry the lid off Jack Caldwell's brain and see what kinds of neurotransmitters were in there and how well they were regulated, we could alter the situation just as we would regulate the windup clock. The lid notwithstanding, that's pretty much what the antidepressant drugs do. Reregulate.

One class, of which Prozac is a member, keeps the nerve tips from being so hasty about taking serotonin up, we believe. Prozac and its kin, then, affect those nerve functions in which serotonin takes part (among other things). We call this class of drugs SSRIs, Selective (meaning they affect only one thing) Serotonin Reuptake Inhibitors.

Another class, we believe, blocks the uptake of both serotonin and norepinephrine. These are called tricyclic because their chemical formula when drawn as a picture shows three rings of carbon. These are the TCAs, the Tricyclic Antidepressants. They have a wider effect because they are not selective. However, because they serve more functions, they also produce more side effects than do SSRIs.

A third class of antidepressants indirectly affects the amount of neurotransmitters by blocking the action of the enzyme used to take them back up into the nerve tips. MAOIs, Monoamine (acids with one amino component) Oxidase (the enzyme that allows rapid oxidation at body temperature) Inhibitors, have been around for a relatively long time and are still the drug of choice in certain situations.

Drugs such as tetracyclics (four rings in the formula), trazodone, and others might save the day when more common substances fail to do the job.

When prescribing a drug for a patient, doctors consider the severity of the drug's possible side effects as much as the drug action itself.

## Side Effects of Antidepressants

Different drugs cause different side effects. The Appendix of this book contains a detailed list of side effects. If you are about to undergo a treatment of antidepressants, thoroughly review the Appendix to familiarize yourself with possible problems.

Two possible side effects we want to mention here are priapism and changes in sexual response. Persons who experience either of these side effects should contact their doctor immediately!

**Priapism.**   Males on trazodone who experience an unintended, uncomfortable erection, should get medical help immediately. You must have medical intervention within four to six hours or the condition can cause permanent, irreversible damage. If the doctor or clinic attendant is uncertain what to do, call this number for Bristol Myers: (800) 321-1335.

Priapism is a rare condition, but when it does occur, the drug being used may be trazodone.

**Changes in sexual responses.**   Some people also report changes in sexual responses—either more or less interest in sex, delayed or altered orgasm, or impotence. Altering drug dosage might solve the problem, but let your doctor decide. Don't adjust the dosage on your own.

Instead of altering dosages, doctors may prescribe another drug if the patient's current medicine interferes with sexual interest and performance. Wellbutrin, for example, may save the day for people who are having trouble on the SSRIs, such as Prozac.

In addition to side effects, patients should be aware of how much of a drug constitutes an overdose.

## Drug Overdose

An overdose of antidepressants can be lethal. A recent article in the *Dallas Morning News* tells of a woman who apparently died of an overdose of amitriptyline taken along with a second drug. The matter involves suspicion and is under investigation.[1]

People who attempt suicide with overdoses of antidepressants are the depressed people with a high tendency toward suicide in the first place. Because of this possibility, doctors frequently prescribe small amounts of the drugs that the patient must have refilled weekly. A week's dosage probably isn't lethal. Because antidepressants are effective most of the time, suicide rates go down in the population using them.

Furthermore, toxicity from an overdose of these drugs may take twelve hours to build. That gives the patient plenty of time to have second thoughts about the probable results of overdosing. If doctors can't stop the toxic climb (for instance, it may be too late to pump the stomach), they can put overdosed patients in a hospital where life support can see them past the crisis.

The big problem with antidepressants, as with any drug, is keeping them out of the hands of young children. Roughly 10 to 15 milligrams per pound of body weight can be lethal in a small child. Anytime a child ingests an antidepressant, obtain medical help at once!

## Putting Antidepressants in Perspective

The majority of persons using antidepressants will experience few or none of the side effects listed in the Appendix. We made that long list to inform you of *possible* problems. By being an informed consumer, you can better determine if something is not right for you.

In a way, it is unfortunate that these drugs are called antidepressants. The term conjures up notions of happiness pills or substances that artificially change a person's basic personality. Those notions are false. Perhaps a more accurate term would be *regulatory* medications. These drugs correct a biochemical flaw in regulation of neurotransmission—they restore good cell function.

We cannot emphasize enough the multifactorial nature of what we call depression—biochemical, psychological, spiritual.

Too, some people are genetically more prone than others to serotonin-regulation problems. Appropriate drugs may well solve the biochemical problem (and usually the genetic tendency thereby). If there are underlying causes which can be dealt with, it is obviously important to deal with them as well.

A comprehensive treatment plan considers all these factors and more. Because many people don't understand this, fewer than half of the people with mood disorders receive any treatment whatever. Often it is because they attach a social stigma to the disorder, something they would never do with diabetes or other physical disorders.

Unfortunately, depression causes stress on brain functions. For instance, depressed people often show hyperactivity in the limbic region of the brain, which gives emotional tone and meaning to experience. Persistent hyperactivity can permanently alter the brain functions. So can other stresses that press unrelentingly on a person. In other words, you want to nip depression as early and as quickly as possible. That means dumping the social stigma.

### Framing a Treatment Plan

Jack Caldwell, like so many Americans, is not a patient man. He wants results *now!* In his case, however, he had an actual deadline and it was a tight one. He had to have results within the thirty days' probation his parish had allowed him or he would lose his ministry. If Jack relied on counseling alone without the aid of an antidepressant, it may have taken him months to achieve the desired results, if counseling worked at all. So very frequently, we find, counsel offers limited or no real relief from depression.

Jack needed something with a reputation for being fast out of the starting blocks. Ideally, this drug would produce minimal side effects; Jack had to go to work without having to deal with drug-induced problems.

He showed no indication of bipolar disorders, psychoses, or other such problems, and his family history recorded no incidence of such disorders. Prozac was the drug that met Jack's particular needs and criteria.

The best dose is the least amount that still does the job, so we started Jack on a low dosage with the intent of increasing it if necessary. By and large, perhaps one-third of patients receiving drug therapy (and they constitute only one-third of patients diagnosed with depression) take too low a dose for too short a time, and therefore they see little or no good effects. *Does the job* is the key phrase here.

Along with the drug regimen, Jack commenced psychotherapy. If monsters lurked in the inner sancta of his mind, they ought to be brought out into the open. In any case, Jack would learn whether they even existed.

The goals of his therapy, then, were:

1. to stop the effects of depression as quickly as possible so he could get on with his life as a father, husband, and pastor
2. to find any root causes for his problem and deal with them
3. to take whatever steps were necessary to prevent major depression in his future

These are the appropriate goals for any depression treatment.

## Other Uses for Antidepressants

If the SSRIs block the reuptake of serotonin, and the TCAs serve a similar purpose, it is probable that they might affect any problem involving serotonin levels.

Because the FDA carefully ascribes only certain uses for certain drugs, if a drug proves to have additional beneficial effects other than what it was prescribed for, these new effects are found serendipitously.

Used alone or with other substances, various antidepressants may be able to:

- alleviate chronic pain
- ease the symptoms of Attention Deficit Disorder (ADD)
- regulate weight (Some substances facilitate a weight gain in certain people, others seem to cause weight loss. Prozac, for example, causes weight loss in 10 to 20 percent of the people who take it; imipramine does the opposite.)
- alleviate panic disorders, such as agoraphobia and anxiety
- help children control bed-wetting (imipramine especially)
- help control sleepwalking
- help reduce night terrors
- ease borderline disorders
- alleviate symptoms of narcoleps
- break the vicious circle of obsessive-compulsive disorder
- occasionally work wonders with the imbalances we attribute to hormones (for example, premenstrual syndrome)
- alleviate migraine headaches

## The History of Antidepressants

In the early 1950s, the French developed a drug that successfully treated some psychoses. Chlorpromazine, marketed in this country from 1954 on as Thorazine, was a true miracle drug. Psychosis, once virtually untreatable, could at last be controlled.

Immediately, pharmacologists began searching for other antipsychotics, hoping to manage psychosis in people for whom Thorazine had limited or no effect. One of the drugs they tried, imipramine, produced a curious effect on people who tested it. It lifted the spirits of people who were extremely sad.

Up until that time, the only mood-altering drugs were ones that could not be recommended medically—alcohol, opium, hemp (marijuana). And none of these drugs did what imipramine did—lift a person's mood without causing more problems than it solved. Imipramine was nonaddictive,

so there were no withdrawal problems. It had no tolerance—
that is, a person didn't need more and more of it as time went
on in order to maintain a certain level of relief. And it seemed
to work in a fairly natural way; it didn't dope people up.

Meanwhile, other researchers were seeking drugs to control and relieve tuberculosis. They were working with
MAOIs (Monoamine Oxidase Inhibitors), oxidase being the
enzyme that affected serotonin and norepinephrine uptake at
the synapses. People with TB took MAOIs and felt happier.
What was going on here? Penicillin won the laurel wreath for
bringing TB to bay, at least for a while, but MAOIs became
famous on their own as antidepressants.

Scientists also began looking at a new form of antidepressant, SSRIs (Selective Serotonin Reuptake Inhibitors). By the
late 80s, they had become all the rage in Europe. This is the
same drug we know today as Prozac. Prozac was not approved
for use in the U.S. until 1987. It became popular seemingly
overnight. People started reading about it, writing about it, re-
futing it, extolling it, arguing about it, and most of all, using it.
Today, Prozac is the number five drug on the world market.

Besides providing doctors and their patients with treatment
options, these varieties of medications have what might be called
subspecialties. A doctor often can tailor the drug regimen to specific needs concurrent with depression, the primary target.

Do they work? Tests with severely depressed patients
showed that just over three-fourths (76 percent) of them
improved with imipramine medication, and 18 percent
showed improvement with placebo. (A placebo is an innocuous substance that looks like the medicine being tested but
has none of the medicine in it.)

Many times, these bonus effects were discovered by pure
chance. Whether a researcher discovers the bonus effects of
a drug by chance or design, imagine his or her pleasure in
finding other ways to help thousands of people with one of
these miracle drugs.

Enhancing the friendship aspect, minimizing the foe aspect—the search goes on and on.

# A List of Antidepressants

Here is a list of common prescription drugs used to treat depression. Some of these drugs cost three to seven times what others cost. But the price of the drug is not the only "cost" to consider. If the drug produces serious side effects, the cost (financial and emotional) of alleviating them must be factored in. If one drug takes longer to work than another, lost productivity should be factored in. If one drug requires more visits to the doctor's office than do others, that should be added in. In short, an expensive drug such as Paxil, which requires minimal attention to side effects and doctor's visits, may well pay for itself and then some when total costs are calculated.

## Tetracyclics and Other Drugs

**Effexor** (venlafaxine HCl) is structurally unrelated to the other drugs on the list. It inhibits the uptake of most neurotransmitters. Effexor may cause side effects in patients with high blood pressure.

**Luvox** (fluvoxamine maleate) is new on the American market and seems to work as well as other drugs in treating depression. It does not produce the unpleasant sexual problems (primarily abnormal ejaculation) that imipramine does. Although it is an SSRI, it is unrelated chemically to other SSRIs. It is effective in treating obsessive-compulsive disorders (OCDs and depression often go hand in hand).

**Serzone** (nefazodone HCl) also is structurally different from the other antidepressants, and it inhibits uptake of several different neurotransmitters. It is especially good for relieving the anxiety that often accompanies depression. It aids sound sleep, although it is not a sleep aid as such, and it often does not produce the sexual dysfunction side effects that some other antidepressants do.

**Desyrel** (trazodone HCl) seems to selectively inhibit serotonin, but it is not specifically an SSRI. Male patients should familiarize themselves with possible problems of priapism before commencing use of this drug.

**Ludiomil** (maprotiline HCl) has some effect on anxiety as well as depression.

**Wellbutrin** (bupropion HCl) is in a chemical world all its own. About four in one thousand patients using Wellbutrin may suffer seizures. It is contraindicated therefore in anyone with a history of seizures.

## The Tricyclics (TCAs)

In general, a patient should not use tricyclics within two weeks of MAOI use. The two together in the system can cause severe problems. A patient switching from MAOIs to anything else should let the MAOIs dissipate before going to the new regimen.

**Adapin** (doxepin HCl)

**Anafranil** (clomipramine) is especially good for treating the chemical component of worry in many people.

**Asendin** (amoxapine) may help depression and certain psychoses simultaneously.

**Aventyl** (nortriptyline) See *Pamelor*.

**Elavil** (amitriptyline HCl)

**Endep** (amitriptyline HCl/Roche)

**Etrafon** (perphenazine and amitriptyline HCl) combines an antidepressant with a tranquilizer.

**Janimine** (imipramine) is much like Tofranil.

**Limbitrol** (chlordiazepoxide and amitriptyline HCl/Roche) combines an antidepressant with an agent to relieve tension and anxiety. It generally works better than either ingredient used alone.

**Norpramin** (desipramine HCl) in many people works faster than the standard, imipramine.

**Pamelor** (nortriptyline HCl) seems to affect the heart in some cases. Monitor cardiac action if using this drug.

**Sinequan** (doxepin HCl) should not be used by people showing signs of glaucoma or having difficulty with urination.

**Surmontil** (trimipramine maleate) contains an anxiety-reducing sedative component.

**Tofranil** (imipramine HCl) also helps children overcome

bed-wetting. Imipramine is the standard by which all other tricyclics are compared, particularly during trials.

**Triavil** (perphenazine-amitriptyline HCl) is a combination drug for treatment of psychosis, anxiety, and depression.

**Vivactil** (protriptyline HCl) can take effect quickly in many people. Usually close medical supervision is required.

## The Selective Serotonin Reuptake Inhibitors (SSRIs)

A patient should not use SSRIs if MAOIs are still in that person's system.

**Paxil** (paroxetine HCl) seems to be more potent than other SSRIs at binding to serotonin reuptake sites.

**Prozac** (fluoxetine HCl) remains in the body for weeks after use is discontinued. This is called long elimination half-life (the period of time in which half of the original titer of the drug is still present in the body). This is a drug we the authors have used extensively. We like it because of its overall low side-effect profile and its effectiveness in treating a broad range of disorders.

**Zoloft** (sertraline HCl)

## The Monoamine Oxidase Inhibitors (MAOIs)

These drugs require close monitoring; they can have potentially dangerous side effects, especially if used in combination with certain other medications and even some foods.

**Nardil** (phenelzine sulphate) can be used for treating people with atypical depressions. Doctors prescribe it to patients who fail to respond to the more common antidepressants.

**Parnate** (tranylcypromine sulfate) is an alternative drug which may be used when other antidepressants have failed.

## CHAPTER 3

*I watch the other kids sitting there and they do their stuff and they're done, and they go outside to play, and I can't even get three problems done. I'm so stupid I can't stand myself.*

A DISCOURAGED ELEVEN-YEAR-OLD

# THE WILD CHILD: ADD AND ADHD

"I'm so stupid I can't stand myself." Corey Boggs, in the fourth grade for the second time, was reciting what his teachers had been telling him for five years.

Since the age of seven he had run a trapline in the woods behind his family's farm in Alabama. The woods sprawled out into swampland bordering a pleasant little river, so Corey took muskrat, skunk, nutria, raccoons, and an occasional otter. He designed and built the traps and deadfalls he used for taking squirrels and rabbits uphill of the wetland. He earned hundreds of dollars every winter off his traps.

In the spring and summer he hired himself out to the surrounding farms to buck hay bales, run the combine, and drive the tractor. He plowed, tedded, and harvested. He helped the farrier shoe the feisty Shetlands some wealthy retired men raced in sulkies. In Corey's eyes, those miserable, spoiled ponies weren't worth beans, but it was good money. It wasn't legal, but he skipped school a lot during spring planting and when the farrier was shoeing around Memorial Day (his teacher didn't report him as truant because when he was absent, the day went so much better).

In the fall he skipped a lot, too. He picked up windfalls for the local cider press—hundreds of pounds of apples. He walked miles of corn-stubble fields, gleaning the fat yellow ears the pickers cut, husked, and then dropped. Corners of fields where the machinery turned were especially rich in fallen corn. He sold the gleanings to the local pig farmer.

He built birdhouses and bird feeders out of old roofing shakes. City people bought them mostly. "Weathered shingles, how quaint," they crowed.

Corey rented his retriever Sky Pilot to the city men who came into the farm country to hunt upland game birds. Corey's pa claimed Sky Pilot was smarter than Corey.

Corey gave his mom all the money he made. Sometimes putting in a fourteen-hour day, Corey Boggs kept his family going during hard times.

And his teachers claimed he was stupid.

## Identifying Attention Deficit Disorder (ADD)

Parents and teachers tremble when they hear the words *Attention Deficit Disorder*. Sunday school teachers despair at the thought of having an ADD kid in their classes. Grocery store managers wince to see one come into the store. Librarians would rather not have them in the library.

These reactions are unfortunate because ADD kids are among the most gifted children in the world. Many successful athletes, businesspeople, doctors, lawyers, and police officers have attention deficit tendencies and capitalize on them.

Some would say that between 5 and 15 percent of children exhibit symptoms of Attention Deficit Disorder. That percentage seems to be increasing, perhaps because of the frenetic lifestyle in our country. These people claim that in 30 to 50 percent of cases, children carry Attention Deficit Disorder right through adulthood. It does not always go away with maturity.

In order to conform to the expectations of parents and teachers, most of these children learn to get by. They mask their symptoms with coping behaviors.

We distinguish two forms of attention deficit tendencies: Attention Deficit Disorder (ADD) and Attention Deficit with Attendant Hyperactivity (ADHD). ADD kids have difficulty remembering something they learned just minutes before. ADHD children have memory problems as well, but they also bounce off the walls. Their inability to remain still, even for short periods, drives people around them nuts. A leading medical journal report on ADHD said, "Attention Deficit Hyperactivity Disorder (ADHD) is one of the major clinical and public health problems in terms of the morbidity and disability of children, adolescents, and adults. Its impact on society is enormous in terms of financial costs, stress to the family, impact on schools, and potentially damaging effects on self-esteem."

Morbidity and disability? Because ADHD children can't always think logically or practically, and because they are excessively active, they are often the kids you'll find in the emergency room being patched up because they weren't thinking, weren't watching, weren't careful. They suffer a disproportionate number of accidents, a few of them fatal.

ADHD kids contribute to stress in the family. As a defense against being called dumb, they perfect the caustic comeback, the acid retort, the irritating behavior. They constantly need supervision and reminders. Because parents get frustrated with the behavior, they often yell at the children. And because the children are told frequently that there's something wrong with them, they develop a poor self-image.

These children do not fair any better at school because few schools are geared to handle ADHD children.

Many problems mimic the symptoms of ADD/ADHD,

making it one of the most misdiagnosed disorders in the world. When a child suffers trauma at home—friction between parents, death or illness of a loved one—the child may well act out in ways that look like ADD/ADHD. Sometimes depression takes the form of inattention and hyperactivity. Anxiety certainly does. The anxious child can mimic every symptom and sign that the ADD/ADHD child displays.

Persons who are not trained in the behavioral sciences cannot easily assess these alternate possibilities. So how can a parent determine if a child exhibiting symptoms is ADD/ADHD or not?

## Signs and Symptoms of ADD/ADHD: Five Questions to Ask

Perhaps someone has applied the term *attention deficit* to your child or another child you love. How do you determine whether that person's opinion is justified?

The following questions can help parents identify the symptoms of ADD/ADHD. Although adults also are subject to ADD/ADHD and exhibit the same symptoms, here we will concentrate on the disorder in children. You need not see all these in a child to make a preliminary judgment. An ADD/ADHD child may display few or even only one. We'll refer to Corey often, because he typifies ADD/ADHD children in many ways.

### 1. Does the Child Have Trouble Paying Attention?

You repeat instructions and they go in one ear and out the other. You say "Don't go out into the street," moments before the child thoughtlessly runs out into the street. Motion, idle noise, a picture on the wall, and seemingly nothing at all distract the child.

Kids with attention problems cannot concentrate on schoolwork. Try as they might, they can't keep their mind on the subject for more than a few moments. Long after their classmates have finished a page of math problems, they're still halfheartedly trying to decide which one to do next.

They understand the first two sentences of a history lesson but miss the rest. Their thoughts wander during play or physical education, and they get bonked with a ball. They get distracted by a leaf floating outside the window and miss the classroom movie on polar bears. In short, they are easily distracted by external things.

## 2. Does the Child Daydream Excessively?

Internal things also distract ADD and ADHD kids. Woolgathering, building castles in Spain, sailing on the high seas— whatever the fantasy the point is clear, the child's mind drifts.

Everyone daydreams. The brain's synapses are constantly connecting in various ways. Most people can block out the random thoughts and concentrate on the thought or task at hand. ADD children and adults cannot. The random, unrelated thought intrudes, lingers, and distracts.

Corey would try to stay with the reading lesson. As his classmate read aloud in halting singsong, Corey would follow the text for a sentence or two. And then he'd remember that he ought to run the traps down by the creek tonight. And he saw a new squirrel nest in the maple by the big rock. He'd like to get a litter of pups out of Sky Pilot; she was too good a dog not to breed. And what about that guy with the moustache who paid top dollar to use her last weekend? And . . .

When it became Corey's turn to read, he didn't know where his place was.

## 3. Is the Child Unusually Impulsive?

These are some of the signs we look for to indicate impulsivity:

**The child acts without thinking.** "The child doesn't think!" Corey's mom told the doctor when Corey broke his collarbone at age five. She said it again when Corey sprained his ankle, and again when Corey was seven and needed six stitches on his forehead.

**The child flits from one activity to another.** The child may be enthusiastically involved in one activity, when suddenly something else seizes her fancy. The child abandons the first activity and delves into the next adventure just as enthusiastically. She can't finish a project because another project always beckons before the first one is completed.

In some cases a child may have problems with both flitting and concentrating too much. The child might become so engrossed in something—a Nintendo game, for instance—that he cannot be pulled away. The child lacks control of his attention and impulses at both ends of the spectrum—can't pay attention, can't break attention.

**The child has trouble organizing homework/schoolwork.** Corey would forget to do his homework. Or he'd do it and forget to take it to school the next morning. He'd forget his lunch. Forget a pencil. Forget where he put his boots and gloves. He couldn't outline and had trouble writing coherent reports.

At home, Corey did not relate well to routine chores at all. His parents were constantly yelling at him for failing to feed the calves, forgetting to bring in stove wood, or forgetting to milk the cow in the morning.

"Corey," wailed his mom, exasperated, "how can you *not* remember that the cow needs milking? She's needed milking every single morning for four years!"

**The child requires constant supervision.** Corey's mom constantly was riding him, coaching him, reminding him. At school, Corey's teacher hovered over him like a vulture. If she did not, she claimed, he would leave assignments unfinished and would forget half of the simplest instructions. Without someone constantly nagging him, Corey could not stay on track. To quote his mom, "If you don't keep on his back, he just goes skipping off somewhere."

**The child is unduly impatient.** Corey was constantly

breaking in line at the sliding board or climbing up the slide against the tide. If Corey knew the answer to a question (and that didn't happen often), he couldn't wait for the teacher to call on him, he blurted it right out.

## 4. Does the Child Have Difficulty Adjusting Socially?

Impulsivity and braggadocio can wreck a child's social acceptance. ADD kids usually have trouble fitting in at school and at play. Too often, adults shun them as well.

Corey honed aloneness to a fine edge. Most of the time he engaged in activities he could do by himself. His decision to play alone was not a conscious one.

## 5. Is the Child Hyperactive?

These points can help you gauge hyperactivity.

**The child can't be still.** Child, thy name is Fidget. The hands and feet move constantly. The child squirms continually. While other children sit quietly in church, the ADD child bangs his heels against the pew, gets on all fours and crawls around on the floor, whispers so loudly that heads turn in his direction.

Corey's family did not attend church, which helped the whole congregation pay better attention to the service.

**The child always is set on *go*!** Corey was on the go from waking (he was an early riser) to bedtime (he was a night owl). He never slowed down. His father claimed he got exhausted just watching the boy.

"When he finally does get to bed and settle in, he just crashes," Corey's mom said. "In spite of all the tossing, he sleeps so deep you can't wake him hardly. If the house ever catches fire in the middle of the night, we're going to have to drag him out by his heels. He sure isn't going to wake up and walk out."

**The child thrashes during sleep.** Every morning Corey's bed looked like a rototiller had gone through it. As the Boggs family grew, the kids started having to double up in beds. Corey, though, slept alone. No one—*no one*—would sleep with Corey. Not even Sky Pilot.

Remember that excessive activity is not a surefire sign of ADD. Hyperactivity can have many other causes and components, such as medical problems or anxiety or any combination of factors.

Based on the signs and symptoms expressed in the questions above, does it appear that the child about whom you are concerned has attention deficit problems? The child may display some, but not all, of the signs we've discussed. Hyperactivity is a case in point.

## When Hyperactivity Is Not a Symptom

Although people commonly associate hyperactivity with attention disorders, many attention deficit people do not exhibit hyperactivity. Children who do not display hyperactivity may instead act "spacey." They lose track of their own thoughts. Other children may call them airheads. Unlike the hyperactive kid who becomes the focus of attention in the classroom, the spacey child is quiet and often goes unnoticed. He or she daydreams the school year away and makes poor grades. Because these children aren't disruptive in class they may not receive the attention they need.

Now that you're familiar with the characteristics of Attention Deficit/Hyperactivity Disorder, let's look at the psychiatric terms and classifications for the variations of attention disorders:

*Combined Type ADHD*—Both attention deficit and hyperactivity are present.

*Predominantly Inattentive Type ADD*—Characterized by daydreaming and spacey behavior.

*Predominantly Hyperactive-Impulsive Type ADHD*—These are the children or adults who are always on the go.

*Attention-Deficit/Hyperactivity Disorder NOS*—NOS means Not Otherwise Specified. People may display many of the characteristics for the disorder, but not enough to be considered full-blown ADD.

So these kids are misfits and we want to make them normal, right? So we pop them a miracle drug and . . .

Whoa! Not so fast. It's not that simple.

First we must make a careful assessment of the child's (or adult's) problems, if any, and how these problems are affecting the child's life, if at all. Then we consider what we can do to ease the deleterious effects without messing up the good effects.

"Good effects?" you ask. "What can be good about ADD/ADHD?"

ADD/ADHD confers some wonderful advantages. Look at Corey. He has characteristics you don't ever want to change.

## The Valuable Effects of ADD/ADHD

Corey, a true-blue hyperactive, got a lot done. He was making a contribution to his family.

Children tend to feel overly responsible for everything in the world, right or wrong (we call that "global guilt"). Corey strongly felt that way. As his overweening sense of responsibility drove him, his hyperactivity became a great blessing to him and to others. A more sedate child could never have accomplished all that Corey did.

And look what it did to his sense of self-worth! People might have labeled him stupid (children accept without question their teachers' and parents' opinions of them), but boy could he deliver the goods. He laid great importance on his financial contribution to the family, and with good reason: his work *was* important.

Although ADD/ADHD people have trouble concentrating, they usually are extremely good at seeing the big picture around them. They are alert. Unusually observant, Corey noticed things most people would not—the new squirrel nest in the maple, the way the corn picking machines dropped ears of corn on the turns. He made a lot of money trapping because he observed and understood the habits of the animals he sought.

As a rule, ADD/ADHD people are highly creative. Corey made birdhouses and bird feeders from discarded roofing shingles. He designed and built his own deadfalls and snares. He was creatively brilliant and a mechanical genius! A whiz!

When adults assess children and other adults, far too often (in fact, we'd venture to say almost all the time) they consider only one kind of intelligence, the kind that comes from sitting quietly in school and learning from books. But there are many kinds of intelligence. Manual dexterity, creativity, and a good mechanical sense are kinds of intelligence that are just as important as book-learning. In some situations, such as Corey's, they are more so.

Were Corey to be transformed somehow from his rambunctious self into a more sedate, "normal" child, he would lose much of the very stuff that makes him so valuable to his family. His hyperkinetic energy and entrepreneurship would be blunted. His family would lose his contribution, and he would lose a large part of his source of pride and his sense of self-worth, the only positive things going for him at this stage of his life. He would lose his Corey-ness.

Corey's value as a human being does not lie in his precociousness, his economic contributions to his family, or his help to the farrier and others. It lies in the fact that he is a unique human being, a child in God's image. His value as a human being is intrinsic and requires no justification.

Transform Corey? Never! Help him do better in school? Now that is a possibility.

## Treating ADD/ADHD

Corey did have a problem learning in school, and that would adversely affect him all his life. He needed two things:

the learning and skills that a good education provides, and the psychological boost of making good in an area in which people had labeled him inadequate.

When initially considering treatment, we assess the child's or adult's situation from many angles. What are the specific problems? Diagnosable ADD? School? Home life? When we know the problems, we can work toward the best solutions. We have at our disposal a wondrous arsenal of solutions, and only a few of them involve the miracle drugs.

## When Are Drugs Necessary?

Brett was having trouble in school. At age seven, he had none of Corey's advantages. He could not contribute to the family directly, he did not live on a farm in the country where he could run wide and far and help with farm work, he did not have a teacher who liked him best in absentia. Brett's teacher was going to "sit him down and make him learn."

When he wasn't at school, Brett spent a lot of time watching television. TV held his fleeting attention, and his harried mom reasoned that TV was educational—well, sort of.

Because Brett lived a mile from school and the bus routes didn't pass near his house, his mom drove him to school each morning. She usually made three trips daily—one to take Brett to school, another to take him whatever he forgot to take with him, and one to pick him up after school. Sometimes she went back to the school a fourth time to get something Brett forgot to bring home with him. And some days she had to make yet another trip to the school to meet with the teacher or counselor.

When Brett's teacher suggested that drugs may help Brett do better in school, his mom steadfastly refused. Brett was all boy, but he wasn't sick. She believed in healthful foods, routine at home, and taking medicine only when disease required it.

That soon changed. The routine fell apart first. Brett could not adhere to a routine at home. He could not remember to do chores and duties. He fought bedtime. He could not sit still through a meal.

Healthful foods fell by the wayside also. Brett put up such a fuss in the grocery store that his mom ended up buying sugarcoated cereals and snack foods to appease him.

When the teacher again urged Brett's mom to consider a drug to control the attention disorder and described the wondrous transformations the drugs can make, Brett's mom's resolution began to waver. *Maybe Brett does need medication to help him,* she thought.

The school counselor suggested Ritalin. The counselor wisely urged Brett's mom to go to a doctor who specialized in ADD and provided a slate of therapy of which drugs were only a part.

The counselor knew the statistics. When a behavior-altering drug is used for ADD children without the backup of counseling and other therapy, no lasting benefit accrues for the vast majority—80 percent by most estimates. Drugs alone are a stopgap, a temporary measure. True, they help the children do better in school, and the children will carry that academic knowledge throughout life. But these kids must learn to cope with their uniqueness and to get along with other people. That comes from counsel, training, and positive experience, not a drug.

## How the Miracle Drugs Work

"Two weeks after the doctor put Brett on Ritalin, he was a changed child," Brett's mom said. "He's been transformed. Now he can sit still through a meal. He can concentrate on his work and start to catch up on what he missed in school. It's a miracle!"

Miracle, yes. Transformation, no.

Recall what you learned about neurotransmitters in Chapter 2. Essentially, they are the switches that connect nerve ends and allow for the flow of thought processes and ideas.

To be frank, we have no clear concept of just how these drugs work, particularly on children. It may be that by raising a level of awareness, they make it easier for the children to concentrate. It may be that they work by increasing the presence of neurotransmitters, especially dopamine. With more neurotransmitters to use when the occasion demands, the brain cells can keep thoughts connected and thereby control thoughts better. Controlling the random thoughts and distractions is a key to curbing inattention and impulsivity and improving concentration.

The change in a person with ADD then is not a transformation. It is a correction. A child who is naturally outgoing will not suddenly become introverted, although a child who is socially hobbled by ADD may grow to be more outgoing as he or she becomes better accepted. The child is not changed; the child is reaching a natural, innate level, which ADD had until now made unattainable.

The vast majority of kids like to learn. When learning becomes onerous for a child, that's a big red flag. Ritalin and other behavior-modifying drugs help the child restore the enthusiasm for learning by making the act of learning easy enough to be a positive, uplifting enterprise. The drugs do not create the enthusiasm.

## What Treatment Entails

Here at the Minirth Meier New Life Clinics, we never ever pop a drug into a child and turn him or her loose on the world. Often we can achieve lasting improvement without drug intervention. When we do employ drugs, Ritalin primarily, to help the child buckle down, we make that a part of extensive therapy, which helps the child develop coping mechanisms.

In Brett's case, Ritalin worked wonders. Moving him to another class at school helped, too. Brett's initial teacher believed adamantly that true learning happens only when a child sits quietly at a desk under bright light. Not only was that not Brett's style, the bright light and lack of movement worked viciously against him. Brett's needs were diametrically different because he was wired differently.

His second teacher, who had grown up with ADD herself, understood about different learning styles. She let her students work anywhere they felt comfortable. She allowed children to use "crutches"—for example, using a finger to follow along a line of text. They may be crutches to some children, she knew, but ADD/ADHD kids may need them. She used color coding and pictures a lot. She allowed her more active kids to work at cubicles where they would be less distracted. Her classroom looked like chaos to the casual observer, but a whole lot of learning was going on.

Brett worked in his cubicle when he had to concentrate on a heavy reading project. He sprawled on the floor to do math. He paced the back of the room when memorizing his spelling words. He went from making D's to making A's.

Many excellent books on the market address alternative learning styles. We won't get into them here, except to suggest you start with the excellent book by Dr. Paul Warren and Jody Capehart, *You and Your ADD Child*.[1] Parents of an ADD child should bone up on these concepts to be able to talk intelligently with the child's teachers.

### Parental Guidance

While Brett was tackling school with renewed vigor, we also counseled his parents. Parental guidance is crucial to a child's success. We explained the unique ways ADD/ADHD kids look at the world and helped Brett's parents see things from his viewpoint. They could then adjust expectations and ways of enforcing discipline. At no time did we suggest they go easy or give up. That is not what we mean by adjustment. We helped them redirect their parenting.

Here are some of the suggestions we offer parents:

**Draw the lines.** It's important to be kind, but parents must also be firm. The philosophy is, "Here are the ground rules, these are the lines, and if you cross them such-and-so will be the consequence."

We don't discuss punishment. We talk about cause and effect. If the child chooses a specific course of action, a specific result will happen. ADD/ADHD kids do not understand consequences as well as most children do. They have trouble linking cause and effect. But they catch on.

Remember to discipline the behavior, not the child. "You're a bad child!" sticks in the child's mind far longer than the consequence does, and it shapes the child more insidiously. "That was a bad thing to do!" is more accurate and less damaging.

**Keep things simple.** ADD/ADHD kids have a lot of trouble processing more than one thing at a time. The idea is to give them only one thing at a time. One order instead of a series of orders. One decision. Limit the choices the child must make by taking them in tandem. Rather than ask Brett what he was going to wear to school the next day, his mom might ask, "Which pants?" "Which shirt?" "Which shoes?" Taken one by one, the choices become manageable.

A parent also must keep instructions simple. Don't say, "Go upstairs, wash your face, brush your teeth, and go to bed." Give the child one instruction at a time. "Go upstairs" counts as one instruction in the ADD/ADHD child's mind.

**Ask for and honor the child's opinions.** ADD/ADHD kids don't get much respect. Any time Brett's folks value his thoughts, it builds him up as nothing else can.

ADD/ADHD kids have trouble fitting into social situations. The family is the first and most intimate environment for socialization. Making the child a valued member of that social group paves the way for him or her to socialize in the wider world.

**Don't haggle over small stuff.** There will be plenty of big stuff to handle without having to deal with the minor power struggles. Shine through the little problems.

**Keep things immediate.** ADD/ADHD kids have a poor sense of time. They are immediate creatures with no concept of tomorrow or even of two hours from now. Confine rewards and consequences to the present.

Give the child chores with immediate consequences. By that we mean you assign the child tasks around the house.

Chores engender responsibility. If the child fails to complete them, a privilege is revoked for a short time, not a long time.

**Accept the child's absentmindedness.** Parents must live with their ADD/ADHD child's absentmindedness, with the not-so-comforting thought that it will not change because physically it cannot. Nagging, punishment, yelling—nothing can alter the child's basic wiring.

We do not suggest that you dismiss instructions or commands. But we beg you to be gentle, firm, and forgiving when it seems that instructions go in one ear and out the other.

One way to get your child to remember an order or instruction is to say, "Tell me what I just said." As the child repeats the instruction, the instruction is more likely to stick. Another idea is to give the order and then ask, "How are you going to carry it out?"

Accept that no technique works 100 percent.

**Don't allow loud and unruly behavior in public.** Reasonable guidelines should bestow a veneer of civilization. Society will better receive the child, and the child will learn what social expectations are.

This is not "My child must appear well-behaved so that I look good as a parent." Rather this is "My child should know what constitutes proper and decent behavior for his or her own sake." To make the parent look good is never a child's purpose in life.

**Maintain a routine.** Brett benefited immensely from a large poster tacked to his bedroom door. It listed chores and activities he must complete each day. He received a star for each satisfactory completion. The first assignment was "get out of bed in the morning." Easy to accomplish, and a bright star with which to begin the day.

Brett's bedtime was the same each night except Tuesdays, when his parents allowed him to stay up until 9:30 to watch a favorite TV program. In other words, the routine was flexible but firm. Dinnertime varied between five and eight o'clock because Brett's father worked odd hours. But times for breakfast and lunch were consistent every day. These meals were routine in their regularity, and the dinner hour was routine in its irregularity. Brett's world had a rhythm to it.

**Use caution when considering home-schooling.** Home-schooling and private tutoring can be excellent ways for ADD/ADHD children to catch up on missed schoolwork. It's not always advisable for the parents to be the teachers. Parents are too close to the child, too concerned with the nonacademic aspects of the child's life, to view school learning objectively. Also, when parents are the teachers they are with the child twenty-four hours a day. A non-ADD kid gets annoying; ADD and ADHD kids are extremely so. Parents need a break.

**Extoll the child's strengths.** Parents get so wrapped up in managing an ADD/ADHD child's weaknesses that they forget to celebrate the strengths—the global vision, the creativity, the enthusiasm.

Explore your child's strengths. It's one of the most important things you can do.

Parental understanding is a key to the treatment of ADD/ADHD. Parents learn how these children are wired differently, what special circumstances benefit them, what limitations they must work within. Then the parents can help them learn to cope with the differences.

Most of all, the parents must slather the children with love. Love is the key.

## Side Effects and Shortcomings of ADD Drugs

Every silver lining has a cloud. Ritalin and the other drugs prescribed to ease the effects of ADD and ADHD do have their dark side.

Ritalin has evidenced little indication of chemical dependency or addiction. That's the good news. It is rapidly absorbed and metabolized. That's the bad news. A therapeutic dose of Ritalin lasts only three or four hours. That's usually not a full school day. New products, such as Adderal, are being designed to rectify this shortcoming.

If taken too late in the day, Ritalin and the other drugs can promote nervousness and insomnia. Insomnia in an overactive child is not an ideal situation.

Although some of these products, such as Cylert, must build up to a therapeutic level over a course of several weeks, they are rapidly absorbed when taken. The body gets rid of Cylert by metabolizing it in the liver. Persons with impaired liver function should not take it.

Sometimes psychotic or potentially psychotic kids who take these drugs can go off the deep end. It doesn't happen often, but it does occur. Social disturbances and thought disorders, things that are supposed to be alleviated by the drugs, occasionally worsen. We call it a paradoxical reaction.

The drugs can precipitate or worsen Tourette's syndrome and other tics. Tourette's syndrome is characterized by sudden, involuntary movements or blurted sounds or words, even profanities. We repeat, *involuntary*.

Tolerance builds when people unwisely use these drugs, and some people can become hooked on the psychological effect. Yes, amphetamines and methamphetamines are the same substances peddled on the streets by drug dealers. That does not make the drugs evil. Used properly and carefully, they are a blessing. Look at it this way: it is tragic that thousands of people die in automobile accidents each year, but the accidents do not make automobiles evil. They are an advantage to people who use them carefully and wisely.

An overdose of amphetamines and related substances leads to any or all of these symptoms: vomiting and diarrhea, extreme agitation and tremors, hallucinations, delirium, euphoria, headache, sweating, flushing, rapid respiration, cramps, rapid heart rate, and abnormally high blood pressure. Extreme poisoning can terminate in convulsions, coma, and death.

Amphetamines and their related drugs are also used to control obesity and ease the problems of narcolepsy and cataplexy.

# The History of ADD Treatment

Once upon a time, say twenty or thirty years ago, children with problems such as Corey's and Brett's were diagnosed with MBD, Minimal Brain Dysfunction. They weren't seriously learning impaired as such, but some little thing in the wiring wasn't right. The name eventually was changed to ADD, Attention Deficit Disorder, with the recent addition, when appropriate, of ADHD, Attention Deficit Hyperactivity Disorder.

Ritalin was used in the 1930s as a respiratory stimulant. In the 1960s, Ritalin and its kin were used also as appetite suppressants for weight control. The FDA decided that Ritalin was being used too casually for too many disorders, and it tightened restrictions on it.

The effective drugs for ADD and ADHD were found, more or less, by accident. No one in his right mind would have guessed that a stimulant could correct hyperactivity. Yet hyperactive, inattentive, impulsive children who received these stimulants for other reasons appeared to settle down. They could concentrate better.

Working backward, researchers figured out the probable neurotransmitter improvement. Now they had a point of intervention. That's a fancy way of saying they found a place where they could insert a medicine and interrupt the problem or disease.

Knowing at last how to tackle the problem, drug companies have developed a variety of products we use today. Cylert, for example, came into use in the 1980s. They also are finding applications for drugs used for other problems. Tricyclic antidepressants serve some ADDs, major tranquilizers may help when all else fails, and even a blood pressure medicine, clonidine, causes improvement in some people.

## Medications for Treating ADD/ADHD

**Cylert** (pemoline) is structurally similar to amphetamines. Cylert takes awhile to get going; sometimes three or four weeks elapse before a person sees evidence of its action. Therefore one cannot easily go on and off the medication. Because Cylert is metabolized in the liver, it is not appropriate for people with impaired liver functions.

**Dexedrine** (dextroamphetamine) is available in a sustained-release capsule and has been used much.

**Ritalin** (methylphenidate HCl) should not be used by a person with tics; it can increase them. Marked anxiety and agitation and sometimes psychotic episodes are other problems made worse by Ritalin. Ritalin provides a very short-term effect; it hits fast and lasts approximately four hours. It is available now in a slow-release form that lasts eight hours. (Incidentally, never chew slow-release tablets; it destroys the slow-release action.)

Because Ritalin comes and goes readily with few lingering effects we can discontinue it now and then to see how the child does without it. We call these "drug vacations." (Parents may use a stronger term for them!)

## CHAPTER 4

*They kept telling me, "It's all right, get hold of yourself." But I simply could not bring myself under control. And besides, it wasn't all right!*

VICTIM OF A PANIC ATTACK

# ANXIETY

"There is nothing to be afraid of," Sue Martin told herself. "I am a professor in a major university. I have traveled through Europe and Australia. I do my own income taxes, handle my own investment program. I am a competent person."

Competent, yes, but Sue Martin was also terrified. Everyday events, like driving on the freeway and shopping at the mall, caused her to panic. It wasn't the everyday events per se that frightened her. Sue could not put her finger on the actual cause of her terror. She thought she was losing her mind.

And then came the health scare.

Sue Martin, a professor of cell biology in a university teaching medical center, liked her office even though it was in the building's basement and had no window. Spacious and bright with its white walls and fluorescent ceiling lights, it provided welcome respite from the hurly-burly of teaching, research, and publication. She had it carpeted at her own expense just so she could kick her shoes off at the door and hang loose, wiggling her toes in the pile.

In the office two doors down, a colleague working late one night was assaulted and raped. Sue went ballistic when she learned about it the next day. Wild fear gripped her. Horrific thoughts clamored in her head. A basket case, she missed the next three days of work.

She experienced tachycardia, a rapid heartbeat and fluttery feeling inside her chest. She felt stifled, unable to breathe comfortably. Fear pressed so hard on her she trembled uncontrollably. Only when she managed to get her office moved to the second floor did she feel any real measure of relief.

A week later Sue and her husband had an argument. It was only a minor spat, but she came unglued. Her reaction was totally out of proportion to the situation. Sue's response angered her husband even more, and their little spat turned into a royal row.

The next morning, alarmed by a sudden onset of rapid heartbeat and dull pain in her chest, Sue saw her doctor on an emergency appointment.

The doctor paternally patted her hand, smiled, and said, "Now, Sue, it's nerves. Take deep breaths, lay off the coffee and tea awhile, and find some way to relax." Sue couldn't believe his reaction.

"But it feels like I'm having a heart attack. It's like an elephant's sitting on my chest," Sue said.

"Not in a woman forty-seven years old. It's just nerves," the doctor replied. He sent her off with a prescription for tranquilizers.

*He thinks I'm a hypochondriac*, Sue thought to herself. But the dull pain frightened her. She drove to the emergency room at the medical center. One of the doctors interning there, Gail Estanado, was a friend. Gail would reassure her without patting her hand.

Without wasting time, Gail helped Sue onto a gurney,

treating her as an acute cardiac patient. Anxiety, which is what Sue was experiencing, can at times feel like a heart attack. All too often, Gail knew, the anxiety and the cardiac emergency can occur simultaneously. Gail responded to the worst possibility first, cardiac difficulties. The multiple-lead electrocardiogram (EKG) showed what Gail suspected. Either because of anxiety or in addition to it, Sue was indeed experiencing a heart attack. The swift, aggressive action on Gail's part minimized the damage to Sue's heart, and may have saved her life.

## Identifying Anxiety

When fear has a logical source it is not termed anxiety. For example, if you're being chased across an open pasture by an angry bull, you're feeling terrified, but psychologically speaking, you're not experiencing anxiety. There's a logical source for your fear, and your terror is a normal, logical, expected reaction to the situation.

Anxiety is not normal, logical, or expected. It is terror without a clear cause. It may surface as a wild panic reaction, as it did in Sue's case, or as a vague, dissatisfying, edgy feeling you cannot identify exactly.

In fact, Sue's case is both typical and extremely rare. Very often, because of the cardiac flutter, the person undergoing an anxiety attack fears a heart attack. That adds greatly to the anxiety and is totally unwarranted. Almost never is a cardiac problem involved in anxiety, which is what made Sue's situation so very rare.

Everyone experiences a degree of anxiety occasionally. But for Sue, the problem had become an overriding part of her life, damaging her relationships and her effectiveness at work. She knew she needed help.

Sue's physical reaction to her anxiety, a heart attack, is a worst-case scenario. This type of reaction is rare. But anxiety attacks can feel like heart attacks, and the only sure way to tell the difference is to run an EKG.

Anxiety is more a crippler than a killer, and its crippling effects can be devastating. It can curtail a person's lifestyle so that the person is afraid to leave the house. It can destroy close relationships, including marriages. It can dump a career in the ditch in a hurry. It angers and frustrates not just the victim, but everyone around the victim as well.

There are a variety of disorders under the umbrella term *anxiety*. Psychologists and psychiatrists consider these disorders separately.

## Panic Attacks

Sue can tell you about panic attacks. The one that nailed her when she heard about her colleague's rape was a doozie. It came on suddenly and within ten minutes was racing full-tilt beyond control. Her panic attacks were characterized by physical, mental, and emotional symptoms.

### Rapid Heart Rate

The heart speeds up, pounds, flutters (we call that palpitation, meaning that you can feel it inside your chest). It may feel like a heart attack, and the person may fear that the heart will give out from all the frenetic activity.

### Irregular Breathing

A person may feel smothered or like he or she is choking. It may be characterized by shortness of breath, as if the person had been running uphill for a mile. This inability to breathe is terrifying.

### Irregular Body Functions

Sweating. Trembling. Shaking. Nausea. Diarrhea. Chills. Hot flushes. Dizziness or faintness. Numbness. Tingling. Chest discomfort or chest pain—the kind you read about in the American Heart Association's warning literature. The body runs amok.

Again, a heart attack brought on by anxiety, especially in women Sue's age and younger, is rare. However, when an acute myocardial infarction (AMI, the technical term for heart attack) occurs, doctors can reverse some of the heart damage if they can deal with it within the first few hours. Survival rates soar when the AMI is caught early.

How do you know when to let the panic attack pass and when to head for cardiac care? Tough call. We can't really answer that question because every person is unique. We can only explain the situation to you and suggest that you weigh all the factors and go with your gut feelings, erring on the side of caution. In a later section we'll discuss the fears precipitated by a panic attack, which compound the anxiety and the prospect of another attack. The reassurance that these symptoms definitely are *not* an AMI in progress, no matter how like one they may feel, may help stem the next wash of panic. Ruling out the possibility of an AMI (an EKG will do that) can ease the anxiety.

### Mental and Emotional Instability

Sue's reaction to the spat with her husband was way out of proportion. Emotionally, she was on the edge.

Panic attacks may also be characterized by a person's strong feeling that what is happening to her isn't real. The person may feel detached from circumstances and out of control at the deepest level. "I'm losing my mind" is a frequent comment of persons experiencing a panic attack.

Be aware that a person in the throes of a panic attack may not display all of the symptoms we've listed. Overriding the signs and symptoms of the attack is the undefinable fear.

Sometimes people experience exaggerated, inexplicable, and illogical fear over a particular object or situation. We call these manifestations of anxiety phobias.

## The Phobias

### Agoraphobia

More than two thousand years ago in Greece, the broad, open central meeting area called the *agora* was the center of public activity. It was the marketplace, the political center, the social heart of the community. It was where news was disseminated and public announcements were made, the place to see and be seen. In psychiatry we've borrowed the term *agora* because it is so encompassing. *Phobia* is Greek for fear. Agoraphobia is an irrational fear of being in a crowd, of leaving the house alone, of traveling, of being surrounded by people in a wide open space.

Agoraphobics may feel terrified of becoming trapped in a public place or situation, where if something went wrong they could not escape. They may fear the embarrassment of having a panic attack among people.

One fellow we know, Larry, lives in San Francisco and is terrified by the possibility of the Big Quake. He is absolutely certain that when the Big Quake strikes and the San Andreas Fault scrapes its way closer to Alaska, he will be riding in the BART tunnel beneath the bay. He hates that tunnel. Fears it. But he rides through it every day on his commute to work. His fear does not impinge on his normal daily activities. It is manageable. He can even joke about it, albeit sardonically. His is not an agoraphobic.

Agoraphobia restricts a person's movements and lifestyle. The person will not leave home without a companion. He avoids travel. When travel or social contact is unavoidable, anxiety and marked distress prevail.

## Social Phobia

You've probably experienced stage fright—butterflies in your stomach, nervousness at the thought of friends or strangers scrutinizing your performance or appearance.

Social phobia is stage fright multiplied beyond reason. People who suffer from social phobia will move heaven and earth to avoid a social situation, whether it is dating, being in a group of people (either standing before them or mingling among them), facing authority figures, or simply making conversation. They may assiduously avoid eating in public or using public rest room facilities. They can experience symptoms of anxiety just thinking about such an event.

They suffer from inner conflict: their better reasoning tells them their fears are unfounded, but another voice in their heads insists that they will make complete fools of themselves in social settings.

## Claustrophobia

People who suffer from claustrophobia fear being in tight, enclosed places. They take the stairs rather than the elevator. They can't stay in small rooms, particularly ones without windows. They don't like flying in airplanes, and they don't like driving through tunnels.

## Acrophobia

People who are acrophobic are afraid of heights.

Our friend Jean discovered just how acrophobic she was when she accompanied a dozen teenagers to the top of Half Dome in Yosemite National Park.

Half Dome is exactly that—half a granite dome. To reach the top, one must ascend the gentlest of the steep shoulders that form the back of the dome. Much of the route requires hand-over-hand cable climbing.

"Ain't nothing between you and God but a billion cubic miles of wind," Jean claims. "Bare air! We got above tree level, and suddenly I realized I was hanging out there in the open and I panicked. I closed my eyes and kept climbing and told the kid behind me, 'Talk to me!' I needed to hear a human voice.

"Once we made it to the top, strangely enough, it wasn't as frightening. The top of Half Dome looks round and narrow from below, but it's really very big and flat. As long as I didn't go near the edge, I was okay."

That Jean kept climbing despite her fear was a good sign. As panicky as she felt, she, and not her phobia, remained in control. She wasn't afraid to discuss her phobia with the teenagers when they reached the top. Come time to descend, a couple of the guys guided her over the side while she kept her eyes tightly shut. As long as she faced the granite and didn't think about "all that eagle territory" out there, she made it down all right.

Her acrophobia was not debilitating. It didn't keep her from participating in life's adventures.

## Animal Phobias

Some people possess an inordinate terror of certain animals. We believe most of these animal-triggered phobias begin in childhood.

Meg, age seventy-five, was terrified of bats. After her husband, Bert, died, she lived alone in their old two-story farmhouse. One night a luckless little bat got in the house. When Bert was alive, if a bat flew in the house he would shoo it out while Meg hid in the closet. She didn't have Bert now.

Meg ran outside screaming. Wrong move. Not only was she a quarter-mile from the nearest neighbor who could help her, but more bats were out there in the dark. Timidly she went back inside. She thought about calling her son to come by after work to help her, but she couldn't stand the thought of the bat being in her house for hours. And what if it hid and they couldn't find it?

Meg covered her hair with a stocking cap and pulled it down low over her forehead. She donned a bulky coat and gloves. With her "armor" on, Meg grabbed a broom and began to chase the tiny creature from room to room, screaming as she did it.

When the bat paused to rest on the archway molding between the dining room and living room, she nailed it. She beat it to the floor with her broom and finished the job with an unabridged dictionary.

When her son came by later to visit, he found her sitting at her kitchen table, trying to drown her anxiety attack with hot tea. He disposed of the bat for her.

From earliest childhood Meg had been told that bats were filthy, they all had rabies, and they liked to nest in people's hair (none of which is true). Meg's illogical fear of bats probably stems from what she learned in childhood.

## Nature Phobias

Storms, lightning, earthquakes, tornadoes. You rather expect destructive forces of nature to be a source of fear.

What we're talking about here is *illogical* fear. Some people are terrified of thunder, yet thunder can't hurt them. A surprising number of adults are intensely afraid of the water and won't go near it. Quite often these people had a terrifying experience with water in childhood. As adults, their responses are irrational.

In our practice we have counseled people with various kinds of phobias, including space phobia, in which persons are afraid they will fall down if they move away from the wall, sturdy furniture, or some other support; and situation phobia, where persons are afraid of particular situations, driving for example.

One woman we counseled, Kay, was irrationally afraid of germs. She avoided social situations because she was afraid she would catch a disease from the people around her.

When the newspapers reported that some travelers contracted tuberculosis during airplane flights, her worst fears were validated. But she dismissed all the evidence that negated her fears.

# Other Triggers of Anxiety

While phobias are among the most popularly recognized triggers for anxiety attacks, there are other circumstances that trigger the physical, mental, and emotional symptoms characteristic of anxiety. One is body shocks and insults.

Joe was mowing his lawn one day when he inadvertently extended his foot too far forward and the whirling blade caught his toe. As is often the case in such trauma injuries, there was little blood. His wife wrapped shoe and all in a towel, shoveled Joe into the car, and drove to the emergency room.

Joe was all right until the towel and shoe came off and he saw his severely mangled big toe. At that point he went glassy-eyed, his breathing became rapid and shallow, and he sat mute and frozen on the emergency room table.

Joe was experiencing a form of shock called a vasovagal response. The doctor's first step in bringing Joe out of it was to hide the injury from Joe's sight. Meanwhile, Joe's wife took one look at the toe and went into a panic attack.

Neither of these reactions was justified by the extent of the damage. Joe's injury, although gruesome, was not life-threatening. The usual causes of traumatic shock, such as a great loss of blood, were not present. In fact, Joe acted just fine until he saw his foot. And Joe's wife? She wasn't even hurt.

We find that atypical reactions such as a panic attack or a vasovagal response very often run along family lines. If others in your close family faint at the sight of blood, so might you.

Another trigger for anxiety is obsessive-compulsive disorder, which we will discuss in detail in the next chapter. Others are extreme stress, extreme worry, and post-traumatic stress.

Now that we've identified some of the anxiety disorders and what sets them off, let's look closely at the signs and symptoms that characterize anxiety. When making a psychiatric diagnosis we look for at least three of these symptoms of anxiety.

## Signs and Symptoms of Anxiety

As Sue Martin lay in her hospital bed, cardiac monitor wires pasted all over her torso, she had a lot of time to think. Heart trouble at age forty-seven? Panic attacks? She was going to have to make some changes, and the first one that came to mind was to divorce her husband. Relations between Sue and her husband had been deteriorating. The AMI might not have happened at all if it weren't for that argument. Perhaps, for her sake and his, she ought to hang it up. And yet . . .

*Why is all this happening to me so suddenly?* she thought. Were Sue to educate herself about anxiety or seek professional help, she would learn that her present problems did not pop onto the horizon without precursors. The panic attack was one manifestation of her distress. But the signs and symptoms of her anxiety had been with her for quite some time.

Anxiety can be focused in some way or quite generalized. It can erupt or simmer. And it may produce some of these components.

## Worry

Worry is built into the human mind and serves a useful purpose. It alerts us to possible problems so that we might either evade them or act upon them. But once worry has done its job, and that doesn't take long at all, we are supposed to dismiss it. Sue could not. Against her will, worry ate at her.

Psychiatrists define worry as an apprehensive expectation. You're afraid something bad is going to happen. We count worry as a serious problem when it plagues its victims constantly for six months and longer and the worries concern a number of subjects or activities. Facing a tough court case and worrying about it excessively doesn't count. Although the worry won't help a thing, it is natural and expected.

On the other hand, Sue worried about a number of things, from driving on the freeway to shopping at the mall. Her worry was extreme and unmanageable. This unmanageable worry is often accompanied by irritability.

## Irritability

Sue didn't think she was all that cross and grumpy. Certainly she wasn't any worse than anyone else. Her husband and kids complained about her, though, frequently and unfairly, she believed. They accused her of snapping at them about ordinary matters, of losing her temper instantly, of being too demanding. "When you're strict, you just aren't appreciated," Sue lamented.

## Edginess and Vigilance

For months Sue had felt restless and on edge. Even before the attack on her colleague, she was constantly on guard and scanning her surroundings. If someone inadvertently startled her she became excessively angry.

She attributed it all to the press of research combined with teaching duties plus raising two teenagers. That's a lot of stress.

On the other hand, she experienced an awful lot of constant agitation. Other people with her load didn't seem that edgy. No doubt it was this constant nervous tension that contributed to her muscle tension.

## Muscle Tension

"Sue, why don't you relax?" a colleague suggested one day. "You're standing there like someone just stabbed you with a pin."

The comment had infuriated Sue. It was none of her colleague's business.

As she lay trapped in this hospital bed, she recalled the comment and it still infuriated her. However, she had to admit she did have trouble relaxing. She felt tense and rigid a lot of the time, as if she were poised to strike or flee. Sometimes her muscles knotted painfully. It wasn't hard to understand why she felt tired so often.

## Fatigue

Sue couldn't remember a day when she didn't feel tired, when her energy didn't set before the sun did. Her doctor explored the possibility that she suffered from mononucleosis or chronic fatigue syndrome, but neither checked out.

Despite her weariness, Sue had trouble sleeping, which exacerbated the fatigue.

## Sleep Problems

Too many times the restlessness that plagued Sue during the day pursued her into the night and she slept fitfully, tangling the covers into knots. She might wake up at 2:00 A.M., and that was it for the night. Or she might not get to sleep for hours after she lay down. You would think that as tired as she was she would sleep soundly. Lack of sleep would explain her concentration problems.

## Concentration Difficulty

Absentminded professor—Sue despised that term! But she, a professor, was absentminded far too often. She had trouble concentrating on a project; her mind kept flitting. Once in a while it went blank. Someone would be talking to her and she'd tune out. Worse, sometimes when she was talking, the thought she was in the midst of articulating would evaporate.

## Other Physiological Signs

We've already discussed the physical symptoms Sue experienced during her panic attack—heart palpitations, irregular breathing and bodily functions. But some of these same symptoms may appear in persons who are experiencing anxiety, but not a full-blown panic attack.

At this point you may be thinking that anxiety-related disorders are peculiar to adults. But children also suffer from anxiety, although their symptoms often differ from those of adults.

# Identifying Anxiety in Children

It is difficult to identify anxiety in children because children don't often react the way adults do, and they usually cannot articulate their fears or feelings.

Children are not able to think reasonably and logically until about the age of seven or eight. Up to that age they often display what adults would characterize as excessive fear. But this fear is normal in young children, for whom the world is a new and interesting, yet sometimes scary, place.

Children may be exceedingly frightened of adults. From the child's perspective the adults hold the reins of power. When we evaluate social phobia in children, we must see evidence that their age-appropriate relationships with peers and familiar adults are affected by their anxiety. Interactions with adult strangers are invalid.

Children express anxiety with crying, tantrums, disorganized behavior, agitation, and clinging. "Wait a minute," you say. "All kids act that way at times." Rather, what we look for are these kinds of behaviors in excess or in circumstances when the behavior is not logically warranted.

To give you an idea of how children display symptoms of anxiety, we'll consider the case of young Roger, who is suffering from separation anxiety.

## Symptoms of Anxiety in Children

When a child is separated from someone or something that means a great deal to him or her, the child may suffer what we term *separation anxiety*.

Seven-year-old Roger worries about being separated from his parents. His anxiety is characterized by several symptoms.

**Excessive worry.** Kids are worrywarts under the best of circumstances. We become concerned when the worries are excessive in both recurrence and scope. Roger worries constantly about being separated from his parents. He worries that his mom and dad may die in a drive-by shooting or be killed when the facade of a building falls on them (he saw a television report of that happening during an earthquake). He worries that he will get lost or kidnapped and become separated from his parents forever.

**Illogical reluctance.** Roger is reluctant to go to school and leave his parents. He is exceedingly reluctant to be alone at any time. There is no basis for his reluctance; his parents never leave him alone in an unsupervised situation. His fear surfaces even when his parents are in a different room of the house. He refuses to go to sleep at night if one of them is not at his side. Understandably, his parents are getting frustrated with his behavior.

**Nightmares.** Although nightmares are common to children (and adults), Roger has nightmares frequently concerning his illogical fear: being separated from his parents. For example, he often dreams that he gets separated from them in a large crowd of people.

**Physical symptoms.** Tummyaches, headaches, vomiting—these symptoms almost always show up when a separation is discussed or imminent. For instance, Roger gets ill when his parents just talk about leaving him with a sitter while they go out to dinner. He's not faking; the symptoms are real. And these symptoms tell the parents, "You can't leave me when I'm sick like this." It almost always works.

The signs Roger exhibits are characteristic of unmanageable anxiety in children. Most kids experience fear to some extent. We consider it a serious problem if it persists for at least a month and if it causes problems with schoolwork, social life, or the quality of relationships. Clearly Roger is suffering from severe anxiety.

## Treating Anxiety

We cheated a bit when we described Sue Martin's symptoms. She did not actually exhibit all of them. Most people with an anxiety problem do not show every one of the signs. We consider a diagnosis of anxiety if the person exhibits about half of them. If we're treating a child, one symptom is sufficient.

So once we've made the diagnosis, where do we go from there?

At her husband's insistence, Sue Martin began seeing Dr. Meier to treat her anxiety disorder. When he suggested a drug therapy as a possibility for relieving some of her symptoms, Sue snapped.

*"Drugs!"* Sue screeched. "Absolutely not! Forget it. I'm not *that* anxious." And on and on she roared in protest. She ranted about the cases of addiction she'd heard of. She raved about being turned into a smiling zombie. She thundered about the misuse of drugs such as Valium that had been going on since the early sixties and how it was men's way of sedating women, of bringing them under control lest they speak their own minds.

Dr. Meier sat quietly, waiting for the din to subside.

She continued, "When my doctor recommended psychiatric counsel, I was furious. I'm not crazy. I'm here only because my husband insisted. If I'd known he was telling me to go visit a shrink who drugs people up, I never would have come." With that the din seemed to have abated.

Paul nodded. "An honest attitude. So tell me, is the reaction you just made—more than five minutes of shouting and protesting—is that your usual response to a casual suggestion?"

She opened her mouth and closed it again. Opened her mouth and closed it. Finally she asked, "What's your point, doctor?"

"Back when I was a child, every Saturday afternoon our local television station would broadcast very old westerns. I mean very old. Colonel Tim McCoy. Ever see one of his western movies?"

"No." Sue sat rigid, her spine straight as a frozen carrot.

"He always walked around ramrod straight. He never relaxed. In every movie they'd show him pushing through the swinging doors into a saloon in his fancy shirt and tall white hat. Then they'd take a close-up of his face. His head wouldn't move, but his eyes would dart from side to side. I guess they were telling you he was on his guard, expecting trouble. It looked absolutely ridiculous. Even as a child, when I accepted just about anything I saw on TV, I thought it looked ludicrous.

"Now I'm not saying you look ridiculous like Colonel Tim McCoy. But what I am saying is that you look like you're expecting trouble—you're on guard. Is that usual for you?"

"Well, not exactly, but—"

"Earlier, you told me about your panic attack. That's not a usual response either."

She softened a bit. "I see your point."

"Would you like to break this pattern of being tense and irritable all the time? Ease the specter of another panic attack? Would you like to get restful sleep and feel good again?"

She said nothing, which Paul interpreted as a yes.

He continued, "Let me describe to you what drugs are available these days and how they work."

## The Course of Treatment

Have you ever told a friend, "Don't worry, everything's gonna be fine"? Did it work? Did your friend stop worrying?

Talking a worrier out of worrying seldom works. Counsel, however, can be of use in helping phobics shake their phobias. The drugs intercede when the worry, the anxiety, the phobia have much too firm a grip on the person for reasoning to take effect. Sue was a research professor in cell biology. Obviously her reasoning mind was well-honed, even brilliant. Yet it might not be able to control her emotions or anxiety.

The problem is that anxiety often is neither generated nor governed by the reasoning mind. Reasoning, therefore, may not be able to alter or dislodge anxiety until it is alleviated. Although anxiety starts out as an emotional reaction, the body's chemistry alters and makes anxiety a medical condition. Oftentimes the body can restore the balance spontaneously and the anxiety abates. Counsel can help here. When the body cannot restore itself, the person feels guilty that he or she cannot talk the self out of the problem. How unfortunate. That's like attaching a rope to a tree and another to a wagon, then handing the rope around the tree to someone and telling him to move the wagon. When anxiety becomes a medical problem, it usually must be treated medically.

Picture two well-trained Percheron horses galloping around a circus ring. In sequined finery, riders perform flips and handsprings from the back of one horse to the back of the other. The key to the act is the horses' training. Once they begin to trot, they keep going at a constant pace and speed so that the vaulting riders know exactly where their horses will be at any given moment. The tent may fall down, but the horses will continue trotting around the ring, on and on.

So it is with anxiety and worry (and also obsessive-compulsive disorder). The disorders just keep cycling and cycling. And the problems can multiply; anxiety feeds upon itself. A person who experiences a panic attack for the first time must immediately contend with still another worry: "This is uncontrollable! What if this happens again, maybe when I'm at work or out in public?" If that worry embeds itself deeply enough, it can precipitate the very panic attack the worrier wants to avoid.

We can usually stop the horses of anxiety with one of a carefully tailored array of drugs. That is the first step. It is not the whole course of treatment by any means. Drugs hardly ever constitute a long-term treatment, either. Once the grip of the disorder is broken, we then use other means of therapy to manage the anxiety. By analogy, we get rid of the circus ring altogether, so that cycling will not recur.

Until you ease the causes, and conversation between therapist and patient oftentimes accomplishes that, the anxiety is likely to return. Being addictive, many of the drugs to curb anxiety should be used only for a short while.

## Examining the Psychological Aspects of Anxiety

We at the Minirth Meier New Life Clinics see a general pattern in anxiety patients. They come to us wound as tightly as garage door springs, and they don't know why. The moment we tell them that anxiety is usually fear of looking at one's problems, they get nervous. No one wants to look at conflicts and pain. This attitude differs from what psychologists call denial, but it arrives at the same conclusion: the patient is not allowing the self to look at the truth.

Paul Meier recounts the story of a young woman who experienced a panic attack while she was driving on the Santa Ana Freeway. Sally, a financial advisor with a major bank, was accustomed to being in control. When she told CEOs to do something, they did it; their bottom line was at stake, and they knew it. She saved many an executive's hide with timely advice and financial planning.

Terrified by her uncontrolled panic, she drove directly to her doctor's office and demanded that he see her. The doctor put Sally on BuSpar, and the anxiety symptoms abated. Sally was happy, her family was happy, her colleagues were happy . . . until Sally's Aunt Janet died.

Sally liked Aunt Janet, but the woman was not by any means a beloved favorite relative. Still, Sally plunged into a wild swirl of panic. More BuSpar. Sally was happy again until the Northridge earthquake hit. She exploded in a ferocious display of panic. Her family, frustrated with her episodes, sent her to our New Life Clinic in Laguna Beach.

Therapy uncovered the reasons for Sally's anxiety.

Sally was the eldest child in an out-of-control home where Mom languished in a slough of perpetual depression, Dad drank too much, and Sally's brothers abused her physically, though not sexually. Sally learned early that she had to take control of her life and direct her own fate. Like many people who experience similar childhood circumstances, she became perfectionistic, which fueled her drive to achieve and succeed.

Sally functioned normally, quite well in fact, until the panic attack on the freeway, the death of her aunt, and the subsequent earthquake: all of them circumstances beyond Sally's control. Sally possessed a violent fear of losing control. In Sally's case, the BuSpar performed the important service of restoring her to normal function temporarily. The intensive counsel, cleaning out her closet of fears, resolved the anxiety permanently.

## How Drugs Control Anxiety

Picture how a fire spreads across a field of dry grass. A spark from a faulty exhaust or a match carelessly thrown on the ground ignites a few brown blades. They melt down as they burn, igniting every grass stem they touch. Suddenly there's a circle of smoky fire two feet wide. Grass torches grass; the fire flares up and out. In moments, a big patch is burning.

That's called *kindling*. You don't need an independent spark to ignite each grass blade and stem. They set fire to each other. Picture a similar process within your nervous system. For some reason (a chemical reason, because this process is all based upon chemistry), thoughts "ignite" thoughts in ways you don't intend. The fire spreads even though you don't want it to.

Kindling can cause the cyclic thoughts and behaviors we see as obsession and compulsion. Kindling can work in expanding ways, driving a person's thoughts and behaviors far beyond what is appropriate. The results can be rage or emotional overload or, at the extreme, convulsions.

Antianxiety medicines, particularly those that control obsession/compulsion, must damper this kindling effect of nerves inappropriately stimulating each other or responding cyclically.

Different classes of antianxiety medications function in different ways. We believe that the benzodiazepines attach themselves to specific nerve receptors that govern the flow of necessary chloride ions into a neuron. To be technical, they augment the action of an inhibiting neurotransmitter called GABA—gamma-aminobutyric acid. This slows down or inhibits nerve activity. There are several related yet differing receptor sites. Some drugs bind to one but not another. Thus, by tailoring treatment we can control very closely the effects of the various benzodiazepines, such as Librium, Valium, or Ativan.

The barbiturates, such as Seconal or Nembutal, are nonselective: they depress the whole central nervous system, slowing everything down. We control their effects by controlling dosage. A very low dose produces mild effects. Heavier doses induce sleep or even coma, and overdose can be lethal. High therapeutic doses are used to prepare a patient to receive anesthesia.

A problem with the barbiturates has been their tendency to make the person look, act, and feel doped up. This was why Sue was afraid of becoming a zombie if she took Valium. The benzodiazepines offer a bigger, better margin between minimum therapeutic dose and zonk-out. Moreover, a one-time-only dose of these drugs can be helpful in quelling an anxiety attack or even a psychosis.

## Things to Consider About Drug Therapy

Patients who take antianxiety medications may also be taking other medicines. When persons are taking antianxiety agents, we carefully inform them about possible interactions between the different medications.

An antibiotic often used for bacterial infections, erythromycin, can work synergistically with antianxiety drugs to raise sedation to dangerous levels. So can antihistamines, substances often taken during hay fever season. Antacids can lower absorption of the antianxiety medicine.

Long-term medication to correct other disorders may alter the effective level of an antianxiety drug. Tagamet (an ulcer medicine), Dilantin (an epileptic medication), and estrogen (a female hormone) raise the antianxiety drugs' blood serum level. Tegretol (an anticonvulsant used also for trigeminal neuralgia) depresses levels, making them less effective.

Although alcohol does not alter the effectiveness of some medications, it does alter the effectiveness of most antianxiety drugs. Alcohol essentially acts physiologically on the body as a depressant. The person who is using Valium, for example, and drinks alcohol will multiply the sedating effects of both substances. You may have heard tales of people on antianxiety medicines who take a couple of stiff drinks and relax in the hot tub, only to slide quietly beneath the surface and drown.

When choosing a drug with which to begin treatment, we consider how the drug does its job, its interaction with other substances, its side effects, the age of the patient, and tolerance, dependence, and withdrawal. Tolerance means that you have to increase the dosage over time to maintain the desired effect. Dependence is addiction. Withdrawal refers to the patient's reaction when the drug treatment ends. We must consider withdrawal effects carefully. Abruptly stopping benzodiazepines can cause vomiting, cramps, convulsions, seizures, depression, paranoia, and delirium. The effects vary according to the dosage and length of time the drug has been used. Stopping barbiturates cold can cause delirium and convulsions and, at extreme, death. These dismal effects are minimized when dosages are kept small, and usually are eliminated when the drugs are tapered off carefully and gradually.

Elderly patients with anxiety problems should receive reduced doses because the metabolic rate in their livers is lower, and the medicine remains in their systems longer. On the plus side, the lower dosage works better on them.

We advise against the use of antianxiety medicines during pregnancy, particularly in the first trimester.

Sue Martin was still unsure about taking a drug to alleviate her symptoms. "What do these drugs do?" she asked. "Transform me into a pussycat who just purrs when she's taken advantage of?"

Dr. Meier smiled. "No. No miraculous transformations. Your basic personality doesn't change, but your ability to relax does. Some of these drugs can stop a rampaging elephant, but it's still an elephant. Often they offer dramatic relief from anxiety. Dramatic!"

Sue's scowl hardly softened. "Much as I hate to think about all this, I realize I have to do something. Things can't go on the way they are."

Sue asked a battery of other questions (intelligent questions), and then consented to a cautious course of drugs and counsel.

Because she was obviously concerned and interested, and because now she knew a little something about the drugs we use, we filled Sue in on some history.

## The History of Anxiety Control

Around the beginning of the twentieth century, if anxiety became a serious problem a patient might receive one of the bromide salts to control it. Nasty stuff, bromine and its salts. If the dosage was off, the patient could suffer skin rash, mental damage, and muscle weakness. But it did sedate.

In the 1940s, doctors began using chloral hydrate. On the street, chloral hydrate dropped into a drink of liquor was known as a Mickey Finn (knockout drops). Used medicinally, therapeutic doses could sedate and relieve the terrors of anxiety.

As barbiturates were developed in the 1950s, they took over the major role as antianxiety drugs. Seconal (secobarbital), for example, was very popular to ease anxiety and to promote sleep. They worked fairly well. They were also addictive.

In the 1960s, pharmaceutical companies discovered the value of the benzodiazepines, and Valium, Librium, and their ilk were born. Although technically they are addictive and can be abused, they present a much, much lower risk of misuse than the barbiturates. For a time, Valium was the world's top-selling drug.

Some of today's array of drugs can be listed according to their potency and duration. A high potency/short duration drug, for example, can knock down an acute attack, whereas a lower potency drug with greater duration is best for the long haul.

# Antianxiety Medications

## High Potency, Short Duration Benzodiazepines

**Ativan** (lorazepam), like many of these drugs, is adversely affected by light. It is best to keep it stored in a carton.

**Xanax** (alprazolam) is the drug of choice for cutting short an anxiety attack. It usually hits fairly fast and hard.

## High Potency, Long Duration Benzodiazepines

**Klonopin** (clonazepam)(formerly Clonopin), is used for both anxiety and seizures. It may help in controlling obsessive-compulsive disorder, and may also help in treating Tourette's syndrome and mania.

## Low Potency, Short Duration Benzodiazepines

**Centrax** (prazepam) is a general central nervous system depressant.

**Serax** (oxazepam) is especially useful in treating older patients. Gentle but effective, it is intended for short-term relief. The first of a new series of drugs related to the benzodiazepines, it manages a wide variety of anxiety and irritability symptoms. Alcoholics can also benefit, particularly when they become anxious as they sober up.

## Low Potency, Long Duration Benzodiazepines

**Librium and Libritabs** (chlordiazepoxide) affect the limbic area of the brain where emotional responses are managed. Withdrawal symptoms usually do not pose a problem if the drug is discontinued by degrees over a period of time. It is also used in managing delirium tremens (DTs), to which alcoholics are subject.

**Tranxene** (chlorazepate dipotassium) offers a rapid response to anxiety in general. It also relieves alcohol withdrawal symptoms.

**Valium** (diazepam) can often alleviate acute seizures and unusual situations such as laryngeal dysfunctions in which the windpipe spasms closed. Available in oral doses and injectables, Valium is often used for skeletal muscle spasms, (such as tetanus), cerebral palsy, seizures, and other disorders wherein the muscles knot up or tighten uncontrollably.

**Valrelease** (diazepam) is a slow-release form of the oral Valium medication. This medication does not help psychosis.

## Other Useful Drugs

**Adapin, Sinequan** (doxepin HCl) is sometimes used for elderly patients in low doses.

**Atarax, Vistoril** (hydroxyzine HCl) may react synergistically with Demerol and other barbiturates but not with the belladonna alkaloids such as atropine. Nor does it interact with digitalis, which cardiac patients take. This antihistamine may decrease anxiety.

**BuSpar** (buspirone), a relatively new drug in use since 1986, is totally different from the classic benzodiazepines, barbiturates, and other sedative medicines. It has no effect on GABA receptors and does not produce dependency. We think it might reduce anxiety through its effect on serotonin, one of the brain's neurotransmitters. Not a sedative, it does not impair performance. It is currently among the top one hundred drugs prescribed around the world.

**Ludiomil** (maprotiline HCl) is actually an antidepressant, but it may help people with anxiety associated with depression.

## More Drugs

We are beginning to pile up a body of evidence suggesting that TCAs and MAOIs, and perhaps SSRIs as well, also help persons with anxiety problems. Panic disorders, general anxiety, and social phobia have all responded well to these drugs.

## CHAPTER 5

*I wish over and over that I had the knowledge when I was starting out that we have today about obsessive-compulsive disorder.*

DR. FRANK MINIRTH

# OBSESSIONS AND COMPULSIONS

*Frank Minirth shares this story:*

I was a young resident in psychiatry, just starting out. Now you know how first-year residents are. Wise and all-knowing. They've got all the knowledge and all the good grades, and now they're going to score 100 percent, righting problems and curing ills. "Just lead us to the problem and we'll solve it!"

So in walked a problem.

Her name was Dora, and she really did resemble Dora. Remember the frail child-wife in Charles Dickens's *David Copperfield*? She looked pale and undernourished, ready to blow away any moment. She had one of those heads of hair that always hangs in strings, no matter how many times you wash it. Idly, nervously, continually, she twisted a lock of hair around her finger, then untwisted it, twisted it and untwisted it, twisted it and untwisted it. She drove me nuts just watching her.

But we residents were above being irritated by a client, of course. I smiled at her: "The receptionist says you are concerned primarily about a medical question. Germs. Are you sure you want psychiatric counsel? Your doctor—"

"My doctor asked me to come. He says he can't help me. He heard you were a Christian—and that's very important to me—and thought maybe you could."

I couldn't argue with that. The reason Paul Meier and I went into psychiatry was to bring that medical discipline together with Christian principles, to help people at both medical and spiritual levels. Here before me sat a lady who needed exactly what we were preparing for.

Elated, I nodded in that wise, all-knowing way that very young residents have and sat back, ready to solve my first big challenge. "What is your problem?"

She beat all around Robin Hood's barn for maybe ten minutes, touching on peripheral things. That's the way most clients do. They sort of sneak up on what's really bothering them. The crux of her problem, when she eventually go to it: She found herself terrified of any kind of germs.

Now that's a laudable enterprise, avoiding contamination, assuming it's done sensibly. But she carried it to extreme and she knew she did. She was doing it moment to moment with always, essentially, the same thought: *There's no good germ.* She kept getting these thoughts; she kept trying and trying to get rid of them, over and over and over.

She washed her hands many times a day, and I mean *many.* She refused to touch doorknobs; she had become adept at turning them with her forearm. Public restrooms, which she used only in extremity, were The Enemy. She carried rubber gloves with which to handle stall doors and latches. She lined the toilet seat. She pushed dryer knobs with an elbow.

She handled money only with rubber gloves, too.

Now I was a particularly lucky young resident because I was wise and all-knowing, not just in the field of psychiatry but in spiritual matters as well, having also been trained in seminary. I sat forward, elbows on my knees, fully prepared to solve her problem. "Dora, can you tell me what First John 1:9 promises us?"

She sure did. "Do you want it in King James, New American Standard, or the Amplified?"

That should have been my first clue that this was not going to be an easy walk to success.

We argued spiritual matters extensively. No progress.

So then I started explaining about good germs and bad germs and how they're spread. This was before AIDS, remember.

Not a glimmer of progress.

Then she interrupted me to launch into a five-minute explanation of why all that didn't really apply to her.

To make a long story not quite so long, I worked on her six ways from Tuesday, using logic, using commonsense, using book passages, even falling back on a paternalistic *"Now Dora, your doctor and I are both medically trained. If we tell you . . ."*

Nothing.

Nothing worked. When she walked out of our lives, she was still seeking to evade germs sixty times an hour because somehow they were going to breach her defenses and do something. She simply would not listen to us, would not accept our reassurances or counsel.

If only I knew then what we know today. If only I had the tools then that we have today. We could have helped that unfortunate woman in a matter of weeks.

## The Nature of Obsessive-Compulsive Disorder

Dora was caught in a biochemical trap, and until the biochemical aspect was corrected, neither her reason nor ours could ever break through her repetitive, cycling, terrifying thoughts.

Obsession is a mental fixation with something, thoughts

you can't shake. In our culture, if you listen to the songs, "true love" is an obsession. "Can't Get You Out of My Mind." "You're My Everything." "Night and Day." A laudable emotion, love is stretched to a damaging extreme.

Compulsion is an irrepressible urge to do something, usually something unnecessary or repetitive, or to behave in a particular way. Hair pulling and nail biting are often compulsive. A colleague tells of a ten-year-old child whose compulsion was to clean up her room. She spent hours a day dusting, sweeping, putting everything in precise order and arrangement. She never invited friends in because they would mess something up. A commendable activity, cleaning one's room was stretched to a damaging extreme.

Obsessions and compulsions are not weird thoughts and behaviors. They are ordinary thoughts and behaviors constantly recycling, magnified by repetition into something weird. They intrude and will not be banished. They become damaging when they impede our social lives, interfere with daily living, and destroy happiness and contentment. At the very extreme, particularly when augmented by other mental problems, they can lead to violence, crime, and self-destruction.

Ten years ago, we thought obsessive-compulsive disorder was rare. We also believed that it started in late adolescence or early adulthood, and that once a person was diagnosed as obsessive-compulsive, that person's prognosis was very poor. Boy, were we wrong!

Obsessive-compulsive disorder (OCD) affects perhaps 2 to 3 percent of Americans. We see it now as a rather common psychiatric disorder. Some call it the Hidden Epidemic. It is probably underdiagnosed, because OCD sufferers often do their best to keep their problem concealed. It's a secret disorder, rife with shame, which translates as a lifetime of misery, worry, and isolation.

One-third of OCD victims experience onset before age fifteen. Another considerable percentage fall victim in their thirties. Dora, age thirty-three, was such a case. Moreover, today we can effect a cure in nearly any of these victims, young or old. The prognosis for complete recovery is very good in most cases. That was certainly and sadly untrue when, as a rank beginner, I sat down with Dora.

## The Mechanics of OCD

In Chapter 4 we introduced the concept of kindling, the phenomenon by which nerves misfire and touch each other off, causing a reaction that far exceeds the response needed. A similar phenomenon can influence cyclic thinking and cyclic behavior, the crux of obsession and compulsion.

Something triggers a thought, and that thought triggers the same thought, which triggers the thought over again, and so on. It may be a rapidly cycling thought, as when a fragment of a song gets stuck in your head. Notice that complex music usually does not get stuck. You don't keep hearing the whole of Beethoven's ninth symphony; only the "Ode to Joy" keeps intruding.

It may be a fairly slow thought or behavior cycle, taking a day or longer to complete. For example, there was Jerry. Jerry kept his car up. He checked the oil, made sure the turn signals worked, topped off the gas tank, vacuumed it, did the windows, and touched up the perpetual wax job.

Every day.

Every single day.

His ragged determination is typical of persons with a compulsion run amok. It becomes all-consuming.

## Identifying Obsessive-Compulsive Behavior

The case cited above is an extreme example of obsessive-compulsive behavior. However, mild, innocuous forms of OCD are common. People, including you, can slip in and out of something akin to OCD very easily. Some OCD characteristics are actually normal in everyday life.

## Normal Repetitive Reactions to Life

**The song that gets stuck in the mind.** A friend of mine complained of hearing the theme song to *Gilligan's Island* playing over and over in his head. "I tried to shake it by sheer force of will," he said, "but that didn't work. Finally, it went away by itself."

Getting a song "stuck" in your head is a common example of an obsessive condition in normal, everyday life. So is the nagging memory of an irritating television commercial.

**Preoccupation with tasks and details.** Often we become obsessive-compulsive with life's minor tasks and details: vacuuming the rug at a set time on a set day each week; balancing the checkbook the minute the bank statement comes in the mail.

Even leisure activities can become compulsive. I knew a fellow who spent an hour and a half each morning compulsively reading the morning newspaper. He couldn't even finish breakfast until he'd gone through every section and done the crossword. His actual obsession (other than the crossword) was that he might miss something of interest. He couldn't skim; he had to read every article word by word.

His wife, a no-nonsense woman with a dour, dry sense of humor, suggested that he clip the puzzle out and do it on the bus to work and read the rest of the paper standing up.

Desperate to cut his time loss, he took her up on it and broke his compulsion. He wasn't as eager to dwell on every little detail when he had to stand up while reading.

**Gnawing uncertainties.** A television advertisement several years ago played heavily upon this common obsession. In the ad, a husband and wife are embarking on a car trip. The wife tells her husband to turn around and go back home so she can make certain she unplugged her iron. Apparently this happened quite often, because the husband pulls an iron out from behind the driver's seat and says, "There. Satisfied?"

"That's not the iron I use," she responds in alarm. They

return home to find their house ablaze and the fire department trying to save what's left of it. A firefighter accusingly holds up the apparent cause, a fried iron. The ad was for an iron that turns itself off after a certain period of time.

All of us have gnawing uncertainties that plague us. Irritating and frustrating as they might be, these subacute reactions to life are manageable. At the very least they dissipate eventually.

However, multiply these common little quirks many times over until they disturb your thoughts constantly, render you practically immobile socially, torment you, prey upon you every waking hour—then you have an obsessive-compulsive disorder.

## The Characteristics of True OCD

Dora's head was disconnected from her heart, you might say. What she "knew" rationally and what she "knew" emotionally were altogether different things. Reason and obsession/compulsion—O/C—work at cross-purposes.

**The O/C is senseless.** Remember the childhood ditty, "Step on a crack, you'll break your mother's back"? How often we as children assiduously avoided stepping on a crack, not because we believed the ditty might actually contain some truth, but . . . but there wasn't really any reason. We just did it.

That is exactly the case with an OCD. A logical reason for the behavior doesn't exist.

We once counseled a man who *had* to step on every crack in the sidewalk. In reference to the childhood ditty, he shrugged his shoulders and said, "Maybe I have something against my mother." He didn't, not that we could find. However kooky it would have been, resenting his mother would at least have been a reason of sorts. He couldn't identify any reason for his compulsivity.

**The O/C can seem destructive.** All too frequently, we find OCD victims fearing they will shoot themselves in the foot, so to speak. Their compulsive behavior threatens to cause them great pain or embarrassment. A nice Christian woman was tempted to swear profusely on the telephone even though such speech habits would ruin her business. A fellow working in an office completes less than half the work expected of him because he runs to the men's room a dozen times an hour to wash his hands. He's been told his job is on the line, but it doesn't slow his compulsion down a bit.

**The O/C cannot be suppressed.** Dora repeatedly claimed she couldn't stop her bad thoughts about germs. No matter what she did, no matter how she tried to distract herself, they intruded. Very well, we suggested, simply ignore them. She couldn't.

The compulsive hand-washer cannot long deny the urge to wash his hands. "Yes," cries the rational friend or counselor, "but if you just tried a little harder—if only you wanted to badly enough."

It is not a matter of will. These urges and thoughts cannot be quelled by the mind.

**The O/C pits reason against reality.** Picture yourself riding a horse along a forest trail. You're not all that comfortable with horses, but you are with a group of equestrians and besides, it's a lovely day. Someone yells, "Look out!" Before you know what's happening, your horse bolts forward. You hang on for dear life, but that isn't helping your plight. You must stop the horse. You pull on the reins, but the horse doesn't stop or slow down. Free of control, the horse takes you anywhere it wants to, which just happens to be underneath low branches that swat you in the face and threaten to pull you off the horse.

The OCD sufferer is riding a runaway horse, powerless to change the situation and knowing all control is lost.

This is the real heartbreaker of obsessive-compulsive behavior: the victim knows the O/C is irrational. He feels the urgent call to resist this ridiculous or dangerous behavior. Almost never does the victim rationalize the behavior as being normal. Still he keeps trying to quell the disorder, or wants to.

Although it functions beyond the victim's control, OCD usually takes some predictable form. We see the same compulsions, the same or similar obsessions over and over in our practice.

## Signs and Symptoms of True OCD

Sufferers of obsessive-compulsive disorders usually exhibit one or more of the following symptoms.

### Obsessive Mind-Sets

Fear and disgust can take on obsessive proportions. A person may feel fear (*strong* fear, not just wariness) or disgust concerning bodily functions, particularly those of an excretory or sexual nature. Body secretions and wastes are not just unpleasant but are unbearably revolting.

A person may fear contamination or infection by someone or something. We frequently encounter persons so terrified of contracting AIDS that they repeatedly have themselves tested for HIV, even though they are subject to virtually no possible exposure.

Persons may be preoccupied with symmetry or exactness. We knew one couple who spent five years (the length of their marriage) rearranging a display on a living room table. She favored a casual arrangement, eccentric yet balanced; he needed the lamp, figurine, and decorative ashtray set in a perfect unilateral triangle. He would arrange it his way. She'd come along the next morning and change it. That night, he'd change it back. Do you know how hard it is to wear out an ashtray? They came close to doing it.

A fear of crime, disaster, or harm may be coupled with a fear that the OCD victim is somehow responsible for it. We've dealt with people driven by a repetitive thought that they might commit a theft; they might hurt or even kill someone; they might commit sexual assault; they might give someone their cold, even if they have no cold. Is this nonsense? Absolutely. Yet it is very real.

Persons fear that they might say the wrong thing, blurt an obscenity, or insult others. They may develop a morbid fascination with certain sounds, words, numbers, or mental images.

All these diverse mind-sets share the commonality that they prey endlessly on the person's thoughts.

## Ritual Behavior

Grooming compulsions, such as tooth-brushing or showering, take on a ritual meaning quite apart from cleanliness. Or the ritual may evidence itself as a need to repeatedly clean certain items in the house—the silver, the glassware, the carpet, the garage.

The person may be compelled to check things. It's prudent to check the locks on the doors and windows before going to bed, but the O/C victim checks them fifty times every night before bedtime.

The person may touch certain things in a ritual manner. For example, one elderly lady rapped on the jamb each time she went out her kitchen door (and that could be dozens of times a day in summer). "That's to chase away the wood sprites," she fondly told her grandchildren. She had the grandkids believing in druidic woodland creatures for years. Later, her family refurbished her house, took out the rotting wooden door frame, and installed aluminum.

Hoarding, a rather arcane ritual, can become compulsive. Paul Meier tells of a man named Roy who retired and moved from Kansas City to Phoenix/Sun City. Before the move, his neighbors came by to help him and his wife pack. Roy's wife, an inveterate knitter, had seven large cartons of yarn, which was a bit excessive but not irrational. But Roy's stash? Piles of not-yet-read magazines were stacked head-high in the corners of the rooms.

Anyone can get behind in reading, but Roy also hoarded stacks and stacks of unread newspapers, some dated three years earlier. He claimed there were articles of interest he intended to clip, he just hadn't got around to it yet. Frustrated when Roy refused to dispose of anything, his neighbors started boxing and labeling cartons "trash." When he got to Sun City, he rented two public storage bays for the reading matter he was going to get to one of these days.

Some O/C persons may count repeatedly to a particular number. Call it an O/C mantra without spiritual meaning.

Children develop rituals unlike anything you've ever seen. They're good at repetitive activities, magical thinking, and worrying. Dora was an amateur compared to the average O/C child who thinks the world and God all pivot around the self. Children may develop as a ritual or obsessive-compulsive behavior the need to receive approval. All children need approval, of course; we're talking here about extreme cases.

## Religious Doubts and Obsessions

In our practice we come across religious obsessions very often. One such obsession can be forgiveness, a common worry among people with religious obsessions.

Similar to the ritual of asking for forgiveness is the need by some O/Cs to ardently confess their sins. A person may have spent the last four days sick in bed but she will have something serious to confess nonetheless.

Another common fear involves salvation. Am I truly saved? Have I lost God's grace toward me? People raised in the Christian church may become obsessed by a fear that they have committed an unpardonable sin, though they cannot define it. Religious leaders point to the healthy nature of doubt. Doubt drives us to seek the truth, and in so doing we emerge stronger—to a point. When O/C doubts dig in, a person's faith crumbles amid the cyclic sick thinking.

## Obsessive Slowness

"That's my husband! Slow!" snorted a woman acquaintance. "The kids and I are long finished with dinner, but he's just barely getting started. To keep him company, I'll get out my needlework and work at the table. I've crocheted whole afghans just waiting for him to finish his dinner. And he doesn't even take second helpings very often."

While the woman exaggerated about completing an afghan at one sitting, her point is well made. Still, this isn't what we mean exactly by obsessive slowness.

Obsessively slow persons may take twenty minutes to brush their teeth and two hours to vacuum out the car. They may lose time at the start of the workday because they must carefully and perfectly arrange every object in their work area before they can begin working. They may slip out repeatedly to wash their hands or perform some other ritualistic time killer. Whereas everyone else is off and running, these people are still getting organized two hours later.

We consider persons to be obsessively slow if they require three or more times the number of minutes to complete a task than does the average person.

## Related Disorders

A certain percent of OCD victims will develop a rapidly cycling nerve-muscle behavior, such as a motor tic or a grimace. So is hypochondria, wherein the person obsessively believes the worst regarding his or her health. Related body-dysmorphic disorders plague victims with obsessive thoughts that their bodies are defective.

Tourette's syndrome, marked by eruptive motor or vocal tics, is a form of compulsion with no obsession driving it. A Tourette's patient may burst forth with animal-like grunts or obscenities, or display a dip of the head or a jerking motion. Tourette's is an example of the widely varied causes for OCD phenomena. One-third of persons with Tourette's will also show other O/C problems, and the O/C difficulties may cause more trouble than the Tourette's itself. A genetic factor may be involved in Tourette's syndrome.

Sydenham's chorea (a nervous jumpiness), certain types of Parkinson's disease, Huntington's disease, and epilepsy seem to be linked to OCD. They appear to be basal ganglia disorders, which links OCD to basal ganglia problems.

## Unwelcome Companions of OCD

A significant percent of OCD victims will experience depression at some time. The depression may be triggered by cause and effect or as a reaction to the debilitation of the disorder.

Mania and OCD are rarely seen together. But alcoholism and drug abuse are more common among OCD victims than in the general population.

OCD victims may suffer from anxiety. Technically speaking, OCD may be considered a form of anxiety disorder. OCD commonly appears along with panic and phobic disorders. Personality disorders, such as avoidance, histrionic, and dependence problems, frequently accompany OCD. Tourette's syndrome occurs in 7 percent of OCD cases; that's twice as much as in the general population.

All this is very important when it comes to dealing with OCD. We have to approach the whole person, and that often means tackling more than one disorder at once, ideally to conquer them all. The miracle drug that helps one problem, though, may not touch another, or worse, it may exacerbate the other problem.

## The Causes of OCD

How did Dora become so tangled up in her persistent bad thoughts and attendant worries about forgiveness? What did she think about that started the whole tragic mess? What triggers in her world touched off her OCD?

A generation ago, our understanding of things like OCD was limited to psychological and behavioral theories. Behaviorists suggest that OCD is a wild, maladaptive attempt to reduce anxiety about something. The person feels threatened by a thought or situation that is beyond that person's control. To gain some sort of control, however irrational, the person comes up with a magical response, which becomes the obsessive thought or compulsive ritual.

In the last few years, however, we've been developing increasingly sophisticated ways to examine the molecular anatomy and biochemistry of the brain and nervous system. From these methods, we're learning fascinating things about the chemical basis for strange behavior and thought.

## The Biological Basis for OCD

**Brain imaging and functioning studies.** PET scans, MRIs, and CT scans—they sound like something out of *Star Wars*. We use these techniques to build computer images of what is happening inside a living, working brain.

PET is positron-emission tomography. With it we can see how glucose, a sugar, is used in different regions of the brain. Sugar is the cells' primary energy source. Where it is metabolized fastest is where the greatest activity is taking place. We have learned from PET scans that a lot seems to be happening in the frontal lobes and basal ganglia of OCD patients.

MRI, magnetic resonance imaging, is used for many different diagnostic tests. It too seems to point toward action in the frontal lobe and basal ganglia. So do electroencephalograms, the tests where wires are attached all over the skull.

**Cause and effect observations.** A patient being treated for depression may, for example, also respond with reduced OCD symptoms. Not always. But often enough that doctors take note. **Anafranil** (clomipramine), **Prozac** (fluoxetine), **Luvox** (fluvoxamine), **Paxil** (paroxetine), and sometimes **Zoloft** (sertraline) are among such drugs.

An elaborate and extensive medical literature records how people respond to the various treatments they receive. Although drugs and procedures are designed to tackle one problem, we take note if they make some other problem better or worse. We try to understand why the body responds the way it does to these various treatments.

People who recover from rheumatic fever occasionally develop a neurological problem called Sydenham's chorea.

These people are far more likely to also display OCD than the general population. The chorea is a chemical problem in the basal ganglia. This datum becomes one thin strand of evidence that OCD also has a basal ganglia factor. When that strand is woven in with the strands derived independently from PET scans and other studies, it adds to a strong rope of evidence pointing to a biological basis for OCD.

Sometimes, when worse comes to worst, doctors will surgically create a lesion in the brain to stop effects of OCD that cannot be stopped any other way. Because these surgical interventions work at least part of the time, we can assume that some of the unwanted activity takes place in that particular frontal lobe area of the brain where the lesion is placed.

OCD patients respond so markedly to specific serotonin reuptake inhibitors—these are the antidepressants such as Prozac and Zoloft—that we believe there is a strong connection between OCD and the way the neurotransmitters function.

Biochemistry, however, is not the only seat of OCD.

## Psychological Considerations in OCD

We see several psychological factors that weigh heavily on the cyclic thoughts and behaviors of OCD.

**Displaced anxiety.** Many psychiatrists find that OCD may be linked to anxiety. Dora was an anxious person. Perfectionistic behavior may appear, and she was a perfectionist at home—all the dishes arranged just so in the cabinets, all the cans lined up just so in the pantry, and woe to anyone who rumpled one of the decorative pillows on the sofa.

Worry enters in. Dora was a worrier. Worrying about whether God truly forgives is a heavy concern for people who were taught Christian tenets, for God's forgiveness is a cornerstone of the faith.

The problems of OCD, then, unite with others to form a solid bastion against reality.

**Defense mechanisms.** Unrelated to OCD, strictly speaking, is the obsessive-compulsive personality disorder. We make the distinction but laypersons often do not. We include discussion of it here not because OCD and Obsessive-Compulsive Personality Disorder are related but because the lay reader may well confuse them.

People who treat patients with Obsessive-Compulsive Personality Disorder examine the defense mechanisms these patients set up. They usually are remarkably similar. Again and again we see isolation and displacement, reaction formations, and magical thinking.

Isolation and displacement mean something a little different in this context than they do in popular usage. Let's say Dora was employing this defense mechanism upon the unexpected death of her father. She isolated herself not so much from the world around her as from her own feelings. They hurt too much, so she separated from them. She displaced them, put them aside.

People commented favorably about her composure at the funeral, about her iron control of her emotions. The truth is, she wasn't controlling her emotions; she had isolated herself from them. She knew the facts of the situation: Daddy was dead and about to be buried. But she did not feel the anxiety, the anger, the depression, the sorrow. She kept herself above and beyond the emotionally loaded situation. To the unknowing observer, she appeared a pillar of strength, a person on whom others could lean. Certainly her composure helped the other family members through the funeral, but it wrecked Dora. Had she openly acknowledged her pain, she could have dealt with it in a healthier manner.

**Reaction formations.** Another fancy psychiatric term, *reaction formation* is the development of a personality or character trait that is the opposite of the patient's reality. For example, when a person's life gets messy and difficult, the person reacts by making the manageable world incredibly neat to make up for the uncontrollable messiness. Dora did that. She became a superneatnik.

To some extent, "Step on a crack, you'll break your

mother's back," is a reaction formation. It's the opposite intent of what you really want.

Reaction formations are tricky to identify and analyze, but they say a lot about the person's mental health.

**Magical thinking.** Throwing a pinch of salt over your shoulder when you spill some is magical thinking. Although you may think no one takes that kind of thing seriously, when O/C grabs hold of a person, strange magical thinking becomes unmagical.

Dora's magical thinking went like this: "If I can somehow avoid all germs and contamination, I will feel safe and in control of my life."

The good news is that the people who are enmeshed in magical thinking are not psychotic. In fact, this coping mechanism is an excellent defense against psychosis.

**Emotional makeup.** We look carefully at the anger, fear, and love the patient displays. We look also for secret loneliness, perhaps a quest for certainty (an O/C in itself). How is the patient handling these universal emotions? To what degree are the emotions under control? Are they exerting control over the patient?

**Ambivalence.** In determining the psychological components of OCD, we look at the interplay between strong emotions, especially love and anger. This can be a powerful force in a person's life, creating great emotional stress.

Dora loved her father, but she was intensely angry with him because now he was gone and beyond her influence. She couldn't love him anymore or get mad at him or hold him.

But everyone has these feelings. Why would it hit Dora the wrong way? Because many other factors that contribute to OCD were also nailing her. When a series of factors pile up together, OCD is one way the human psyche might respond.

All these lines of evidence are gathered together and considered as we seek new ways to deal with OCD.

# Psychological Triggers of OCD

Dora never asked the question she ought to have asked: "What got me started on this?" When she came to us we didn't know enough about OCD to help her.

What tips OCD victims over the edge into the cyclic behavior? If it's an exterior event or situation—that is, something that happens to them from outside themselves—why can't OCD victims save themselves by force of will? Apparently, however, it was force of will that got them into it.

Researchers have come up with several triggers that seem to precipitate O/C thoughts and behaviors. Chief among them are sexual difficulties and marriage problems, loss of a loved one or near loss (for example, a stroke or other catastrophic illness), and pregnancy and delivery. Frustration and overwork can tip a person into O/C problems.

A few researchers claim that behavior such as obsessive slowness or time-consuming rituals (hand-washing, arranging the paper clips) may be a passive-aggressive resistance to what the persons feels is intolerable or unacceptable work.

Many medical writers have noted that stress is a big factor. Interestingly, they also noted that when the tension was either reduced or changed drastically, OCD patients sometimes improved spontaneously. For example, people who enter wartime military service may show improvement in OCD symptoms.

Once the psychological trigger allows some little response to get going—hypochondria, real or imagined pain, anxiety, weak feelings, depression—the problem begins to feed on itself. Brain chemistry adjusts to the new reality. The symptoms dig in and worsen. The brain chemistry adjusts further.

The brain's chemistry, incidentally, is always changing and adjusting to the outside world. When you go to a funny movie and laugh your head off, your brain's chemistry is changed for the better. "Laughter is good medicine" has a basis in biological fact. When you are in mourning, your chemistry shifts accordingly. When you are super-cold or super-hot, the chemistry does its best to allow for the changes.

These changes are usually temporary in that they constantly fluctuate as conditions alter. But if something like an O/C sits down and camps, the unwelcome change the O/C precipitates can become harder to correct. The longer you are locked into the cyclic thoughts or behavior, the harder it is going to be to adjust the chemistry back to normal.

We take all this into account when designing a treatment, and we're starting to understand what works well and what doesn't. Miracle drugs? Miracles indeed! They play a big part in achieving a successful treatment. They may often multiply the good effects of treatment based upon strategies such as behavior modification. What used to be a terrible expected outcome for people with OCD has become a very good one, by and large.

## Treating OCD

If Dora were to walk into our offices today, what could we do for her that we could not do five or ten years ago?

### Step 1: Break the Cycle

By the time the patient comes for professional help, the O/Cs have been cooking away for a long time. OCD is not something people trot right to the doctor with immediately.

Dora was certain she could whip this thing if only she tried hard enough. A part of her certainty came from her advisors and counselors. They all told her she could. They assured her that it was in her head, and her head could cure it.

Dora spent years fighting her obsessive thoughts. During those years, the O/C had plenty of time to become so deeply ingrained that a water cannon could not blast it loose. When she finally came to us, the cycling was impossible to reach with normal psychotherapy.

Incidentally, we've found that the usual psychoanalytic approaches don't work well with OCDs. This is why the prognosis was so poor in the past. Simple behavior modification techniques don't cut it. The relaxation techniques that work so well with phobics don't help OCD. Children are particularly prone to OCD and particularly refractory to any psychological attempts to dislodge the O/Cs.

The only way to reach the patient is to break the ingrained cycles. The only good way to break the O/C cycles is with drugs. Once the damaging cycles are broken, then the patient can take over mentally and work on the underlying problems.

When Dora came to us, either we did not yet have those drugs or we didn't know the drugs we had would help OCD the way they do.

## Step 2: Find and Deal with Factors Affecting OCD

Had we worked with Dora today, we could have identified several factors. The untimely death of her father was one. That she had a two-month-old infant at the time her father died was two.

Occasionally, psychological factors combine with medical or genetic factors to influence the patient's problem. But exploring such things rarely influences the cycles. We would have found causes perhaps, but the effect—the OCD—was an independent monster in itself.

There are two medical responses to OCD that are used only as a last resort. One is electric therapy. It may provide a temporary improvement. Another is surgery to clip connections in certain portions of the brain. We'll find ways to help, but these are options of the most drastic sort for the most drastic cases.

Let's say a compulsive hand-washer comes in for help. In fact, just for illustration, let's say it's you.

Until you were fired from your job, you tried to keep your hand-washing compulsion under wraps. Now, with your life in shambles, you've come for help to stop this maddening behavior.

After we've used drugs to break the cycle of constant

hand-washing, we go to work on your deep-seated anxieties and other problems.

"I don't have any," you insist. "I can handle the things that come my way. They aren't any different from anyone else's, and everyone else gets by okay."

Pride—we get past that first. You persist in the idea that you are a weakling because you can't break the cycle all by yourself. Can you control how your gastrointestinal tract digests its food? No? Well, neither can you control your brain chemistry; same thing, different chemical system.

We find you are incredibly germ-conscious. You yelled when your spouse failed to wash the table grapes to your satisfaction. You don't let the kids handle money. Before you lost your job, you kept a disinfectant spray at work and sprayed your phone anytime you suspected someone else had used it. You go through an elaborate sterilization ritual in public bathrooms. All is designed to keep other people's germs from getting to you. (Hey, it's hard to open the washroom door with your elbow.)

We deal with the underlying psychological causes by several means.

**Behavior therapy.** This has been one approach. We help you desensitize to the object of your O/C. We may use exposure or response prevention. Or, some may use aversive conditioning.

For example, Jane experiences a terrible fear of ants and avoids any place where ants might be. She won't even sit on her patio. Her phobia develops into an O/C when she begins mentally fixating on the possibility that ants are crawling around behind her back. Three or four times a day, she paints cayenne pepper water on her baseboards because an environmentally conscious neighbor told her cayenne pepper infusion drives away ants. Imagine her terror and dismay when she finds a whole line of ants between her kitchen sink and the sugar bowl, merrily disregarding the cayenne.

Jane's compulsive behavior had not yet become ingrained, so we might be able to forego drug intervention. It's always preferable. Desensitizing Jane would involve talking about ants, looking at pictures of them, possibly visiting the entomology department at the local university, and eventually sitting out on the patio while ants scurry about. Whereas some people profit from a course of Valium while undergoing desensitization, most, like Jane, don't need it.

Certainly we draw the line at ants in Jane's house, as does she. But now she does not turn her baseboards sticky brown with cayenne pepper infusion. When she sprays, she does so for the normal reasons people don't want ants in their kitchens and not out of phobia and O/C. Desensitizing has helped reason master the O/C behavior.

Aversion therapy makes punishment the immediate consequence for doing something you want to quit doing. If every time you wash your hands or take a puff of a cigarette, you get a mild but noticeable electric jolt, that's aversion therapy. To be effective (and some claim its effects are very temporary at best), the aversive reaction must follow immediately on the heels of the behavior to be stopped.

**Stress reduction.** Many O/C thoughts and behaviors either are brought on by stress or are exacerbated by stress. Any reduction of stress that we can achieve helps the patient. We preach stress management techniques to most of our patients because most are adversely affected by stress, but OCD patients are especially affected.

**Insight-oriented therapy.** Psychiatrists and psychotherapists have been debating the efficacy of insight-oriented therapies in the medical literature. We use this therapy because we've seen it work.

When Anxiety A expresses itself as Anxiety B or an obsession or compulsion, we try to work backward through B to A, then deal with A. This covers all the bases and helps the patient emerge victorious. The people for whom this method works best are those who enjoy learning and accruing knowledge; they're likely to take an objective look at their own problems, gather insights about those problems, and thereby become better able to deal with them.

Because your urgent need to wash your hands is held in abeyance, we appeal to your intelligence. You had trouble breaking the cycle, but now that it's cracked you can smash it altogether, all by yourself. This appeals to your pride and ego, and rightly so. Reason at last has a chance to make a dent in your responses.

We go beyond the compulsive behavior to your obsession with germs. In several sessions we both listen to your perceptions of your attitude toward germs and insert facts that would be useful to you. Because you are rational, the facts help you see your obsession. "Yeah, I really do go overboard." Then we might use some behavioral therapy, desensitization perhaps, to help you work past your obsession. Cognitive therapy frequently can make a difference.

But it doesn't end there. What are the deep, deep reasons for your anxiety and its manifestation as an OCD? If you do not undergo psychotherapy to uncover these deep reasons, you are going to fall back into an anxiety response or an OCD. Like a dandelion that keeps sprouting unless you kill the root, OCD and other anxiety phenomena will just keep reappearing, perhaps in some other context.

Therefore, insist on this final step of recovery, uncovering the roots. It will be painful. It will be inconvenient. But it is imperative to your recovery.

**Support.** Most of all, we build a scaffold of support for the person trying to recover. For example, we engage the family in helping the patient realize when obsessions are surfacing, when compulsions are starting to cycle. It is telling, we believe, that the majority of patients who have problems and suffer difficulty getting past their problems are unmarried or otherwise alone in life. Love and family make a huge difference.

We also support the person with the clinic's resources. The family cannot do everything; we fill in. We cannot do everything; the family makes a vital difference.

## Step 3: Build Spiritual Strength

Many of our clients claim a place in the family of God as well as of humankind. Every person possesses a spiritual dimension, and our Christian patients are particularly aware of that fact. We do not neglect the spiritual aspect, for the spiritual dimension is the most powerful of inner guides.

The fork of our spiritual input possesses five tines.

**Remember grace, mercy, and forgiveness.** In the raucous battles displayed in the media—the Religious Right this and the Christian Coalition that, the forces to promote school prayer here or ban it there—we lose sight of the Cross. The Cross is grace (more blessing than we deserve), mercy (less punishment than we deserve), and forgiveness (total erasure of our confessed sins). In the clinic, we emphasize getting back to the roots of faith: the Cross—its blessings and its burdens. Everything else is secondary to God's work.

**Rest in Christ.** Put aside legalism and introspection for the moment. Jesus Christ the person reaches out to us, His persons. In the clinic we help our Christian clients touch Jesus Himself without the baggage and adornments of dogma. Jesus. Just Jesus. The unbeliever cannot begin to grasp the comfort of simply knowing Jesus.

**Stand on Scripture.** Most of us at the clinic are big on memorization of Scripture. It's not just a pious gesture; memorization possesses very practical advantages. With memorization you have the words of God at your fingertips, anytime you need them. None of us claims memorization is a cure-all. Look at Dora. She knew Scripture inside out. It didn't help her break the cycle. But had we been able to break through and free her from her obsessive concerns, in her freedom she could have used the verses to full advantage.

First John 4:8: "God is love." What a comfort that could be to a person like Dora! John 6:37: "The one who comes to Me I will by no means cast out."

Yes, there's power and comfort in the Scriptures.

**Understand the misunderstood.** The unpardonable sin has been debated for two thousand years. If it is giving you a serious problem, gather the different opinions about it, understand them, study the Scripture, and then let God lead you the way He wants you to go.

Dwelling on some misunderstood detail of Scripture is obsessive in itself. Instead . . .

**Focus on the big picture.** We encourage our Christian clients to do this as much as anything else. A verse is not Scripture. Work on an encompassing perspective. The broader your understanding of God, the better you can rest in Him when stress and triggers and all these other plights descend upon you.

We see then that drugs without other therapy avail little or nothing. Therapy alone may or may not effect permanent, positive change. The psychotropic drugs work to make healing and spiritual insight possible.

## Medications for Treating OCD

You have already been introduced to some of these medications in previous chapters, and you will meet some again in the chapters that follow.

An interesting side note: when researchers test the efficacy of drugs on OCD, they find that placebos hardly work at all.

**Anafranil** (clomipramine HCl) is used in treating depression. It blocks receptors that take serotonin up out of action, thereby making more serotonin available for nerve tips to use as they send messages. When Anafranil is metabolized, the product that results blocks reuptake of norepinephrine, another neurotransmitter. This makes both neurotransmitters more readily available. It takes at least two weeks, usually more, to show beneficial effects, but unwanted side effects show up quickly.

Anafranil has been tested on children and apparently can be used safely and effectively on them. It has been used effectively on adults for up to a year. It produces no tolerance and no addiction.

**Prozac** (fluoxetine HCl), one of the SSRIs and the darling of the antidepressants, also does a pretty good job with OCD.

**Luvox** (fluvoxamine maleate) seems to work well as an antidepressant, but it really shines as a drug to break the OCD cycles. Relatively new to the market, it may hold great promise because of its touted limited side effects.

**Haldol** (haloperidol) reduces the symptoms of Tourette's syndrome and may dampen the kindling that encourages OCD. It also serves well as an antipsychotic. It can reduce aggression and explosive excitability in adults and children (you know, when they blow up in your face over some trivial or fancied irritation). Haldol can induce the dangerous side effects called tardive dyskinesia and neuroleptic malignant syndrome.

**Klonopin** (clonazepam), one of the benzodiazepines, helps with seizures and convulsions. It depresses the central nervous system, but it may also quell OCD at times.

**MAOIs,** monoamine oxidase inhibitors, primarily **Nardil** (phenelzine) and **Parnate** (tranylcypromine sulfate), sometimes do not work well, and when used with other psychotropic drugs can cause serious synergistic problems. However, they may occasionally help.

**BuSpar** (buspirone HCl) is very occasionally employed in the treatment of anxiety and the OCD into which anxiety sometimes mutates. When used, it generally augments other drugs.

## CHAPTER 6

*You know the story about Dr. Jekyll and Mr. Hyde? Well, that's me. I'm just as out of control as Mr. Hyde.*

A HOSPITALIZED MANIC-DEPRESSIVE PATIENT

# MOOD SWINGS AND MANIA

The sun was shining, the birds were singing, the mall was open! Trina couldn't be happier. The mall was her natural habitat, and it was her day off from work.

Trina and her friend Patti arrived at the mall just as the stores were opening. Their first stop was the kitchen specialty store, where Trina bought a bread machine. Next stop, the music store (nine CDs), then the Gap (seven pairs of blue jeans and four shirts), then the specialty T-shirt store (birthday presents for five nieces and nephews). After a quick trip to the car to unload some of their packages, they headed next for the new bathroom-and-linen place (new towels, a water bed spread, a brass-and-crystal soap dish, two rugs, and a shower mat).

They paused long enough to eat lunch at the food court, where each had a supersalad, iced tea, and a slice of pecan pie, then it was on to the shoe store. (Trina didn't plan to stop there, but she was getting a blister so she bought a pair of sandals and wore them out of the store.)

Four stores later, their credit cards were warm to the touch. Trina and Patti then caught an afternoon movie at the cineplex, after which they retired from their day at the mall.

At home, Trina was ecstatic over her new purchases. Her happiness lingered . . . until her husband, Rick, came home.

Right away, Rick noticed the new towels, rugs, and soap dish; they had replaced bathroom towels and accessories less than a year old. He noticed unfamiliar music playing on the CD. He walked into the kitchen and watched Trina as she dumped ingredients into her new bread machine.

Rick was furious.

Two weeks later he sat in Paul Meier's office, so frustrated he couldn't clearly articulate his feelings. "It's . . . I don't know how to explain it. Trina goes on binges, and a few months later she turns sensible again. Then in a couple of months she'll go off on another spree. She saves money so well most of the time, but on the binges she spends more than I make."

"*We* make," Trina corrected. "I'm only spending my money, not yours."

"Yeah, but if you make a thousand dollars, you spend a thousand, and I have to pay the taxes on that thousand. And other expenses! You don't allow for—" and Rick took off on what was obviously a well-honed, standard lecture.

Trina dismissed it with, "He's so fussy."

Rick didn't realize it; Trina certainly didn't realize it; but she was exhibiting signs of a disorder labeled "mood swings" or "manic-depression."

What Rick perceived as her normal, sober side was actually a clinical depression. A staid and serious fellow, Rick liked Trina this way. She didn't wildly spend money. But her manic side sent her on raids at the mall, discount stores ("But, Honey! Look how much we saved!"), and flea markets.

To some degree, everybody experiences mood swings. They are the natural way we deal with the vicissitudes of life, rolling with the punches and enjoying the good times. These normal shifts do not seriously interfere with our work, parenting, or life in general.

In two situations, though, mood swings absolutely must be dealt with: if they reach a degree to which they hobble or damage our everyday functions, and if they for any reason pose a hazard to the self or others.

"What can be hazardous about a little shopping?" Trina asked, innocently.

Rick scowled at her. "Does the term 'credit rating' mean anything to you?"

## Measuring the Need for Correction

Trina's problem was a fairly mild form of the disorder. As frustrating as it was for Rick, and as damaging as it was on their bank account, it didn't severely disrupt Trina's ability to make it through life. Counseling and setting guidelines and rules (for instance, no shopping without Rick along) would probably be adequate to halt Trina's periodic sprees. Although the mood swings were present, and they did pose a problem, it was a manageable problem. We would consider medication for Trina as a last resort, when other things such as counsel failed, unless her depressions grew deeper or her manias more manic.

And that oftentimes happens. Frank describes such a case.

Some time ago I counseled a woman who was convinced she was the Virgin Mary. Her exasperated husband had brought her to the hospital because he didn't know what else to do.

"But I *am* the Virgin Mary!" She said it with such earnest conviction, it seemed hopeless to argue with her. She stood before me, arms akimbo, and as much as dared me to contradict her. Her black eyes were piercing. She was a very pretty woman, probably in her late twenties. Her husband, incidentally, was not named Joseph, nor was he a carpenter. He owned a combination bed-and-breakfast and restaurant.

A few things worked against her claim. For one, by her own admission, she had borne three children. For another, she was of Chinese descent; you don't exactly look for that in the mother of Christ. And of course, she was a good two thousand years out of sync with history.

But this young woman was deadly serious, and that made the situation totally serious. You could see the gravity of it etched in her husband's drawn and harried face.

I waved a hand toward the chairs in the conference room. "Please be seated, Mr. and Mrs. Wong."

"It's Mary," she said as she sat down.

"Mary." I chose a seat at an angle to the two of them so as not to appear confrontational.

Her husband looked like he had just chewed a sour pickle. "I'm very sorry for this bother, Doctor. I don't know how to deal with this. I've never seen anything like it before. I need advice, wise counsel," he confessed.

"I'm glad you two came in." I meant it, too. "You can seldom improve a problem by ignoring it. Let's—"

"It's not a problem," Mrs. Wong snapped. She appeared to be a woman who was constantly in motion. She didn't fidget the way a nervous or uncomfortable person would. She simply flowed from position to position, constantly rearranging her limbs, head, and torso.

I would soon get around to asking whether she was on prescribed or covert medications, which is the first thing to look for when a person displays aberrant behavior. First, we sketched out some personal medical history. I asked her husband, "When you say you've never seen anything like this, I presume you're saying no one else in her family—her relatives by blood—have presented problems of this sort."

She interrupted, "It's not a problem! I *am*. He's just going to have to live with that."

Mr. Wong winced. "No. Her mother is often quite depressed and is receiving treatment. Psychiatric counsel. Joan seems—"

"Mary," she said. Her hands danced a tarantella in her lap.

"Mary seems depressed at times. Other than that—no. No one in her family—mine either, for that matter—is, you know, crazy."

The three of us discussed Mrs. Wong's history and background for several minutes. Mary (Joan Wong) chattered in rapid-fire measure. She was not studied in her role. She had not read the Bible, and she did not know, for example, that the original Mary had a cousin named Elizabeth. She did attend church for two years, from age nine until age eleven, while she was staying with her Catholic aunt. She had stayed with her aunt because her father had died suddenly and her mother was incapacitated by grief and depression and unable to function as a parent for two years. Girl and woman, Joan/Mary had always been moody, but during the last few years, her mood swings had become increasingly wild and frightening.

And now this.

"Every once in a while, Joan . . . I mean, Mary . . . gets hyperactive and excitable. She can't sleep. She tears into a project without any warning, like the time she suddenly cleaned out the basement." Her husband shrugged helplessly. "But she never jumped off the deep end before. This began yesterday. I try to talk to her, but I might as well be talking to the wall."

When I counseled Mr. and Mrs. Wong, it was in the 1960s. We were experimenting with the drug properties of a naturally occurring salt, lithium carbonate. I was in on the trials, so I obtained approval to put Joan/Mary on Lithium. Two weeks later, not only was she Joan Wong again, her personality had stabilized. She had become a normal, happy, functioning Joan Wong (with a comfortably cluttered basement).

Her husband was so grateful, he wanted the city to name a street after me.

Joan represented the extreme high end of a broad spectrum, literally and figuratively. Hers was mania beyond all bounds, mania that had slipped into psychosis.

Joan's swing to mania squelched her ability to be an adequate mother to her three young children. She had lost touch with reality. Her problem demanded immediate help, and that help included the use of stabilizing drugs.

People need not swing to Joan Wong's extreme in order to become a hazard. For example, I know of a young woman who was a sheriff's deputy several years ago. A couple of times a year, she'd walk into her sergeant's office, hand him her service revolvers, and walk out. He knew what was happening. She was descending into one of her depressive moods, and she could not trust herself with her own weapons. He would assign her to desk duty, and a few weeks later she'd come back in and pick up her sidearms. The extreme depressive state having passed, she was safe to go back out on the streets.

Her sergeant explained, "I didn't mention any of that to the lieutenant because we were afraid they'd put her on furlough or maybe even dump her. When she's okay, she's such a darned good street cop that we don't want to lose her. She can talk a suicidal person off a bridge."

Added a self-serving coworker, "She's handling it all right. Besides, when she takes the desk work, we don't have to."

No one, including the woman, noticed that when she was at the manic end of her disorder, she took terrible chances, stepping into situations where the more prudent would not venture. Her fellow officers misidentified her behavior as bravery.

Mood swings certainly can disable without appearing dramatic. If they significantly alter your lifestyle, your effectiveness as a parent and spouse, or your work situation, they deserve attention.

Plain old depression and plain old mania are termed *unipolar*. That is, they hang around at one extreme of the spectrum or the other. Manic-depression is *bipolar*—in other words, swinging between two extremes. Let's look at the two extremes individually. Do either of these descriptive svndromes sound like you or someone you care about?

## Signs and Symptoms of Mania

Keep in mind that mania is not a black and white, either/or condition. We're talking about a range of intensity, a matter of degree. A considerable range of time is also involved; swings can last for hours, for days, for months. The diagnostic criteria psychiatrists use declare that the swing must last at least a week in order to be diagnosed as a manic episode.

### Increased Activity

Mania is characterized by a significant increase in activity level. A person functions in overdrive, and the temporarily elevated activity affects work, social situations, and marriage.

Trina felt an elevated sense of well-being. She did not notice her increased activity level because that's just the way you act when you feel good. Go, go, go. Right?

### Rapid Speech Pattern

Persons suffering a manic bout talk rapidly, intently, and constantly.

Rick claimed that Trina babbled nonstop during her ebullient moods. It irritated him. Trina in her quiet, pensive mood was the "real" Trina, the woman he married, as far as he was concerned.

### Racing Thoughts

Thoughts race out of control, like a brakeless semi on a downhill run. Thoughts seem so intense and scattered that you have trouble controlling them. The psychological term is "flight of ideas."

### Increased Distractibility

In a manic bout, persons cannot concentrate on any one thing for very long. They flit from project to project, thought to thought, deed to deed.

Trina did not spend a lot of time browsing in any one store. Instead she flitted from store to store, making purchases as she went.

## Inflated Self-Esteem

The person is ready to take on the world and win, setting high expectations and assuming he will meet them. In reality, the person is a midlevel government worker, but in the manic mode he is Alexander the Great preparing to conquer all the government's problems. We call it grandiosity.

## Shortened Sleep

Persons feel so good they don't want to waste time sleeping. They sleep less because they seem to need less sleep.

Joan was dragging boxes out of her basement at 2:00 A.M. Trina—and therefore, Rick—enjoyed increased sexual interest. Although that in itself was not a bad thing, it cut significantly into sleep time. In her manic mood Trina could take the decreased amount of sleep, but Rick had a hard time with it.

## Daredevil Behavior

During a manic bout, a person may walk too close to the edge, when normally she exercises a modicum of caution. Activities present a high potential for danger or loss. Shopping sprees, sexual indiscretions, reckless driving, foolish or impulsive business ventures are some examples.

One patient we counseled bought six cars in one day! (He subsequently sold three of them—at a loss.)

Another patient, a man who suffered a serious alcohol problem during his depressive states, tried to buy the world during his manic phases. New schemes, approximately two per year, were going to make him wealthy. He lost money in real estate, on a shar-pei breeding farm, at a soap sales scheme. Cried his wife, "Don't you know a Ponzi scheme when you see one? You can go to jail for that!"

The woman who was a sheriff's deputy endangered not just herself with her recklessness, but also other officers and civilians. Although her fellow workers were willing to go along with her manic-depressive flow, the hazard aspect made it imperative for her to seek help.

## Aggressive and Hostile Behavior

This was another symptom in the case of the deputy. If she lost patience with a felon, she was instantly in his face, big time.

Trina, normally quite a conservative driver, became aggressive during her manic phases. She ran stoplights, cut people off, and didn't think twice about maneuvering her little compact car across two or three crowded lanes of traffic in order to get to a turning lane.

# Signs and Symptoms of a Depressive Phase

The other side of the coin, a depressive state, may stand in sharp contrast to the manic state or differ from it only slightly. Again, this condition displays an amazingly wide spectrum of signs and symptoms.

## Feelings of Sadness

In the depressive state, persons feel sad or irritable for no specific reason. If a person feels down because she missed a promotion or lost a loved one, that's logical; there's a reason for the depressed feelings. Persons in a full-blown depressive state have consistent, overall feelings of pensiveness, with no apparent cause.

Premenstrual blues can cause mood swings of quite marked degree. We count them separately, for there's a strong implication of hormone imbalance there. They're explainable, probably even predictable.

## Loss of Pleasure

Favorite activities now hold no pleasure. For instance, sexual interest may decline, cherished hobbies are ignored, enjoyable events no longer hold any joy. Nothing seems worth the effort.

## Decreased Appetite

During a depressed state, a person's appetite takes a dive. Though not sick, she has no interest in eating.

Both Trina and Joan considered the decreased appetite a positive factor because it helped them keep their slim figures.

## Interrupted Sleep

Unlike the manic phase when a person feels like he doesn't need much sleep, persons in the depressive state want to sleep but have trouble doing so. They may wake up several times during the night or too early in the morning, or they take hours to fall asleep.

## Chronic Sluggishness

The person may feel like she's operating in slow motion. Her energy has bottomed out, and fatigue comes on easily, even with no apparent cause for it. It's hard to concentrate and make decisions.

## Low Self-Esteem

Feelings of worthlessness often characterize the depressive phase. A person may feel responsible for everyone else's problems. Guilt grows like mold in a shower stall.

At the very bottom of this sense of reduced self-worth, the person may think he's not worth keeping alive. Thoughts of death are recurrent. The person may think about suicide.

When Joan Wong felt low, she felt very, very low. That worried her husband as much as the mania did. Even more worrisome to her husband—and to her, during her "normal" periods—was the escalation of the mood swings. They were getting worse, her behavior was out of control during the extremes, and the question plagued them, "Where will this end?"

# Genetic Tendencies

When we diagnose manic-depression, we do not just look for the symptoms listed above. They are certainly a large part of it, but family history also plays a large part, both in the disease itself and in its diagnosis.

The tendency toward bipolar disorders seems to run in some families, as does depression. It's certainly not a sure thing, like eye color, for example. But there's a tendency. Relatives of people with a bipolar disorder are affected twenty times more often than are people in the general population. If both parents are bipolar, the children have a 50 percent chance of developing the disorder.

If several people in the extended family have problems maintaining emotional equilibrium, that tells us something about the kind of medication that might be appropriate. Is this a temporary disorder we're seeing, or is it innate? Will the person benefit from a short course of therapy, or is this a lifelong maintenance situation?

## Living with the Bipolar Person

Living with people like Joan or Trina can be miserable. Just ask their spouses. You can do some things, however, to ease circumstances considerably.

### Find a Self-Help Group

Knowing you are not the only person living with a manic-depressive can bring you peace of mind. Support groups provide opportunities to vent frustrations and develop solutions. You can learn a lot of good tips.

### Get a Manic to the Hospital

When mania builds beyond a person's control, he or she can become a hazard to the self or others. Hospitalization will prevent the person from embarrassing or harming self or others.

### Don't Be Fooled by Denial

Denial is intense in bipolars, particularly in a manic phase. Use your own counsel and step in when needed.

## Don't Take Their Anger Personally

In a wild mood swing, a person is ripe for fury, and is quite likely to project that anger onto you. It's part of the disorder, not the person's actual opinion of you. Don't take it personally.

## Monitor the Person's Caffeine Intake

We don't mean you should cut out the person's caffeine intake completely. Caffeine seems to help lithium balance. Completely eliminating caffeine—caffeinated soft drinks, tea and coffee—may cause the lithium level to rise.

## Keep the Doctor Informed of the Situation

A lot of things can mimic bipolar disorder—brain tumors and infections, HIV, multiple sclerosis, thyroid problems. A whole list of drugs can induce the disorder: anything with bromine, amphetamines, cocaine, TB drugs, prednisone. Make certain the doctor knows all medications the person is taking.

All that in mind, rest in the knowledge that bipolar disorder is a medical problem—a chemical imbalance—and medication can produce miracles in many, many people.

# Treatment of Manic-Depression and Mania

Standard treatment for manic-depression employs lithium in the form of a simple salt. As in the case of Joan Wong, lithium can work wonders. In the friend-or-foe balance of things, though, lithium can be a formidable foe. It has a vast and dangerous dark side.

## Lithium's Dark Side

Lithium is the lightest of the chemical elements classified as metals. It's so active and quirky, you never find it in its pure state. It always combines with other elements to form a salt or other compound. Closely related to sodium, lithium can change places with sodium under certain conditions and jump through most of the same chemical hoops that sodium does.

It's awfully hard, however, to build up a toxic level of sodium in the human body. It's very easy to do with lithium. And that is one of its biggest foe factors.

Lithium's toxicity level is very close to its therapeutic level. Stated differently, the margin between miracle and tragedy is a narrow one.

Certain persons are more susceptible to lithium poisoning than are most persons. Because lithium interacts with sodium in strange ways, we exercise great caution if the patient is using diuretics. Diuretics affect the body's sodium level anyway, and the combination of diuretic with lithium causes chemical imbalances. At the extreme, these imbalances can cause emotional or other psychological disturbances.

Because lithium can cause problems almost as easily as it cures them, we may suggest a medical workup before the patient begins medication. The tests include urinalysis, CBC blood count, EKG, thyroid profile, creatinine, and sometimes others. From time to time during treatment we redo the tests, comparing the latter results with the former to make certain the salt is not altering body chemistry in serious ways.

We usually do not give lithium to patients with renal disease or sodium depletion. We are also concerned with cardiovascular disease. Lithium directly affects kidney action because the metal is filtered out by the kidneys. Also, a few patients getting lithium plus haloperidol, a neuroleptic, experience weakness, lethargy, fever, tremors, confusion, and blood chemical changes. In rare instances, brain damage has resulted. Lithium can cause adverse effects on the kidneys and/or thyroid.

The elderly seem subject to adverse reactions more frequently than the general population. And we can never administer lithium to women who are pregnant or hope to become so during treatment, because lithium can harm the fetus.

Lithium can impair mental and physical abilities. If your work depends on fast action and quick reflexes—using dangerous machinery for example—proceed with caution.

## Lithium's Light Side

The good news is, with monitoring, we can often minimize the possibility of problems. Whenever we treat with lithium, we already have at hand the facilities for fast, accurate serum lithium determinations. More frequent checks are sometimes appropriate during the first leg of a treatment regimen. They offer a good assurance that the drug isn't building up to toxic levels. As the person's reactions to the drug become known, we may ease off the close monitoring. We've found that people who are exceedingly manic have a higher tolerance for the drug than do people in a lesser state of mania. So we have to use mood level as a cross-check along with serum checks. We use lab tests as secondary indicators. The primary indicators of how well a patient is doing are always the patient's behavior and any side effects.

Signs of lithium toxicity that we watch for include diarrhea, vomiting, memory loss, or tremors (the shakes). One may experience a mild ataxia, an inability to coordinate voluntary muscle movements. Sometimes drowsiness or weakness occurs. If any of these side effects occur, we stop the lithium treatment immediately. Almost as soon as the patient ceases to take the medication, it begins clearing itself from the system. The lithium level will bottom out in about forty-eight hours.

Patients who halt lithium treatment stand a great chance of relapsing within a few weeks. We therefore maintain treatment for nine to twelve months. If a patient stops treatment and then must return to it, he or she generally picks up again at about the same dosage level. *Lithium is never addictive.* Patients experience no withdrawal effects, no dependence.

Once in a while, we administer lithium for manic-depression or mania and at the same time prescribe another psychotropic drug to help a related disorder. For example, were

Joan Wong emotionally unstable in other ways as well, she might receive thioridazine or another antipsychotic drug.

On the other side of the coin, when antidepressants do not perform as well as we hope, we sometimes prescribe a bit of lithium as well. Lithium often improves the performance of antidepressants, when they otherwise provide mixed results or none at all. This combining of drugs must be done very, *very* carefully, however. It's potent.

All this sounds cut and dried, yet nothing about the human psyche is clean and orderly. We are messy folk psychologically, and that messiness extends into the medication we use. As we monitor our patients on lithium, we discover that within a year, one-third to one-half will stop taking the drug. About 13 percent, mired in a depressive relapse, will go off the drug. A surprising number will quit because they miss the manic state; they get bored being normal and want the high. This is why psychological therapy must be a part of treatment. Drugs alone won't do it.

Administered orally and used carefully, lithium keeps mania from recurring in most patients and, at the very least, reduces the intensity of manic behavior. In Joan Wong it essentially effected a complete cure. That happens with cheery frequency. In many other patients it would relieve the symptoms, if nothing else. The light metal provides a light of hope for the victims of manic-depression.

So far, researchers have not found a substance that can equal lithium's effect on manic-depressives. MAOIs, the antidepressant drugs, sometime help. Some anticonvulsants such as Tegretol seem to help. Still, dangerous as it is, the light metal remains the drug of choice because it works so well.

## Fine-Tuning Lithium Treatment

And we keep searching. No sooner was this miraculous ray of light discovered, than medical researchers and doctors started looking to improve upon it. First they had to figure out how it works.

They still haven't done that. We think lithium alters the

way sodium moves around in nerve and muscle cells. Within the neurons—the nerve cells—it somehow changes the method by which certain chemicals, the catecholamines, are metabolized. And that, folks, is fancy jargon that can be translated, "We really don't understand the specific mechanism."

We may not know how lithium works its miracle, but we know how the body gets rid of it. Some drugs are broken down in the body and their parts used for other things—that is, they are metabolized. Not lithium. The amount you ingest is the amount you will excrete. Usually, about half the lithium you take in will leave your body within a day. About 95 percent of it will be filtered out by your kidneys and excreted in the urine. A little less than 5 percent will leave through your sweat (you perspire even when you don't feel any moisture on your skin; sweat is one of the body's marvelous cleansing systems). Incidentally, some of your sodium leaves your body through sweat. That's why sweat tastes salty.

Other fine-tuning is possible. When we treated Joan Wong at the beginning of lithium's reign, we used the naturally occurring salt because that was all we had. We hospitalized her during the first weeks of treatment in order to monitor her carefully. Not only were we uncertain about the possible side effects and toxicity levels, we were feeling our way along as regards long-term efficacy. Besides, we were keeping careful records. This was the initial trial period, when everything we learned was something new. We recorded success, failure, observations, and problems that ought to be addressed in the future.

One problem is to get lithium into the system without spiking. To understand spiking, think about the legendary sugar high in a young child. The child eats something very sugary. Minutes later, the child starts bouncing off the walls, really hyped. Every cell in that little body has lots of energy. The theory is that the sugars in the sweet treat are blotted up rapidly into the child's bloodstream and are distributed throughout the body. All cells use sugars for energy. As the cells and liver pick up and use the sugar molecules, taking them out of circulation, the sugar level in the blood goes down and activity returns to normal. Some medical people claim there's no such thing as a sugar high. Mothers swear by it.

Similarly, the blood's lithium level jumps soon after the patient takes the dose. The salt is being picked right up into the bloodstream. Then, as it is distributed to all the cells, the salt's concentration coasts downhill until it leaps back up at the next dose. This problem is minimized in some of the controlled-release forms of the salt available now. The medicine goes in, but as it is prevented from being soaked up immediately into the blood plasma, it tarries. Although the stomach and upper small intestine are always the sites where your body takes up the lithium you ingest, less of it is absorbed in the stomach and more of it taken up farther along. The elevation in lithium serum level appears as a soft, casual lump more than a sharp spike. It will all be absorbed eventually, but *eventually* is the key word.

All this sounds complex. How in heaven's name did we stumble across a poisonous metal as a therapy for manic-depression? It's an interesting story.

## The History of Medicines for Treating Manic-Depression and Mania

Lithium carbonate is an ordinary metal salt (sodium chloride; table salt is another metal salt). In the 1940s, the lithium compound was used in veterinary medicine. An Australian in 1949 noted that when excited, agitated animals were given lithium carbonate, they settled down dramatically. (Few things are more dramatic than a one-thousand-pound horse upset about something.)

Eventually doctors tried the salt on human beings and found the same calming effect. Serendipity provided a drug to combat manic-depression and mania. By the early 1960s we were working out dosages and indications for lithium in this country.

Serendipity struck twice. A few years ago, people working on an antiseizure drug, Tegretol, discovered that it sometimes also provided a stabilizing effect for people with mood swings and mania. Doctors may also use certain antidepressants, for example, MAOIs, particularly if the bipolar nature of the patient's disorder hangs more at the depression end. But lithium remains the major agent and is the standard against which experimental drugs are judged.

## Medications for Treating Manic-Depression and Mania

### The Lithium Products

Like shock absorbers on a car, the lithium products cushion the ups and downs. They level the effects of manic-depression.

Slow- or sustained-release forms of the carbonate tend to keep serum lithium levels fairly constant, with fewer sharp peaks. Less lithium is released in the stomach, more in the small intestine. The syrup, the regular salt, and the sustained-release forms all deliver 100 percent of the lithium taken. If you take 300 milligrams, you sooner or later absorb 300 milligrams (sooner with the syrup, later with the sustained-release forms).

**Cibalith-S** (lithium citrate in syrup form—raspberry flavor, incidentally) is the most rapidly absorbed form, taking fifteen minutes to one hour to absorb after dosing. It is also the most expensive form, twice the cost of other name brands, and four times the cost of plain old USP salt.

**Eskalith** (lithium carbonate) is available in a controlled-release form that delivers the salt at a uniform pace.

**Lithane** (lithium carbonate)

**Lithium carbonate** USP is the basic salt, available in tablet or capsule.

**Lithobid** (lithium carbonate) capsules provide a slow-release delivery.

**Lithonate** and **Lithotabs** (lithium carbonate)

### Other Products

**Tegretol, Depakote,** the antipsychotics may provide a

beneficial effect. Lastly we might try the minor tranquilizers: **Klonopin** (clonazepam) is an example.

## Drugs Currently in Research

**Calan** (verapamil HCl) is a blood pressure and heart stabilizing medicine. How it works neurologically nobody knows. But it seems to work and currently is an exciting research field.

**Clozaril** (clozapine) destroys bone marrow in a few susceptible people. It is also used to treat psychosis.

**Risperdal** seems to work with few side effects. It is also effective with many psychotic patients.

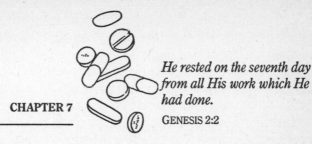

## CHAPTER 7

*He rested on the seventh day from all His work which He had done.*

GENESIS 2:2

# SLEEP PROBLEMS AND DISORDERS

"The same week I got a five-hundred-dollar bonus check for a really successful project, my supervisor caught me curled up under my desk asleep," lamented Dave Saul, who was sprawled flaccidly in the armchair. He melted so deeply into the upholstery, he appeared to have no bones at all.

"She tried to get the incentive award taken away from me, but I fought for it and won," Dave said. "I need that in my file as proof that I'm valuable to the company, because I know from the way my supervisor acted that she's going to try to get me fired."

Gretchen Finglass stared morosely at the decaf in her cup. She stirred the coffee with one hand and jiggled her foot; Gretchen was always moving. "Sorry I can't muster much sympathy, Dave. I'd love to get any sleep at all. If I could curl up under my desk and snooze, I'd do it in a minute."

"Me, too," said a bleary-eyed Sonja Heiss."Ever since that driver slapped the lawsuit on me, I haven't been able to sleep but an hour or two at night."

Dave, Gretchen, and Sonja all complained of sleep disorders, but they didn't share the same problems. And problems they were, too. Dave stood in danger of losing his job, and there didn't appear to be a solitary thing he could do to save himself. Gretchen had suffered from chronic insomnia for years, but some times were worse than others. Poor Sonja was beset by a list of problems and had reached her wit's end. Over-the-counter sleeping pills didn't do a thing for her.

Thirty-three years old and loving his job as a project coordinator, Dave Saul was noted for his innovative problem-solving skills. Once he undertook a project and built his team, he let the team do all the work, while he set up the completion phases and acted as a troubleshooter. He loved nipping little difficulties in the bud before they became work-stoppers, and he enjoyed a rare gift for recognizing them in time. His projects always came in ahead of deadline and under budget.

And he was a whiz on the computer! When his secretary complained about the time it took to process purchase orders and keep track of equipment, Dave wrote her a program that handled it all with one two-minute data entry.

He explained, "When I roll under my desk for a nap, I swear I'm not being lazy. All of a sudden I'm so sleepy I can't stay awake, and I just zonk out. After the nap I'm fine again."

"That's weird," Gretchen said, wrinkling her nose. "Attacked by sleep. And you sleep all right at night?"

"Yeah. Usually I'm asleep by ten or ten-thirty, and I'm up at six." He paused. "Sometimes I zone out. I can't explain it. I'll drive from Mesquite to Richardson and not remember doing it."

"Run over any pedestrians?" Gretchen asked sarcastically.

Dave hunched his shoulders upward in a feeble shrug. "Haven't received any citations in the mail."

Green imps of envy danced in Gretchen's heart. Her whole adult life, she had been plagued by insomnia. She tried all the things people said to do—go to bed at the same time each night, drink warm milk, use a white-noise machine and black curtains—nothing helped. When her doctor told her she was using too many sleeping pills, she switched doctors. Four doctors later and still no prescription for pills, she obtained a street source and no longer had to get her medicine by prescription. Now she could go back to her regular doctor, who assumed that she was sleeping free of narcotics.

If she ever got caught buying from her dealer, she knew it would ruin her. She was the principal of a prestigious Christian academy. A drug bust wouldn't sit well at all with her governing board. At least Gretchen had a source. Sonja was stumbling through life like a zombie.

Six months before, Sonja Heiss had felt on top of the world. Assistant manager in a department store, she not only made good money, she also worked good hours. Her kids spent less than four hours a day in day care. Then the store folded. One of the biggest, most venerable, most elegant old department stores in the country, and it crashed.

The first to be laid off, Sonja finally found a similar job in a chain discount house working lousy hours for half the pay. Her middle son developed pneumonia, and he almost died. He never quite got over all his respiratory problems. When Sonja back-ended a Bronco in heavy traffic—just a little bump at less than walking speed, and her car weighed half what the Bronco did—the driver sued for injuries, damages, and heaven knows what else. How was Sonja going to pay a lawyer? And yet she couldn't win this lawsuit without one. Now her own health was in jeopardy. She couldn't fall asleep before midnight, no matter how long she lay in bed, and when she woke up at 3:00 A.M. she couldn't go back to sleep. If she could just get some rest, surely her health would make it through this crisis.

Sonja's sleep disturbances were her response to the vicissitudes of life. Gretchen's body ought to be accustomed to her sleep patterns by now. And if Dave would set up his own company, he could sleep whenever he wanted to. Did they need medical help?

Yes. The telling point is that these sleep disorders were damaging the well-being and the day-to-day activities of all three persons.

## The Problems with Sleep

Everyone suffers occasional sleep problems. The seemingly simple act of sleeping is actually very complex, with different brain functions taking turns, as it were, to process the day's experiences and prepare for tomorrow. Glitches in the process are bound to happen now and then because there are so many opportunities for something to go wrong. When glitches become commonplace, when mood and attention suffer, when the same old problems recur for weeks on end, and most of all, when the sleep problem disrupts life, it's time to do something about it.

### What Happens During Normal Sleep

"You lie down. You fade out. You wake up. What's so complicated about sleep?" Sonja asked.

The sheer wonder of it is complex!

On the average, most people require between seven and eight hours of sound sleep each night. Some people can do with less, others require more. In that third of a day, amazing things are going on.

There's not much to notice if you are observing a sleeping person. The person just lies there. He or she may toss and turn; in fact, the person will shift body position a dozen times a night, on the average. The only parts of the body that move predictably are the closed eyes. During one kind of sleep, the eyes dart about as if watching an action movie. We call that REM sleep—rapid eye movement. You may have already guessed what we call sleep that produces no eye movement: NREM—nonrapid eye movement.

As a person drifts into sleep, the recordable brain activity changes from short, snappy waves into long, high waves. This is delta sleep. It's easiest to awaken out of delta-wave sleep. The delta phases are associated with the secretion of growth hormones and are probably the periods in which the body is actually rested and restored. Episodes of REM sleep lasting an hour and a half or so alternate with NREM sleep. The mind shunts some memories from short-term into long-term storage and disposes of others. Dreaming happens during REM sleep.

Dreams, most of which you don't remember, are the main mechanism by which the mind processes what happened during the last day or so. Dreams are also the means for processing fears and losses.

In a night of undisturbed rest, the body and mind use sleep to perform all kinds of important tasks. Should sleep be disturbed or curtailed for a night or two, the body and mind will make do. The problems arrive in droves when sleep is routinely disrupted or disturbed over lengthy periods of time. When professionally evaluating dyssomnia—sleep disorders—we expect the various symptoms to prevail consistently for at least a month.

Sleep can go awry in three different ways: too much sleep, too little sleep, or poor quality of sleep (that is, the REM/NREM pattern is disrupted by medication, sleepwalking, or something else).

## Too Much Sleep

Dave was right on target when he suspected his boss was going to try to oust him. She started the paper trail that very day. The best defense is a good offense, so Dave did what he should have done years ago—he went to a doctor.

Too much sleep or inappropriate sleep can be as great a problem as insomnia. It was Dave's problem, and it's not uncommon.

**Narcolepsy.** Dave was one in a thousand. That's approximately the ratio of persons per general population who show signs and symptoms of narcolepsy.

The narcoleptic experiences sleep attacks such as Dave's, wherein he suddenly had to take a nap. It was not a choice for him. His project team members all knew about his involuntary need for naps, and that it was not laziness or a desire to beat the company out of an hour's salary. They also knew how brilliant he was at his job, how much he worked overtime to bring a project home, and how valuable he was in making their jobs possible. So they covered for him as best they could.

Most of them knew Dave's problem began in his last year of college, and that is normal for narcoleptics—adolescence to early twenties is the usual initial onset. The disorder affects both sexes equally.

What neither Dave nor his colleagues knew was that when Dave zonked out in one of his naps, he slipped immediately into REM sleep. Normal sleep begins with a delta phase.

Dave was lucky in that he didn't suffer depression. Most narcoleptics do. Narcoleptics also exhibit at least one of four other conditions.

They may experience *sleep paralysis*. They awaken, and they know they're awake, but for several moments (it seems like ages), they cannot move.

They may experience *hypnagogic hallucinations*. They are relaxed and ready to slip into slumberland. Suddenly they see a vision or feel a touch that cannot possibly be happening. But it seems so real, so vivid. The hallucinations may be so strong that persons feel they are having a psychotic episode.

They may experience *automatic behavior*. Dave had these experiences on his drive from Mesquite to Richardson. His consciousness would sort of check out, and when the episode passed he would have no recollection of the drive or the amount of time that had passed.

Note that this is different from the *petit mal* episode associated with epilepsy. The epileptic having a petit mal seizure sort of goes on hold; he or she will drive off the road or into another car. If the epileptic is pouring milk from a carton when the seizure hits, she will keep pouring until the carton is empty and her lap is full. The narcoleptic will fill the glass properly and set the carton upright, but will not remember pouring the milk.

Narcoleptics may experience *cataplexy*. In a rush of emotion, they fall out laughing or crying or yelling, whatever the emotion may be. Their skeletal muscles suddenly go weak, and they melt to the floor or tumble off the chair or fall facedown into the mashed potatoes. This is not a fainting spell; they retain full consciousness.

A narcoleptic friend shared this story: "Four of us were seated in a restaurant booth. Three of us are cataplectic and the fourth, my husband, Roger, is not.

"Roger knew better than to tell a funny joke in our presence, but he did and it was hilarious, and we all were splitting a gut. Meg went first. She peeled sideways out of the booth and landed on her ear on the floor. Chris dropped forward and flattened the hamburger on her plate. I laughed so hard at those two that I melted and slid off the seat and underneath the table. So here's Roger trying to prop Chris up and drag Meg back into her seat and haul me out from under the table, and all the while he's laughing so hard he has tears in his eyes. Roger's used to these episodes by now. We've been married twenty years."

The friend jokes about her condition—many narcoleptics do—because that's about all she can do. Narcoleptics often die untimely, not directly of the narcolepsy but indirectly because of physical accidents. They routinely fall, break bones, go to sleep at the wrong time (while driving, for example), and "check out" during dangerous circumstances. Although, so far, Dave was getting from one town to another safely, his reflexes and state of alertness were nowhere near sharp, and should a sudden traffic emergency pop up, he'd be in trouble. He was running on borrowed time, on the road and at work.

Dave's supervisor was irate that one of the employees

under her would have the nerve to sleep on the job. She took it as a personal affront, a lack of respect, a disdain for her authority. She built her case and brought it before her boss. She had Dave nailed solid. The guy took an afternoon nap every day and sometimes a morning snooze. She could prove it.

When the big boss called Dave in, Dave pointed out the incentive awards he'd garnered and his record of bringing projects home on time. Then he whipped out his doctors' reports and explained them to the boss. He described what narcolepsy is, complete with recent medical articles. It can be reduced, and he was taking medications to do that, but it cannot be cured. It's a disability, and as such it is subject to ADA—the Americans with Disabilities Act—which expects employers to make allowances for people with disabilities. "Besides," Dave concluded, "my particular problem isn't hurting your bottom line a bit, and I make you good money. It would be a mistake to dump me."

The boss agreed and ordered Dave's supervisor to stay off his back.

Not all stories have a happy ending like Dave's did. Too often, people think narcolepsy is a behavior problem that the narcoleptic can correct with a change in attitude. "If you just try a little harder, you can maintain productivity without a nap." That's like telling a person with a broken leg, "If you just try a little harder, that bone will heal right up by tomorrow."

Narcolepsy is not the only disorder that makes its victim sleep too much.

**Hypersomnolence.** A corrections officer at a juvenile detention facility said, "These kids might come in all hyped and angry and uncooperative, but as soon as you lock 'em down, they flop out on their cot and that's it. Like you pulled the plug. Put these guys in a cell, and they spend all their waking hours asleep." The man frowned, then smiled. "That didn't come out right."

His point is well made. The detainees devote an inordinate amount of time to napping. That's hypersomnolence.

Many different things can cause a person to sleep much more than is normal, which is the definition of hypersomnolence. Almost always, hypersomnolence is a symptom rather than a disease; and it is therefore corrected by correcting the causative disorder.

A major cause of hypersomnolence is anything that disturbs the normal, necessary REM/NREM cycles—barking dogs, loud activity in the apartment next door, alarms or sirens; anything the person does not sleep through *soundly*. Partial awakening is sufficient to disturb sleep. The disturbances keep the person from sleeping well, so he sleeps longer or naps during the day, trying to make up the deficit. The deficit accrues because of the quality of sleep rather than the quantity, so naps won't cure it. Only finding and correcting the disturbance will restore sound sleep.

People who are depressed or dysthymic also may sleep too much. So might people who suffer from a chronic liver, kidney, or thyroid disease. Encephalitis (an inflammation in the brain) or brain tumor can cause hypersomnolence.

And then there's the occasional case where we cannot find a good reason for hypersomnolence. The person needs twelve hours of sleep a day, and that's that. How envious of that person is the insomniac!

## Too Little Sleep

An abnormal inability to obtain adequate sleep is called insomnia. Gretchen had it, and what she wouldn't do for a good eight hours of sleep.

When she was a little girl, Gretchen slept just fine. Her sleep patterns deteriorated in middle school—she was around thirteen years old—and got worse as she went through high school and college. She hoped the stability of a good job would reduce the problem. It didn't. Now she was living on borrowed time, waiting for the narcotics officers to knock at her door, and the tension made her problem even worse. When her doctors suggested psychiatric evaluation, she *really* got scared.

Sonja Heiss suffered insomnia also, but her problem had developed within the last month or two. She either couldn't fall asleep, or if she did she couldn't stay asleep for long. When she awoke at 3:00 A.M. she was up for the day. No matter how tired she felt, she could not go back to sleep. She feared for her health, and with good cause. Lack of sleep can wreck a person.

Each night an average of seventy million Americans have trouble sleeping. Some estimates show forty million Americans suffering from chronic insomnia problems. And then there are the elderly, who are unusually susceptible to depression and probably pursue a lifestyle with reduced activity. A majority of them suffer sleep disturbances. Medicines to aid sleep are the most commonly used drugs in our nation; they are number one.

We categorize insomnia into three major types.

**Transient insomnia.** This type of insomnia lasts a day or two, then the normal sleep pattern reestablishes itself.

"When I fly to Australia and back," a friend says, "the time difference really messes me up. Australia is across the international date line, which means it's tomorrow in Australia. On the flight home I live today twice. It's really weird, and my body knows it. Back home again, I keep falling asleep at two o'clock in the afternoon, and I'm wide awake at two o'clock in the morning, whether I go to bed on time or not. I'm usually back to normal after about three days."

Surgical patients in hospitals may suffer a temporary insomnia because of physical inactivity. Physical activity promotes normal sleep. Temporary disruptions cause temporary problems, which almost always evaporate without further attention. When the bout of sleeplessness extends over several weeks, we label it short-term insomnia.

**Short-term insomnia.** Stress is usually the culprit in cases of short-term insomnia. Sonja was subjected to a number of unusual psychological stresses within a short time. Insomnia was one result of the overload.

The stress of illness can disrupt sleep patterns. So can physical stresses. Short-term or not, Sonja's problem needed to be fixed. The approach to her treatment would differ from the approach to Gretchen's, for Gretchen's problem differed in kind and in cause.

**Chronic insomnia.** This problem lasts for months and months. In Gretchen's case, it was half a lifetime. Her doctors recommended psychiatric counsel because the origins of chronic insomnia usually lie either with a major medical illness or a psychiatric problem.

Chronic pain from arthritis sometimes disturbs sleep. So do leg cramps and "restless legs," when the muscles won't be still. Only walking quiets them. Heart or kidney disease or stroke might be the culprit.

Drug abuse and alcoholism are biggies. Whether or not Gretchen's situation involved drug abuse at the outset, she was hooked now, severely dependent on powerful sleep medications.

Once we rule out medical possibilities we're left with psychiatric problems, with this caveat: it's not a case of either/or. Our patient may be suffering insomnia because of a psychiatric condition in addition to one or more medical problems.

We would treat chronic insomnia differently than the lack of sleep that often accompanies Attention Deficit Disorder.

**ADD/ADHD.** Attention Deficit Disorder, particularly in adults, may have as one of its characteristics a lack of sleep. However, this is probably not pathological. ADD/ADHD people seem to need less sleep than most people, and they relish racing around accomplishing stuff—whatever that stuff is—while we more ordinary folk are sawing Z's. Their need for less sleep can make ADD/ADHD adults extremely productive, successful people. So long as health remains stable, and in these persons it usually does, why tinker with it?

## Poor Quality of Sleep

Finally, sleep goes awry when our sleep is of such poor quality that we do not feel rested.

**Disturbed sleep patterns.** When the normal, necessary pattern of REM and NREM sleep is disrupted, you may sleep your usual number of hours, but you don't feel rested.

Changing from an afternoon work shift to the swing shift can cause temporary sleeplessness or disturb sleep cycles. Common sense says the problem is temporary, and the body needs time to adjust.

A different sort of disturbed sleep pattern is called phase-delay insomnia. The person has difficulty getting to sleep at a decent hour at night and difficulty waking up in the morning. Without an incentive to get up, the person may sleep until noon.

**Sleep apnea.** "When Hank snores, it sounds like a dozen drag racers are revving their engines all at once." That's how Hank's wife Janna described it.

Although snoring is not usually a medical emergency, in some cases it can be a sign of sleep apnea, a serious disorder that can sometimes cause death.

The prefix *a* in *apnea* means "not," "none," or "a lack," and *pnea* means "air" or "breathing." To qualify as sleep apnea, the breathing stops five times or more an hour, and the pauses last at least ten seconds each. We find that afflicted men (and a few women; 90 percent of sleep apnea victims are male) were heavy snorers ten or fifteen years before the onset of the disorder. Among other problems, heartbeat irregularities may develop and become severe enough to cause death.

There are two kinds of sleep apnea. With *central sleep apnea*, the victim ceases to breathe for a time. His respiratory wiring momentarily shuts down somewhere in the central nervous system.

In cases of *obstructive sleep apnea*, the respiratory wiring remains active, but some kind of blockage prevents smooth air flow. We find this kind often among overweight, older men. Left untreated, the disorder can lead to an assortment of problems you'd never guess were sleep related—impotence, personality changes, depression, and headaches.

The snoring that accompanies sleep apnea can prevent a good night's sleep for even the most sound-sleeping spouse. That was Janna's problem. Even when she *could* fall asleep before Hank, and thereby avoid being kept awake, Hank's snoring probably disturbed the kind of sleep she got. Remember, the brain uses REM and NREM sleep to process and renew. Without actually awakening Janna to a conscious level, Hank's snoring could disrupt her sleep cycles, preventing REM sleep and disturbing the delta phase. She would log the appropriate hours of bedtime, but they would not be as restful and productive as they ought to be.

Some sleep difficulties cannot be linked directly to abnormal sleep patterns, but they occur during sleep intervals. These are the parasomnias.

**Parasomnias.** Sleepwalking is a well-known parasomnia. Sleepwalking usually occurs during the first round of NREM sleep. You've seen the cartoon sleepwalkers in their nightgowns and tasseled nightcaps, marching with arms outstretched, palms turned down. Usually a string of Z's wafts back from their heads.

Forget the cartoon stereotype. Most sleepwalkers only sit up in bed or perhaps stand beside the bed. If they do roam, they walk normally. If discovered in their peregrinations, they can be led back to bed. They may talk and appear to be awake, but in the morning they probably will not remember the episode. Sleepwalking is common in small children and normally disappears as they mature. Sleepwalking in adults indicates a psychological problem.

Bed-wetting—technically termed enuresis—is another well-known parasomnia. It's a childhood disorder, but it can signal a psychological problem if it extends into adolescence. Bed-wetting in a preschooler and early grade-school child could be delayed maturation. The complex muscles and wiring to control urine release are not quite mature enough to handle the job 100 percent when, in sleep, the child's attention and guard are down.

Bed-wetting can be devastating to an older child, who may not dare sleep over at a friend's house or invite friends to sleep over at his house. Camping is out of the question. These children are sometimes ridiculed and shamed by adults. The threat of shame alone terrifies a child this age, when appearance and status are so important.

Other parasomnias include nocturnal migraines, nightmares that disrupt sleep, and night terrors. Night terrors can cause profuse sweating, heart pounding, and the victim may awake with a scream. The person cannot recall the dream or cause of the terror, and reassurances by others cannot make the terror abate.

These are all major sleep problems. For lack of space, we have not mentioned a host of minor problems.

So how does one tackle a major sleep disorder? Identifying the causes for sleeping problems is the first step.

## Identifying Causes of Sleep Disorders

Let's pretend that someone you care about has chronic insomnia. Let's further pretend that this person insists nothing is terribly wrong and refuses to consider medical or psychiatric intervention.

How can you intelligently assess the situation? First, familiarize yourself with some of the causes for sleep disturbances.

### Depression

Review the signs and symptoms for depression discussed in Chapter 2. More than 70 percent of chronic insomnia cases arise as a direct result of some degree of depression. It's the first thing we look for. Depression, particularly dysthymia (long-term depression), causes the victim to awake early— 3:00 or 4:00 A.M.—and prevents him from falling back to sleep.

Look for this pattern in your analysis. Remember, if your loved one is teenage or younger, depression may appear as anger, acting out.

## Anxiety

If your loved one is keyed up, tense, wary, nervous, or perhaps even panicky, consider anxiety as the problem. Look over the detailed symptoms of anxiety listed in Chapter 4.

Anxiety frequently leaves its victim wide-eyed at night, unable to fall asleep. Be aware too that panic attacks can occur during REM sleep.

## Obsessive-Compulsive Disorder

Read over the signs and symptoms for OCD in Chapter 5. Repetitive, ritualistic behaviors, bizarre routines, time-wasting activities—any actions done to obvious excess should excite your suspicions. Obsessive-compulsive persons sometimes develop elaborate, repetitive, compulsive rituals that cut into sleep time so deeply that the practical result is too little sleep.

## Mania

Insomnia is frequently a symptom of mania and manic-depression. If your person is zinging along in overdrive, her activity level greatly elevated, familiarize yourself with the signs and symptoms listed in Chapter 6.

## Chronic Worrying

Remember, anxiety is fear or nervousness with no obvious cause, whereas worry has some reason you can identify.

Worry is a real sleep destroyer, because it actually triggers the wake-up system. Worry is identified with transient insomnia, because once the reason for worrying has passed, the victim can sleep again. Chronic insomnia triggered by chronic worry is another matter; that would be a form of obsession.

## Paranoia

Does the person fear or suspect someone or something is persecuting him, out to get him, close to hurting him, suspicious of him? He may be too afraid to relax his guard and fall asleep.

Gretchen developed problems with paranoia. She feared she would get busted for buying sleeping pills on the streets. She knew her actions were illegal, and the paranoia exacerbated her insomnia.

## Physical Illness

Heart disease, pneumonia, and other lung diseases make sleeping difficult. Often the patient must sleep semi-sitting, hardly as comfortable as lying down. Casually ask your loved one if she experiences pain or headache at night. That can curtail sleep.

## Alcohol or Drug Use

You've probably heard people—whether in real life or the movies—say they needed a nightcap before going to bed. For some people, a single small drink in the evening can make sleep come more quickly. That small benefit comes with a price, however, because later in the night sleep is disrupted. In a majority of cases, alcohol causes sleep difficulties with no benefits. We are talking about restorative sleep, the kind in which the brain and body can perform their nighttime tasks undisturbed.

Any drug, prescription or otherwise, interferes with normal sleep. Even the sleeping prescriptions cause insomnia sooner or later. It's called rebound, and Gretchen was experiencing it firsthand. Her sleeping pills were keeping her awake.

You'll want to learn what medications your loved one is taking. Thyroid medicine, if taken in a higher dosage than necessary, can cause insomnia. Steroids, which are prescribed for arthritis, skin problems, and some other conditions, will cause insomnia if their dosage is too high or if it is in the process of being changed. Certain asthma and weight-loss drugs can suppress REM sleep and also cause insomnia. Both problems result in incomplete rest.

Of the antidepressants, tricyclics improve sleep but MAOIs can interfere with it. Drugs for Parkinson's disease may make the patient sleepy or irritable and thereby interfere with the restful sleep.

Drying out, either from alcohol or drug misuse, can trigger insomnia that lasts for months. Using short-duration drugs such as Halcion can worsen the situation. Withdrawal must be done slowly and carefully.

Technically speaking, caffeine is a drug, and for most people, it works very well as a stimulant. Over-the-counter pills to help you stay awake contain nothing stronger than caffeine. Each pill contains about as much caffeine as two cups of coffee. Coffee, tea, and many soft drinks contain caffeine in sufficient quantity to cause sleep disruption. If your person is drinking a lot of caffeinated beverages, the simple step of switching to decaf and noncaffeinated beverages could help immensely. Be advised, however, that quitting caffeine all at once can cause severe symptoms including excruciating headaches. Gradual withdrawal is the best method.

You may be an amateur at diagnosing problems that lead to sleep disorder, but you can get a general idea of what is happening. That idea will lead to either solutions or places to go for help. You also will be able to discuss the problem intelligently with a counselor or doctor, which will help with the professional diagnosis.

## Professional Diagnosis

Professionals look for the same causes identified in the section above. Because we do not know the patient personally at the beginning of treatment, we start at the bottom and go from there.

Let's suppose that Gretchen, panicked by the thought of

being arrested for buying sleeping pills on the street, comes to Frank Minirth or Paul Meier for counsel. One of the first things we ask is, "Was the patient coerced into coming in for treatment?" Gretchen would not be classified as coming in under coercion because she voluntarily sought counsel for her problem.

We begin with an extensive history. We ask her about sleep patterns, waking hours, things that happen during sleep times (or fail to happen), and how sleep or lack of it affects her life. We learn exactly what drugs Gretchen is taking.

Do patients ever lie to us about drugs and symptoms? They sure do. Can we detect when they're lying? Most of the time we can. To quote an old friend, "I was born in the middle of the night—but it wasn't *last* night."

Next, we do a complete medical workup on Gretchen to uncover any heart, liver, kidney, brain, or hormonal problems. Extensive laboratory tests are all part of that. It's amazing how many diseases can generate insomnia or hypersomnolence. During the medical examination, we look for structural anomalies that could cause sleep apnea or make it worse—a deviated nasal septum for example.

We refer Gretchen to a sleep laboratory for other tests. Sleep labs wire you up at bedtime and record your brain and body responses as you sleep. They can tell exactly what happens during delta sleep and REM sleep. They can detect nighttime heart arrhythmias, nocturnal seizures, and other things that we would miss during a daytime examination.

Most important, we do a psychiatric examination and diagnosis. So many sleep disorders, whether aggravated by disease or not, are caused by psychological problems.

Treatment, of course, depends on what the examination uncovers.

## Treating Sleep Disorders

Of all the miracle drugs we've discussed, the sleeping medications can serve as splendid friends that restore healthful rest, or as horrid foes that lock a victim into a miserable cycle of addiction and abuse.

Gretchen was mired so deeply in a cycle of abuse, she could not escape on her own. We needed to hospitalize her and wean her off the medications gradually.

Taking a person off an abused substance is exceedingly dangerous. Many of these drugs cause heart problems and seizures if you don't taper them off gradually, usually with countering drugs. Their sudden removal can be lethal.

Typical of people trapped by the foe nature of these drugs, Gretchen refused to believe she was in danger. "You just want the money," she fumed.

"We just want you to stay alive," we replied.

Gretchen's treatment was three-pronged, and it represents the usual course we follow.

1. *Flush the body of any toxins.* Any drugs we would administer would interact with drugs already in Gretchen's system. This is exceedingly dangerous; no two people react the same to these mixes. Unpredictability plus toxicity equals disaster.

2. *Find the right drugs at the right doses.* The purpose is to ease the symptoms of the sleep disorder and help the person gain the emotional and physical strength that sleep provides.

3. *Employ behavioral counseling to correct insomnia without drugs.* Most of the time, simple changes in habits, behavior, and perhaps foods can alleviate sleep problems. To explore these prospects in detail, see Dr. Minirth's book, *Sweet Dreams*.

4. *Uncover the causes of the disorder and correct them through appropriate therapy.* Some sleep-disturbance victims need this fourth step or they will fall back into a sleep disorder and the destructive patterns of the past.

Let's go through the sleep disorders and briefly discuss their causes and treatment.

Narcolepsy is an inherited physical condition. Parents do not invariably hand it down to their children; rather, they hand down a genetic tendency to it. It doesn't show up in every child, and narcolepsy in a parent certainly does not condemn the child to the disorder. There is no psychological component to its occurrence, although it can cause secondary psychological problems.

Once we find an effective drug, the narcoleptic can plan to remain on that drug for life. Therapy and counsel cannot correct the problem any more than they can correct eye color. Counsel is valuable, however, in helping patients develop a lifestyle that minimizes the influence of narcolepsy (for example, scheduling nap times). You can learn to live with it; you cannot get rid of it.

Most narcoleptics respond well to stimulants such as Ritalin (see treatments for Attention Deficit Disorder in Chapter 3) or Cylert. The drugs raise their neural activity enough to keep them awake and alert during normal daytime activities. Ritalin and related drugs can minimize the forced naps such as Dave Saul took beneath his desk. Cataplexy, wherein the victim loses muscle control, particularly during moments of intense emotion, is often managed with tricyclic antidepressants (see Chapter 2) such as protriptyline.

Once Dave Saul learned what his problem was, he identified narcoleptic tendencies in his father, his uncle, and two cousins.

Hypersomnolence does not respond real well to stimulants unless it is caused by depression. Then we use the antidepressants to good effect.

Sleep apnea is usually a mechanical disorder. We try first to get patients to lose weight and sleep on their side. If the problem is severe, a positive-pressure sleeping mask frequently helps. This is an unattractive little device, sort of like a portable hair dryer with a long, flexible hose ending in a mask held in place by a harness that fits over the patient's head. The machine gently blows enough air into the patient's nose and mouth to keep the nasal passages open. It sounds much worse than it is, and patients see so much welcome improvement they seldom mind the harness or the mask on their faces. If the positive-pressure device does not work, very occasionally we must resort to surgical intervention to improve the airway.

If a child does not outgrow sleepwalking, we start looking for psychological causes. Drugs usually don't help.

Imipramine works wonders with bed-wetting. Before using drugs we make certain the problem is not caused by physical conditions such as immature sphincter control.

Sleep terrors may respond to the benzodiazepines, but they are likely to pop up again following a psychological trauma or conflict. Better to find the root through psychotherapy.

Short-term insomnia can usually be helped by one of the sedative-hypnotic drugs discussed below, probably one of the benzodiazepines. We limit use of the drug to a month or so—the amount of time to bring the disturbed sleep cycle back under control and repair the damage. During that time, we provide intensive counsel on how to reduce stress. If counsel for psychological problems is appropriate, we provide that also.

As we have stressed about medications in previous chapters, the drugs we use to treat sleep disorders do not transform a person's God-given personality. Dave Saul was changed not a whit. He took fewer naps (usually none at work), worked the same long hours, and no longer zoned out while driving. He's still the best troubleshooter in the business.

## Selecting a Treatment

In treating sleep problems, we start with the simplest and safest method first, and this is usually to alter habits and surroundings. A few such steps can make a world of difference.

### Changing Surroundings and Behaviors

**Adjust light, noise, and temperature.** Nearly everyone sleeps better in darkness. People who work at night and sleep in the day can purchase window shades that block sunlight.

When noise is beyond a person's control (street traffic, for instance), white noise often does the trick. A stationary or oscillating fan is a good example.

"Fine," you say, "but temperature's another thing. My spouse loves it warm and I prefer it cold."

Some ways to strike an ambient temperature for both spouses include using an electric blanket with dual temperature controls; stacking extra covers on one side of the bed; or placing twin beds on opposite sides of the room, one by the heater and the other by the open window. (Twin beds aren't so bad; you can still visit each other.)

**Don't loaf in bed.** Use the bed for sleep and marital relations, and nothing else. Don't read, knit, or watch television in bed. You'll only condition yourself to see the bed as another place to be alert.

**Limit use of sleep-altering drugs.** Nicotine, alcohol, and caffeine are drugs, and they alter sleep. And while sleeping pills work for a short time, after a while they start contributing to the problem they were taken to correct.

**Adhere to a routine.** Regular meals, regular bedtimes, and regular wake-up times can make a profound difference in treating a sleep disorder. Pay attention to your body's rhythms and honor them. By all means, if insomnia is a problem, avoid daytime naps.

**Relax—even if you have to work at it.** A little deep breathing at bedtime often helps. So does tightening all your muscles at once so that you're rigid as a clothesline pole, then deliberately relaxing them so that you melt down into the mattress.

Think relaxing thoughts. Pick something that's unique to you. Let your mind dwell on memories of the sensations of soaking in a hot tub, of receiving a massage, of stretching out in the grass under a tree—any scene that's relaxing to you.

When and if these techniques utterly fail, it's time to consider drug intervention. Again, we try the simplest and gentlest first. And always, in drug intervention we look to treat not the sleep disorder itself but any underlying causal disorders.

## Specific Drugs for Specific Causes

If the root cause of a sleeping disorder is anxiety, as in Gretchen's case, we treat the anxiety and the insomnia abates. Lorazepam or diazepam usually work well. So does Valium. We also might try BuSpar or Vistoril.

If depression is the underlying cause, we treat the depression. But we can't use just any drug to do that. MAOIs, for example, are often useful in treating depression, but they may aggravate insomnia.

When acute or chronic pain reduces sleep, we may suggest Prozac. Although it is technically a medicine for depression, it also possesses analgesic qualities that will raise the threshold of pain enough to permit sound sleep. Amitriptyline works similarly.

Elderly persons suffering dementias such as depression delirium can sleep better with antipsychotics to ease the delirium; examples are Thorazine or haloperidol.

Although the drugs of choice listed in the chapters on depression, Attention Deficit Disorder, anxiety, and mania are also used in treating sleep disorders, we will not repeat them in this chapter. Instead, we will list only the drugs that serve a particular use in the treatment of sleep disorders. Most of them act by altering the work of neurotransmitters such as serotonin and GABA (gamma-aminobutyric acid).

Before we list the medications we currently use to treat sleep disorders, let's look at the history of these sleeping aids.

# The History of Sleeping Aids

Considering that human beings need seven or eight hours of sleep each day, on the average, it seems strange that sleep has been the neglected stepchild of medical research for so long.

Until electroencephalograms and related instruments became sufficiently sophisticated to read small differences in brain activity, we generally assumed sleep was nothing more than the body shutting down for a while. We hardly guessed at all the work done during sleep. Treatment consisted of finding a sedative strong enough to bring on the outward physical appearance of sleep. We didn't know that although the person lapsed into reduced consciousness, the work of sleep may not be happening; REM sleep, for example, does not occur during some drug-induced slumbers. We couldn't understand why the person who "slept" awoke unrefreshed.

Narcolepsy was not recognized at all until relatively recently. Generations of narcoleptics were accused of laziness, stupidity, or madness. We are just now beginning to unravel its causes and treatments.

Sleeping potions, however, have long been the staple of alchemists, folk medicine, and herbalists. Plant decoctions, such as chamomile tea, have been used for millennia. They actually work quite well for mild and temporary problems.

Bromide salts can sedate. At the turn of the century, they were the drug of choice. In the 1940s, chloral hydrate could either put you gently to sleep or slam you into a coma, depending on the dose. These are the infamous "knockout drops."

In the 1950s, pharmaceutical companies tamed the barbiturates somewhat. They were still highly addictive, but the worst side effects were reduced. Seconal became a very popular sleep-inducer. In the 1960s came the benzodiazepines, which treat both anxiety and sleep problems.

As we learn more about the intricacies of sleep, we can better tailor medications to treat what is wrong without messing up what is right.

## Medications for Treating Sleep Disorders

### Benzodiazepines

These products tend to alter the quality of sleep, decreasing REM sleep (except Restoril) and dragging out the time it takes to reach REM (except Dalmane). Their main use is to increase the total sleep time. They are used extensively because it may be harder to overdose on them, they don't depress the central nervous system as badly as do barbiturates, and although they are not as addictive as many substances, they may be addictive.

**Restoril** (temazepam) is absorbed slowly. It doesn't help you get to sleep so much as it helps you stay asleep. Intermediate in action, its effects don't last as long as some, and it produces no morning hangover headache. Do not take the medicine unless you can expect seven or eight hours of uninterrupted sleep. It can cause temporary memory loss, which of course doesn't matter so long as you are snoozing. A few cases have occurred of people taking Restoril in order to sleep on an overnight flight. Awakened at their destination four or five hours later, they can't remember where they are or why.

**Dalmane** (flurazepam) offers rapid relief and long duration, but it produces headaches in some people. It does its best work two or three days into use.

**Halcion** (triazolam) has received a lot of publicity, some of it possibly true, most of it not, about the way it sometimes exacerbates psychiatric illness or increases daytime anxiety. Used with care, it provides fast relief of short duration—just what some patients need. It does well for short-term treatment (seven to ten days); but if it is used for several weeks, rebound insomnia begins to cancel its good effects.

**Doral** (quazepam) works similarly to Dalmane, but it is slow to be metabolized. This could pose a dosage problem in the elderly, whose metabolism is slower anyway. Doral does not change REM sleep significantly, but it decreases the delta wave phase.

**ProSom** (estazolam), like the benzodiazepines in general, can make people feel drowsy during the daytime, particularly older people. Monitor reactions closely.

**Klonopin** (clonazepam) is used mainly for controlling seizures. But it often also helps insomniacs and people who suffer with leg cramps at night, producing a mild sedative effect and controlling the cramps. It's addictive, so you can't use it as a long-term preventative.

**Ativan** (lorazepam) injectable, with its strong antianxiety action, helps people with both anxiety and sleep problems. Patients report relatively low side effects.

**Versed** (midazolam HCl) injectable is used in hospitals where respiration and heart action can be closely monitored.

## Barbiturates

Barbiturates are addictive. We generally discourage their use, knowing how quickly and sneakily they can get a grip on patients. They depress the central nervous system, slowing down everything from thinking to reflexes. They act in one hour or less and perform their magic for six to eight hours. They reduce REM sleep and may cause nightmares when they are withdrawn. Although there is some variation among them as regards effectiveness and side effects, they are enough alike that we'll only list them.

**Alurate** elixir (aprobarbital)
**Butisol Sodium** (butabarbital)
**Luminal** (phenobarbital)
**Mebaral** (mephobarbital)
**Nembutal** (pentobarbital)
**Phenobarbital**
**Seconal** (secobarbital)

## Drugs That Act Like Barbiturates

**Chloral hydrate** works great for a few nights. Then the body gets used to it and its effectiveness fades.

## Other Substances

**Ambien** (zolpidem tartrate) is new in this country. An imidazopyridine, it ought not be taken during or right after eating; food delays absorption. Ambien acts within thirty minutes and does not seem to affect the various stages of sleep or their length. Rebound and hangovers are minimal. Overdoses can cause coma but death is unlikely, unless other drugs are involved as well. So far it does not seem addictive. Time will tell.

Sometimes, when all else fails, we try drugs that are not, properly speaking, hypnotics or sedatives.

**Benadryl** (diphenhydramine) is an antihistamine that acts as a sedative for mild insomnia in younger patients—not the elderly. It is not addictive.

**Desyrel** (trazodone HCl) is an antidepressant that helps people who suffer sleep problems because of their depression. In fact, at relatively low doses, it may help sleep problems in people who are not depressed.

**Diprivan** (propofol) injectable is used in hospitals and delivered intravenously to provide temporary rest and sedation.

**Mepergan** (meperidine HCl and promethazine HCl) injection combines two ingredients to produce a morphine-like painkiller with an antihistamine sedative. Usually used to prepare a patient for anesthesia, it may also serve when pain is a factor in sleep problems.

**Phenergan** (promethazine HCl) injectable is an antihistamine that also controls nausea. It lists sedation as a side effect, but in these cases, that's the effect we want.

**Sinequan** and **Adapin** (doxepin HCl), related to the tricyclics, lift mood by altering the serotonin balance. We often use them when sleep disturbances are interlocked with depression.

**Unisom** (doxylamine succinate) is an over-the-counter antihistamine that just happens to have sedative properties. It's not as fast as the barbiturates, but it does nearly as well as some of the benzodiazepines.

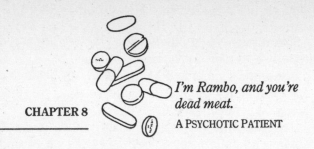

**CHAPTER 8**

*I'm Rambo, and you're dead meat.*

A PSYCHOTIC PATIENT

# PSYCHOSIS

In an urban setting he'd be called homeless. Out here in the desert of southeast California, they called him eccentric. He lived in an abandoned adobe hut with a blue plastic tarp for a roof and cooked over an open fire, which translates that he didn't cook at all in rainy weather (not to mention that his roof leaked and periodically dumped its accumulation of rainwater into his home). Personal hygiene? Persistent rumors claimed that he was forced to wash his hands once, and when he did he found the pair of mittens he'd been missing for two years.

The permanent residents of the small town thirty miles from his shack accepted him as he was, so long as he stayed downwind. He called himself Shoshone, although he picked up an army pension check under another name. The postal clerk never told anyone what Shoshone's real name was. On the other hand, no one ever asked. Shoshone received neither respect nor disrespect. He simply existed, coming and going, muttering a lot, buying beer and grocery staples.

The little town's permanent residents become a minority during the winter months when the snowbirds flock down from the north. Trailer camps and RV parks sprout like crabgrass and spread twice as fast. Suddenly, twenty thousand people need dump stations. They all want to turn a buck, too. The road is lined with rickety fruit and vegetable stands, jewelry peddlers, "antique" dealers, and kitschy craft sellers with crocheted doodads and airplane mobiles made out of aluminum cans. Come April or May, when Easter has passed and temperatures break one hundred, the winter visitors head back north, leaving the bruised, trampled desert behind.

Curious thing about that burgeoning winter crowd: they are an exclusive bunch. Nearly all retired or on disability pensions, they keep to themselves and never associate with the locals. Especially an undesirable local. They cut no slack for the likes of Shoshone; they all assumed he was a criminal. They wouldn't tolerate an eccentric old man.

Shunned by the snowbirds, Shoshone shunned them right back. Things might have remained pretty much at a truce, provided the wind was right, but one day one of the winter visitors engaged Shoshone in conversation at the post office.

"They're trying to brainwash me," Shoshone told the man.

The visitor opined to himself that if that were the case, it must be the only part of Shoshone that ever got washed.

The eccentric continued, "The CIA. They can broadcast right inside my head. Ain't nobody except me hears their voices, so I know that's what they're doing. They've been after me, persecuting me, ever since I got back from Nam."

*Nam*, the visitor thought. *It figures. These vets . . .*

"I was with the medical corps and I know secrets. Do I ever! I could sink the country if I told everything I know. That's why they're after me. But I'm ready for them if they come. Got enough firepower to blow away everybody in the state. Everybody!" With that, Shoshone picked up his army pension envelope and headed out the door.

Ten years ago the visitor would not have felt particularly alarmed. But this was another age, when the TV news routinely reported rampages in which deluded men opened fire in offices and restaurants. Who knows what this kook might do? The only thing the visitor knew for certain was that this loony-tune had to be locked up, or nobody was safe. By luck, the snowbird also knew something no one else did, for he had seen the full name on Shoshone's pension envelope.

Acting on the visitor's formal complaint and backed up by a SWAT team and a battalion of mental health professionals, sheriff's deputies took Shoshone into custody for psychiatric evaluation.

When all the snowbirds went back north, quiet returned, and dogs could again cross the near-empty streets safely. But Shoshone was gone, too. No one had to stay upwind anymore. A charming, legendary bit of local color faded to black. Permanent residents who had never realized they cared found themselves mourning Shoshone's departure.

## Identifying Psychosis

When people think of someone going nuts or being crazy, they generally mean psychosis. The Napoléons and George Washingtons in the psychiatric wards are psychotic. In Chapter 1, we described the problems of James Henry, the seminary student with delusions of grandeur. He was psychotic. So was Shoshone.

Basically, psychosis is losing touch with reality. It's been around for—well, for as long as there have been people, probably. In the Hebrew Scriptures, 1 Samuel 18—31 describes the severe delusions of persecution suffered by Saul, the first king of Israel. He was convinced that his most staunch supporter, David, was out to get him. Saul drifted in and out of his psychosis and died in despair by his own hand.

Another biblical psychotic, Nebuchadnezzar, became a wild

man, living ungroomed and unsheltered. Nebuchadnezzar was a rare exception: he snapped back to reality. So complete was his recovery, he took his throne again.[1]

Nebuchadnezzar's episode lasted seven years, if our analysis of the time spans in Daniel is correct. Psychoses may not last nearly that long. Patients who suffer a *brief psychotic disorder* are jolted out of reality by an intense emotional shock, then return to reality once the trauma is passed.

Long before psychosis was clearly defined, its precipitating factors were known. So dreaded was the doom disorder in the past, hundreds of Victorian writers used descent into madness as a major plot element in their novels. Usually the trigger was the loss of a loved one—a sweetheart, a spouse, a parent. Charles Dickens, for instance, employed the drama and despair of psychosis in his character Miss Havisham in *Great Expectations*.

But what causes someone to break with reality? A variety of things can tip a person into psychosis.

## Causes of Psychosis

Intense, overwhelming anxiety or stress lies at the heart of most psychotic episodes. Some psychological disorders, such as chronic depression and manic-depression, can bring on psychosis as a secondary effect. This apparently results, at least in part, by altering brain chemistry.

Physical stress or trauma can precipitate psychosis as well. In rare instances, a difficult childbirth or stillbirth or an acute reaction to drugs (for example, in surgery patients) can bring on psychosis. Very occasionally, persons receiving psychotropic drugs to alleviate one emotional or psychological problem become psychotic when their body reacts paradoxically—that is, the opposite of the way it's supposed to.

Brain injuries can also spur psychosis, as can alcohol, drugs, syphilis, encephalitis, epilepsy, and some dementias.

# Signs and Symptoms of Psychosis

Psychosis varies in degree from mild to severe. Several key indicators tip us off that the person in question has lost contact with reality.

## Delusions

Delusions are vigorous beliefs in things that can't be true. Shoshone was strongly delusional. He believed the CIA was out to get him because he knew damaging secrets that could topple the government. As it turned out, he was delusional about his firepower, also. When the sheriff's deputies searched the ruined hut and its surroundings, they found a battered .270 with a duct-taped stock and maybe a dozen rounds of ammunition. That explained all the scattered mule deer bones—Shoshone ate venison.

Delusions take many forms. Shoshone, believing he had the power to topple the U.S. government, and pseudo–James Henry, who believed he was Ollie North, suffered from *grandiose* delusions. In our psychiatric practice, we regularly encounter patients who believe they are Jesus Christ (once in a group session we had three of them). People who claim to be U.S. presidents and other famous historical characters line the halls of many psychiatric wards.

*Paranoid* delusions are convictions that you're being persecuted or chased. Shoshone's conviction that the CIA was after him was a paranoid delusion.

Here's an illustration: Let's say you purchase a lottery ticket. If you believe you have as much chance as anyone else to win the lottery, this implies that you know your actual chance of winning is highly remote, which is true statistically. If you believe without a doubt that you are going to win, then your thinking is delusional. If you believe that lottery officials are purposefully trying to keep you, personally, from winning, then you're suffering a paranoid delusion.

Similar to paranoia is the delusion that people are talking about you. A whisper campaign is in full cry. A person who suffers this delusion can watch a football game on television and believe the players huddled on the field are talking about him.

*Somatic* delusions have to do with the physical body, usually involving fancied disease or illness. The hypochondriac who is fully convinced she has cancer, even though her doctors have found no cancer, is an example.

Often at the clinic, we see patients who have *jealousy* delusions. These people are certain their spouses are cheating on them. One woman we counseled was absolutely convinced that her husband was having an affair. Her daughter informed us the husband had died unexpectedly seven months before. This traumatic emotional blow pushed the woman over the edge.

Some delusions defy categorization. One patient was certain his car had rheumatism. He dropped an aspirin in the gas tank every now and then. Another patient accused strangers on the street of stealing his watches. When he was hospitalized, he accused the nurses of stealing his watches.

A friend tells of a woman who insisted that the little girl next door (a perfectly normal little girl) was a witch. Witches have "familiars," and in this case it was the woman's own cat, an aged, corpulent tabby. The woman wanted to drown the cat, but she was afraid if she failed the attempt, the witch would take revenge. Besides, cats have nine lives, and what if this was not her tabby's ninth and final? It would come back to haunt her. The woman had an enormously elaborate scenario set up in her mind.

## Complaints of Thought Control

This is a form of delusion deserving its own category because it occurs with surprising frequency. Perhaps it's because of our technological advances in communications, but whatever the reason, the patients are convinced their thoughts are being withdrawn from their heads, or broadcast on the radio or television, or interfered with electronically. They may feel that outside forces are introducing thoughts into their heads and they cannot stop the intrusion. They may feel that television or radio is speaking directly and personally to them.

Thoughts are our most secret and intimate conscious function. To have that intimacy violated is one of our deepest, darkest fears.

## Hallucinations

Auditory hallucinations are very common. Shoshone heard voices. He was savvy enough to realize that no one else heard them. Are the voices real? To the patient they certainly are. They come from within.

Visual hallucinations might take the form of faces projected on a wall, figures approaching, wolves slinking behind trees, or some other sighting. These images are totally real to the person viewing them. If you tell the person the images do not exist, you will do nothing for the situation except make the person suspicious of your motives.

Less frequently, aromatic or other sensory hallucinations may occur. The person is absolutely certain he or she smells, tastes, or feels something that has no basis in fact.

## Loose Associations in Speech

Rambling monologues, illogical progressions of thought, strange comments reflecting scattered ideas—a person's speech may reflect the loose or random nature of his or her thinking. The brain synapses aren't connecting properly to promote straight-arrow thinking. The listener comes away thinking, "Huh?"

Possibly the synapses aren't connecting at all. The person's poverty of thought is exemplified by not having much to say.

## Emotionless Countenance

An expressionless face, a monotone speech pattern, a listless attitude—the person's countenance is emotionless. Depression frequently causes a sad countenance, but this person's demeanor does not have even that much emotion. It's not sadness, it's emptiness.

## Deteriorating Capabilities

Once upon a time, Shoshone was sharp enough to be a medical corpsman. He graduated from high school. He married, he divorced, he earned an associate's degree. Now the best he could do was pick up his check and shoot mule deer and an occasional rabbit for stew.

The person has trouble functioning now at a level he or she mastered at one time. Once a wage earner, he no longer can hold a job. Once a student, she has dropped out. Once a parent, the person now neglects the kids. This deterioration can come on rapidly or gradually, but it does not go unnoticed by friends and family.

## Reclusive Behavior

Shoshone used to come into town every month about the time of the full moon. Toward the end, he'd skip a month now and then, or maybe two. Eventually, he was showing up only when his beans and flour ran out. The ever-patient postal clerk held his checks for him until he dropped by. The locals, people who lived in remote circumstances by choice, admired his independence; the winter motor home crowd distrusted it.

The once-outgoing person becomes reclusive, or the introverted person cuts off interpersonal relations completely. Withdrawn and self-isolated, the person stays at home or in his or her room.

Unlike the agoraphobic, who is terrified of open spaces and crowds, the psychotic is merely indifferent. The person doesn't want or need any company.

## Slack Personal Hygiene

Several disorders are marked by a disinterest or neglect of bathing and grooming. This in itself is not a telling trait indicating psychosis. It commonly accompanies the other traits, however, and should be considered part of the suite of symptoms.

Shoshone's personal hygiene was so slack people couldn't get past it; it was all they noticed. This neglect of basic hygiene and grooming seems to indicate an asocial indifference. Shoshone, like many psychotics, simply didn't care.

## Peculiar Behavior

When the King James Version of the Bible called Christians "a peculiar people," it opened the door to all manner of gags. What it means is "beyond ordinary" (Titus 2:14) or "set apart" (1 Peter 2:9).

When we use the term *peculiar* here, we mean a lot more than that. We mean *really* peculiar: hoarding perishable food under the bed; stashing a deceased goldfish in the freezer because to part with it is unbearable.

Shoshone muttered to himself a lot; that was his peculiarity.

## Magical Thinking

Small children are experts at magical thinking because they are so self-centric. They believe the universe revolves around them. This kind of innocent, unformed association is appropriate to young children. Maturity will guide the child to a more reasonable and less self-centered approach to cause and effect.

As the psychotic increasingly turns inward, becoming more and more self-centric, magical thinking may reappear. Dr. Minirth tells of one man who, every time he entered an elevator, prayed fervently that the doors would open. At the appropriate floor the door would open in direct answer to his prayer, or so he thought. Had he not prayed, heaven knows how many people would be stuck between floors.

A sweet little English woman was absolutely certain that her luck at Patience—that's Solitaire to us Americans—depended totally upon the number of seconds she shuffled the cards. Too much or too little shuffling misaligned them. Magical thinking.

Magical thinking is actually a part of our heritage, and there's nothing wrong with it if we take it lightly. To throw salt over the shoulder or to avoid walking under a ladder to avert bad luck are superstitions we grew up with. They are magical thinking and we treat them casually, in fun.

When a person ceases to take these superstitions casually, when they become dogma instead of silliness, they have become a sign of mental disorder.

What do you do if a loved one begins to exhibit signs and symptoms of psychosis? The one thing you do *not* do is wait and hope the signs disappear. As these signs and symptoms persist, they burrow deeper and deeper into the person's psyche, making the disorder harder to reverse. The sooner you get help for your loved one, the quicker and better the chances for recovery.

## Schizophrenia

Readers familiar with the term *schizophrenia* may wonder why we have not mentioned it in this discussion. We avoid using the term because of the misunderstanding so many people seem to have about schizophrenia.

The public has come to connect schizophrenia with split personality and describe it as a person inhabited by two or more personalities. That's false. Multiple Personality Disorder is a different thing altogether. *Schizo* does indeed mean split, but it refers to the separating of a person's reason from reality.

With his paranoid delusions and hallucinations, Shoshone exhibited signs of a subtype called paranoid schizophrenia. Other subtypes include disorganized type, in which the person's speech, thoughts, and behavior are confused and randomized; and catatonic type, in which the patient is either immobile, excessively on the move, plagued by peculiarities such as involuntary jumpiness or grimacing, or totally rigid.

Some schizophrenics cannot be characterized easily within a subtype and are referred to as undifferentiated type. Their disturbance falls short of the symptoms we've enumerated, but the person's behavior is odd. You can't overlook it; things are not quite right.

The characteristic symptoms of schizophrenia are delusions, hallucinations, disorganized speech, catatonic or nonsensical behavior, and what we call negative symptoms—when a person's nature becomes uncharacteristically dull, flat, and directionless, and ambition flees. Frequently this disturbance has some other cause, such as mood disorders, a medical problem, or a developmental disorder like autism. We treat the other cause and the schizoid problem abates.

Again, because of the misunderstanding so many people seem to have about schizophrenia, we use the term *psychosis* here, of which schizophrenia is a part, because it works as well for our purposes.

## Treating Psychosis

It used to be that the vast majority of psychotics, once they lapsed into the disorder, were doomed to remain there until death. In the 1950s, diagnosed psychotics comprised about 3 percent of America's population. Numbering in the thousands, they filled half of all the beds in mental hospitals.

Today, thanks to increased understanding of the brain and its chemistry and new medications and therapies, psychotics have a better chance of recovery and leading a more normal life.

After Shoshone was picked up by the mental health professionals, he was taken to a state mental health facility. His psychiatric evaluation identified psychosis.

The assigned psychiatrist told him, "I think I can get rid of the CIA for you. Will you let me?"

This prospect amused Shoshone, because he knew the CIA was out to get him and that was that. When the doctor said she could change things, Shoshone thought *she* was delusional. He went along with her, just to see what would come of it.

Five months later Shoshone became a taxpayer. His psychosis in abeyance, he landed a night job in the kitchen of a nearby restaurant, and with the mental facility's help he got an apartment. During the day he trained as an emergency medical technician, thanks to sponsoring by the local fire department. From there he went to paramedic training. Two years later, he was working for the ambulance company that served the town near which he had lived before his recovery.

Every now and then in winter, he and his crew would rescue some winter visitor and transport the poor snowbird to the hospital. Shoshone treated the locals with special affection. They had known him when.

## Transformation?

What an amazing transformation in a man who forty years ago would have been locked away for his lifetime. From colorful, kooky eccentric to responsible wage earner and taxpayer in a matter of months—Shoshone looked upon his recovery as a miracle.

And yet, as miraculous as it appeared, his transformation was not a shift from Ugly Undesirable to Desirable New Person, but from his psychosis back to the personality he once had been. Drugs did not create a new Shoshone; they restored him. Essentially, the "new" Shoshone was the original Shoshone, picking up again where he left off when his disorder set in.

Recovering stability does not erase memories. Over and over, our patients tell how they mourn the love and laughter their psychosis robbed them of. Some patients may be able to partially restore the wasted years.

Usually, drugs are the key, and a variety of them are available to work the kind of change that occurred in Shoshone. Generally speaking, cognitive therapy (the kind of therapy in which psychiatrists lead their charges to understand and change what is happening mentally) is not effective by itself. You cannot talk the brain chemistry out of being unbalanced. The chemical balances must be redressed first—dragged back into normalcy, if you will—before the patient can think clearly. Otherwise, the delusions and other difficulties remain in control of the patient. Once they are corrected, cognitive therapy—discussion and talk—can sometimes work additional magic in helping the patient remain stable without further recourse to drugs. Very often, however, the patient must maintain a drug regimen throughout life in order to maintain healthy brain chemistry.

At first Shoshone resisted the idea of a lifelong drug regimen. "I want to fix the plumbing, not hold my finger on the leak forever. Get my mental balance back in place and show me how to keep it there."

Our goal is always to obviate the need for drugs. That goal, however, cannot always be attained by psychotics.

Shoshone had lived with his disorder for years. Had the disorder been caught early, he might have been able to do well without drugs. But time had deeply etched his brain chemistry into the new, unhealthy patterns. As it was, the continual, carefully adjusted drug regimen permitted him to function normally in the world, to pursue dreams, to love and learn and work and play. Not a bad outcome for a man who otherwise would have been condemned to a wasted and uncertain life filled with hostility, suspicion, fear, and emptiness.

Psychosis is a heavy blow to the human mind. Although the vast majority of psychotics today are able to return to a normal life, their disorder usually leaves residual damage—scars not in a literal, medical sense, but in a figurative one. Should these people cease medication, perhaps even for a fairly short time, the psychosis returns.

## When Medicine Doesn't Work

A small but persistent number of patients remain psychotic despite medication. Of these, some (apparently no one knows exactly how many) were put on medication, the regimen was found wanting, and they were turned loose without being helped. No fishing around with different drugs, no experimenting to find one that might work. Sure, they tried Thorazine and the other early medications, but nothing happened. But new products out now, such as Clozaril and Risperdal, attack the problem by other avenues. In the last four to five years, just these two medications have healed one-third of patients resistant to the standard medications. The reason these new drugs have been developed is to serve persons whom the original drugs cannot help.

Others among this resistant group took too little or took it wrongly. You'll remember that doctors estimate that up to three-fourths of their patients do not take medicines according to directions (this is all sorts of medications; not just psychotropics). Play fast and loose with an antipsychotic drug, and you have either zero response or multiplied problems. Most antipsychotic drugs seem to work on a sort of bell curve, with dosage plotted horizontally and maximum efficiency vertically. The effectiveness climbs as the dosage increases, but only to a point. As the dosage continues to increase, effectiveness falls away again, eventually to nothing.

Based on experience and statistics he has seen in several sources, Dr. Meier estimates that a significant number of our nation's homeless people could be helped by medication. Unfortunately, they are the people least likely to have access to new discoveries in a supervised drug regimen.

## How the Drugs Work Their Miracles

Two-thirds or more of patients benefit from medications. How do these drugs perform their magic?

Experimentation and tests indicate that the antipsychotics prevent the binding of a neurotransmitter. Although the blocking action begins immediately when the patient starts the drug course, actual change may not occur for several weeks. Once they find an effective drug, patients do not seem to develop a tolerance for it. That is, after the optimal dose is established, it does not have to be increased as the patient gets used to it. However, the side effects do show tolerance, but the effects often abate with time. These drugs are not addictive; patients don't get "hooked."

The blocking action creates several of the adverse side effects associated with these drugs. Moreover, the different kinds of antipsychotic medicines block other things as well—noradrenergic, cholinergic, and histaminergic receptors—and thus each medicine presents a unique suite of side effects.

When we set a patient on a course of medication, we monitor very closely for several reasons. First, we monitor because treatment is completely individualized. A case-hardened patient like Shoshone is going to need a lifetime maintenance regimen to counteract the ingrained imbalances. Other patients may have suffered a brief psychotic reaction, a single episode, and will recover well following a short course. Dosages are also highly individualized because every person reacts a little differently.

Another reason we monitor is because people can easily get into trouble with these medications. Many of the medicines make the person overly sensitive to heat and bright sunlight. Too much sunbathing can make the patient ill. Patients may take legal or illegal cocaine, amphetamines, or other drugs. This is extremely dangerous; the combinations can actually cause the psychosis we are trying so hard to correct and avoid. People also get into trouble frequently by failing to take the medicine as it is intended or by quitting the drug entirely. We call that poor compliance, and we run into it all the time.

Finally, we monitor to make certain several serious, irreversible side effects don't crop up. Primary among them is tardive dyskinesia, a disorder in which the patient's lips or other muscles twitch uncontrollably. Up to 20 percent of patients on long-range drug therapies—that is, a year or longer—develop the involuntary twitches. If not nipped in the bud, they become irreversible. Danger is less with the newer products such as clozapine.

Neuroleptic malignant syndrome, identified as NMS, can be fatal in 15 to 25 percent of the people it strikes. Basically, it's a violent reaction to the neuroleptic drugs. High fever, rigid muscles, sweating, and increased blood pressure and heart rate are some danger signs. Incontinence is another.

The problem is not just that these drugs are potentially so terribly dangerous but that their foe aspect can sneak up on a patient without appropriate supervision. Are they worth the risks? You bet! They revolutionized the lives of thousands of people.

## Other Problems Solved

The antipsychotic drugs, of course, treat psychotic episodes. But they do much more.

An hour or so after taking Haldol (haloperidol), most people who stutter will stop stuttering. Haldol is also effective at controlling a variety of nervous tics. An interesting phenomenon crops up here. We have found that about 80 percent of persons who can correct their stuttering and other tics with Haldol quit taking it. They felt comfortable with their habit and don't want to give it up. Because of the danger of tardive dyskinesia, though, Haldol is not the first choice of treatment.

We find that porphyria, the disease that probably felled King George, the monarch who lost the thirteen colonies, can look a little like psychosis.

Occasionally, other neurological conditions can mimic psychosis. Multiple sclerosis occasionally shows up in that way. So may pernicious anemia and temporal lobe epilepsy. Any such problem involving the dopamine transmitters may be relieved with antipsychotic medicines.

The biggest problems of a schizophrenic or other psychotic usually come from the people around him or her—people who are ashamed, afraid, or simply confused as to how to treat this person. Loved ones may feel angry or frustrated that the patient will not shape up when counseled to do so. We counsel the family members and friends by reminding them that psychoses are primarily medical in nature, just as pneumonia or cancer or the common cold. Psychotics cannot be talked out of their affliction anymore than victims of pneumonia or a cold can. Knowing this, loved ones can treat the psychotic patient with understanding and love.

Considering the span of human history, we have had these medicines a very short time. Psychotics we've had with us throughout time.

## The History of Treating Psychosis

Through most of history, psychotics remained a part of the community, like Shoshone, functioning as best they could, dependent upon others for many things. Generally speaking, their neighbors were fairly tolerant of them, but if the psychotics turned violent or dangerous, they were destroyed. On those occasions when a psychotic recovered spontaneously, he or she simply slipped back into the mainstream.

Then came the notion of locking up the insane to protect themselves and others. People felt that proper, tidy communities need no longer put up with the lunatics bothering decent folk. Families, shamed by a madman in the ranks, now had an acceptable way to hide their embarrassment. The heavy stigma of madness, which entered full flower when institutionalization came into vogue, remains with us today to some extent.

In 1950, Thorazine (chlorpromazine) was being tested for use as an anesthetic. To everyone's startled surprise, most psychotics given Thorazine returned to their right minds. Its use in anesthesia fell by the wayside. In 1954, the drug was approved as a neuroleptic, a drug to improve mental or neural maladjustment.

What a miraculous, glorious awakening! By the thousands, mentally unbalanced people stabilized well enough to go home. The mental hospitals were emptying out, and utopians envisioned a day when one wonder drug or another would render mental institutions obsolete.

But Thorazine did not work on everyone, and even people who benefited suffered side effects. Persons on Thorazine often have a distant look about them. Their socialization skills, damaged by the disorder, remain in disarray. They don't mix with others. These plus other sometimes-severe side effects spurred the search for new kinds of drugs. We have quite an arsenal of effective medications now to correct the chemical imbalances that cause psychosis.

Dr. Minirth tells of a young man, Sam, who was in and out of mental hospitals for a long time. He had tried several medications—Moban, Stelazine, Prolixin, Navane, Haldol. Nothing helped. Sam's family okayed starting him on Clozaril with some trepidation, having heard its reputation for destroying bone marrow. But Clozaril's reputation also includes success when other medications fail. Then Sam's family moved and he came under Dr. Minirth's care. The young man's blood count indeed began to drop, but at just about that time, the brand new Risperdal became available.

Dr. Minirth started Sam on a transition from Clozaril to Risperdal. "I was out of town for several weeks," Dr. Minirth recalls. "When I got back, I saw Sam and blurted, 'What happened to you?!' He was a new person. No more blank, empty facial expression, no more paranoid schizophrenia. The antipsychotics, wonderful as they are, usually don't produce results as dramatic as Sam's. But to him, Risperdal truly was a miracle drug."

## The Antipsychotic Drugs

The sum effect of any of these drugs is to slow a patient down—a calming effect. That means you don't take these when other depressants are present in the system, such as downers or alcohol—*especially* alcohol! But their main mechanism action is to alter the neurotransmitters of the brain so that a person can think more rationally.

These drugs can produce impressive results at times—true friends. They can also carry potentially grave side effects, such as neuroleptic malignant syndrome—foes.

**Haldol** (haloperidol) and Haldol decanoate (a long-acting version for patients needing prolonged therapy) are used to help patients with Tourette's syndrome and certain behavior problems in children (hyperactivity accompanying conduct disorders such as aggressiveness, mood swings, and frustration that quickly get out of hand). An injectable form brings swift relief to acutely agitated patients with severe psychotic symptoms. Haldol has been used in certain kinds of autism. (If the character in *Rainman* had taken Haldol, he possibly might have been closer to normal, but of course this would have loused up the movie.)

**Navane** (thiothixene) is usually administered orally as a pill, but it is also available for injection. This is a blessing in patients who cannot successfully take oral medication. Another blessing: in many patients, Navane acts quickly.

**Stelazine** (trifluoperazine HCl) is available in a fluid concentrate that serves conditions where oral medication is preferred. For most people, it is not as sedating as older drugs such as Thorazine and Mellaril.

**Thorazine** (chlorpromazine) is the grand old original, the drug that started it all, and it is still widely used. It is more strongly sedating than are newer products such as Haldol, Moban, and Navane. Thorazine is also an antiemetic (which is to say it prevents nausea and vomiting). That can pose a problem if the Thorazine masks the nausea symptoms that would warn the doctor that something else is going wrong. For example, a symptom of Reye's syndrome is vomiting; Thorazine might mask that symptom so well that the doctor misses the accurate diagnosis. Thorazine is available as a suppository, an injectable, a syrup, a concentrate, and in tablets.

**Prolixin** (fluphenazine) is available as three different compounds, fluphenazine HCl, fluphenazine enanthate, and fluphenazine decanoate. All are equally effective, but the enanthate and decanoate seem to extend over a longer period of time and are useful for chronic schizophrenia. Prolixin is available as an injectable, a pill, or a syrup. The drug nonselectively hits not only the central nervous system, but the whole body as well. The usual warnings about side effects apply.

**Moban** (molindone HCl) acts quickly; its presence in the blood peaks about an hour and a half after it is taken and lasts twenty-four to thirty-six hours. Patients using Moban rarely have trouble with seizures.

**Mellaril** (thioridazine), taken orally, helps calm agitated patients and children exhibiting out-of-control, explosive behavior. In addition to helping psychotic patients, it may help in depression. Elderly patients who suffer from fears, sleep disturbances, anxiety, and agitation often find relief with Mellaril.

**Risperdal** (risperidone) is an exciting new drug. It seems to work well even in refractory patients (people who do not respond well to most medicines). Risperdal may produce fewer side effects than do many other drugs. Its potential continues to be explored.

**Clozaril** (clozapine) blocks several sites besides the dopamine D-1 and D-2 receptors and seems particularly active in that part of the brain (limbic) controlling emotional responses. Because of its possible side effects (detailed in the Appendix), such as a risk of seizures, doctors try Clozaril only after other drugs have proven ineffective. To minimize the chance of problems, patients' white blood cell count is monitored weekly. As is the case with all these drugs, it sometimes fails to work, but when it does, it works splendidly, including the times when other drugs fail.

**Serentil** (mesoridazine besylate) treats certain brain dysfunctions as well as psychosis. People who do not respond to other medications often come around with Serentil.

**Compazine** (prochlorperazine) is available as a pill, a syrup, a suppository, and an injectable. It is used primarily for

controlling severe nausea and vomiting (thus the suppository).

**Loxitane** (loxapine succinate), available as an injectable
for immediate relief and an oral medicine for long-term use,
possesses a chemistry that differs from other antipsychotics.
Although it acts in a somewhat different way, the usual warnings about side effects apply. Side effects, especially tardive
dyskinesia and neuroleptic malignant syndrome, are described in the Appendix.

**Taractan** (chlorprothixene), in pills or concentrate, slows
you up, as do others. Even brushing your teeth can be a slow
and tedious ordeal.

**Trilafon** (perphenazine) is another antipsychotic that is
also an antiemetic (for you who like the technical data, all
dopamine-2 receptor antagonists do that). By controlling nausea and vomiting, it can mask that particular symptom that
might otherwise warn of other serious problems. It is available in tablets and as a concentrate and injectable.

## CHAPTER 9

*I'm taking care of my two-year-old daughter and my mother, and they both act exactly alike. I'm going crazy. I don't know what to do.*

# ALZHEIMER'S AND OTHER DEMENTIAS

Everyone said that Fred Hannah was never quite the same after his wife, Mae, died. Slim as a pencil all his life, he lost weight he couldn't really afford to lose. He slouched so much that he looked inches shorter than his full height of six feet. His hair got grayer and his wrinkles deeper.

Fred was retired, and he spent a lot of time puttering around the yard of his suburban home, though he didn't actually get much done. He let his magazine subscriptions expire and quit taking the paper. He watched TV a lot, but he didn't have any favorite programs or movies.

Mrs. Murphy, a busybody who had more time than tact, lived across the street. Her day was not complete until she called her gossiping buddies with news of Fred's latest foible.

"Martha, you should see his lawn. What a mess! That Fred mowed half the front lawn then put his mower away. He did the same thing last week. The east side's mowed, and the grass on the Colberts' side is tall enough to hide a pony. His yard is really an embarrassment to the neighborhood. Yesterday he stuffed a bag full of garbage in the mailbox. And his windows! They look like they haven't been washed in two years. I doubt he can see out them anymore."

Fred's son Don started to suspect something was wrong when he stopped by to visit his dad on a trip through town. Don lived about a hundred miles away and didn't see his dad much. Busy. You know how it goes. A few minutes into his visit, he picked up the phone to call his wife and found the line was dead.

"Happened a couple of days ago," Fred said. "I haven't needed it, so I haven't gotten around yet to asking them to come fix it."

"I'll call it in from the gas station when I leave." Don looked around. "Where's your toaster?"

"Toaster?" Fred looked puzzled.

When Don opened the refrigerator for a soft drink, he found the toaster. It was about the only thing in the fridge. "Dad. What do you do for food?"

"Whaddaya mean? You're getting a little critical and snippy, aren't you?"

"No. I just—"

"Well get off it!"

The next morning before he went to work, Don did some calling around. His dad's phone was out because he hadn't paid the bill in three months. Don paid it, plus the charge to restore service. His dad hadn't paid the electricity bill lately either, or the water bill.

When Don called Fred's next-door neighbor, Mr. Colbert admitted he had been putting Fred's garbage out for him; Fred kept forgetting that the truck comes on Tuesdays. Another neighbor admitted signing Fred up for Meals on Wheels so the old man would get a decent dinner now and then.

Don recalled that, during the last six months, whenever he talked to his dad on the phone, his dad seemed a little distant, had trouble tracking a conversation, and said silly things. Don had more or less dismissed the observations as signs of mourning, even though it had been two years since his mom had died. Now Don began to realize the truth: at age 69, Dad's clutch was starting to slip.

Don hung up the phone, stared at the wall awhile, and wept.

## Recognizing Dementia

Fred Hannah is typical of the most rapidly growing sub-class in America—people who are living well past retirement age and facing difficult problems with dementias. Alzheimer's disease alone, only one of the dementias, affects 10 percent of persons over age 65, almost one-fifth of persons over age 80, and nearly half of persons who reach age 90. Complicating the picture is the fact that the elderly form our fastest-growing population subgroup.

Dementia causes suffering not just for the one who has the disease, but also for the victim's loved ones, as they struggle to care for the deteriorating person.

A master of denial, Fred insisted he was fine, maybe just a little slower, that's all. He denied stuffing his garbage in the mailbox instead of the trash can; he blamed it on youthful pranksters. He faulted the phone company for cutting off his phone without any warning. He said the electric bill must have gotten lost in the mail. Well, no, he hadn't reconciled his checkbook lately, but he didn't write all that many checks anyway. Besides, his social security check went in on automatic deposit, so he knew he had money.

As is typical in cases like this, Don Hannah would have a difficult time getting his dad to accept the outside help he needed. Fred would bitterly fight the loss of independence, loss of control, loss of personal dignity, and loss of his home. And like most elderly people suffering dementia, if he did experience these losses, he was likely to give up on life.

Says a friend about the death of her eighty-year-old

mother: "Mom's biggest fear was a catastrophic illness that wouldn't kill her. A stroke. A disabling heart problem. She was terrified of ending up in a nursing home and extremely afraid of being a burden on my brothers and me. She lived alone, independent to the end, even though she probably shouldn't have, and I thank God every day that when He took her, He took her completely. From her perspective, it was the most wonderful gift He could have given her."

Don Hannah faced an agonizing question: When was Dad going to be too far gone to live on his own? How long do you let the man stumble along, a danger to himself and possibly to others, and when do you blow the whistle and take over?

Fred often let pots boil dry on the stove. He left the bathroom heater on, with towels hanging on the rack inches above it. Not long ago, he turned the water on in the tub for a bath and then forgot and lay down for a nap. An hour later, his hot water long since gone, he found the bathroom floor flooded.

Fred still had his driver's license, and that scared the daylights out of Don.

"Sure, Dad's memory isn't perfect, but no one's is," Don told a friend. "After all, I always have to remind my son to bring his bike in out of the rain. And I forget things now and then. How do I know if Dad has dementia? In fact, what *is* dementia?"

## Signs and Symptoms of Dementia

In popular use, "demented" usually means insanity with a macabre twist. Batman went up against demented villains like the Joker. When someone laughs at a joke that makes fun of people who are physically or mentally challenged, we say that person has a demented sense of humor.

That's not dementia in its psychological sense. We use the word to denote deterioration of the intellect—*de* being out of, or away from, *mens* being the mind. Generally, that deterioration is caused by something organic, a physical change brought on by old age or something else.

In medicine we differentiate between presenile dementia—onset before age 65—and senile dementia—onset after age 65. Here's what we look for. Perhaps you can use these guidelines to evaluate someone you care about, as Don Hannah might evaluate his father, Fred.

## Memory Progressively Deteriorates

They say memory is the first thing to go. More precisely, it's the first thing we consider in an evaluation.

We take great care not to judge a person over age 65 too harshly, counting every lapse of memory as a sign of dementia. That kind of harsh judgment of the elderly happens all too often in our society. Everybody, no matter what age, can be forgetful.

Rather, when weighing memory impairment, we look for:

## Difficulty Learning New Information

This can be mental or physical information. For example, a year before her death, Mae Hannah went with her friend Barbara to a clog dancing club. They intended to join the club, and the club members welcomed them. Barbara instantly got with the program. She would watch a step, go through the motions of the step a few times in slow motion, then she had it. Mae just could not get it. No matter how she tried, she couldn't remember what her body was supposed to do from moment to moment. She could not learn the new somatic information.

She had just as much trouble remembering the matching cards when she played Concentration with her grandson. (But then, it's next to impossible to beat a five-year-old at Concentration.)

## Difficulty Recalling Data

Fred could not remember his home phone number. He could not remember the name of the little girl who recently moved in next door, no matter how often he heard it. He used to be able to rattle off his social security number. Not anymore. He no longer blurted out the answers on *Jeopardy*—rather, the questions. He knew the answers; he knew he knew them. They were on the tip of his tongue, but they just wouldn't come.

When weighing learning and recall difficulties, we look for a frequent, continual pattern of memory impairment, not isolated circumstances.

In later stages, the person forgets details of personal history, familiar people's identity, the spouse's name and, eventually, his or her own name.

## Verbal Skills Slip

The loss of skill to use or comprehend words is called *aphasia*. Fred couldn't recall common terms for everyday items. Oh, he knew what the doohickey was, but he couldn't remember the term for it. When Don came by for a visit one day, Fred couldn't think of that, uh, that—you know—there. He pointed to the back of the car.

"The trunk, Dad?"

"Yeah."

As the problem progresses, the person ceases to talk much or talks nonsense, meaning one thing but getting the words wrong. Speech degenerates to nonsense words, soundalike words, and finally to grunts and incoherent shouts.

## Orientation Degenerates

One night Don Hannah got a phone call from Mary Murphy, his dad's neighbor. She told him that Fred had been picked up by the police and taken to the hospital.

"The hospital!" Don said.

"They found him wandering downtown. They didn't want to put him in jail, so they gave him a room in the hospital for a few hours. When the police asked him his name, he couldn't remember it, but they got his name and address from his driver's license. They contacted the Colberts, you know, your dad's next-door neighbors, and Bill Colbert has gone to the hospital to get your dad."

The next morning when Don arrived at his dad's house, the two men got into a big argument. Don had never known his father to be so verbally caustic and abusive before. Fred insisted the incident the night before had been a simple mistake. He got disoriented, and it wouldn't happen again.

As his disease progressed, Fred would become disoriented to time as well as place. He would forget what day it was; forget appointments; fail to realize it was April instead of February.

## Cognitive Skills Degenerate

Eventually Fred would look at something he had been familiar with for years—the refrigerator, for example—and not know what it was. Simple arithmetic would become impossible. In the final phases, he would fail to notice people and circumstances around him. He would fold into a closed little world of his own. Each moment would become isolated, without reference to the moment past or the moment to come.

## The Personality Changes

"He used to be so polite and sweet. I wish you had known him then."

*Used to be.* As Fred Hannah's dementia progressed he became increasingly curt and angry. Part of it was the disease. Another part was fury and frustration about what was happening to him.

There is a period of time between early onset and full-blown dementia when the person is aware that mental processes are falling apart and no one can stop it. Rage is a natural reaction to this realization.

## Motor Skills Deteriorate

Fred's motor functions began failing to coordinate well with what his ears and eyes told him. He had trouble gauging space; he failed to negotiate stairs, missed the step up to the front door, and had difficulty getting out of the car. His table manners became embarrassing to anyone around him. He ate with his fingers, grunted and slurped, and played with his food. Eventually, he would forget such simple things as how to walk smoothly. Seizures and incontinence would signal the beginning of the end.

How bad is bad? We consider memory loss and the other symptoms to be serious if the person's job or personal life suffers. The deterioration can take place in a matter of a few years or over many years. The mental state can deteriorate to the point that the person requires twenty-four-hour supervision, even as the body remains in fair health.

Although society has come to call any of these problems Alzheimer's disease, there are actually several kinds of dementias. All or just a few of the symptoms may appear in any of them. Often, a clear diagnosis of Alzheimer's, as opposed to some other deteriorating disease, can be determined only by autopsy.

## Types of Dementias

The lay observer can benefit greatly by knowing the kinds and causes of dementia. People often are quick to label a loved one's mental deterioration as Alzheimer's. But that's not necessarily the case. Certain chemicals, wrong drugs or wrong doses, physical problems—these and other factors can cause Alzheimer's-like symptoms. And many of the other dementias can be reversed.

In medicine, we sort dementias according to the part of the brain affected. Damage or disease of the cortex, the outer portion of the brain (if the brain were a tree, the cortex would be the bark), is responsible for cortical dementias. Subcortical dementias arise from deeper within the brain.

### Cortical Dementias

**Alzheimer's disease.** The key to this, the most common of the dementias, dangles just beyond science's fingertips. We know so much about it, but the things we must know—what causes it, how to stop it—so far elude us. Imaging techniques on living brains don't show us what we must know. Only after autopsy can we definitely determine whether the dementia is Alzheimer's.

In autopsied brains, we find tangled knots of nerve threads and senile plaques, which are little globs of non-brain tissue. You probably have seen pictures of a normal human brain and thus know how wrinkled the cortex is and how those wrinkles and convolutions are closely packed together. Not in an Alzheimer's patient. The convolutions shrink back, leaving open canyons where once they pressed upon each other.

We have also been doing detailed gene mapping, trying to find if there are genetic anomalies in Alzheimer's patients. In the past, head injuries have been linked to Alzheimer's. People rendered unconscious by a blow to the head seemed at increased risk for the dementia. Also, a particular gene, apo-E4, seems to confer increased risk. Now we are seeing that if you carry that gene *and* get knocked out, your chances go up to ten times what people with neither factor can expect.

And then there's the debate over aluminum. Autopsy reveals an unusual accumulation of aluminum in the brains of Alzheimer's victims. The question: Does that accumulation of aluminum cause the brain's disintegration, *or*, does the aluminum get stalled out there because the brain is disintegrating? Is the aluminum cause or effect? Can you prevent or postpone Alzheimer's by avoiding aluminum?

Aluminum is one of the most common elements in nature, but it is so active chemically that it binds tightly with other elements, making it virtually unavailable . . . we think. We have no idea which aluminum compounds might be metabolized within the human body in such a way that the metal is released as an available ion. Some people will say that avoiding ingested or absorbed aluminum, as for example banning certain deodorants, cookware, and such, is not only a good preventative, but also a possible treatment. At least, they claim, deterioration might slow down.

On average, victims usually live another ten years or so after the symptoms of dementia become clear. Death often comes not from the disease itself but from a secondary infection of some sort. Also, the dementia can be responsible for a fatal fall or misjudgment, the cause of death being recorded not as the disease but as an accident.

**Infections.** Creutzfeldt-Jakob disease is caused by a slow virus. We've discovered several slow viruses, strange little disease-makers that infect early and show no evidence of their presence until much later. Once they invade their host, slow viruses take years to develop. C-J looks like Alzheimer's and acts like Alzheimer's, with about the same onset and manifestations. It brings death after only a year or so, however. Some cases have been traced to corneal or other organ transplants from infected persons. Because the symptoms are so gradual, the infected person would not know the virus was present.

Syphilis in some forms causes dementia or lays background symptoms of dementia behind the more obvious problems of delusion and paranoia.

**Pick's disease.** The brains of people with Pick's disease contain Pick bodies. This means nothing to most people; we detect the Pick bodies only upon autopsy. There are other changes as well, but none the casual observer would see. Otherwise, the disease progresses about the same as Alzheimer's. Death comes in two to ten years.

## Subcortical Dementias

**Multi-infarct dementia.** We understand a little about what happens to cause this, the second most common reason for mental disintegration. Infarct refers to cell death, usually caused by a clog or plug. If the grease trap in your sink infarcts, you can pull the stopper, but the dishwater doesn't drain away. The drain is dead.

You'll recall in the chapter on anxiety, Sue Martin experienced an acute myocardial infarction—a heart attack. Her AMI occurred because a blood vessel feeding her heart became clogged and that particular bit of her heart was starving to death, literally; its cells were receiving no oxygen and getting rid of no waste products. In her case it was a small vessel clog causing limited damage.

When a major clog occurs in the brain instead of the heart, starving the brain cells beyond the clog, we call it a stroke (in medical terms, a cerebrovascular accident, CVA). We believe a multi-infarct dementia is tiny little strokes, tiny blood vessels in the brain clogging up. Lacunes result, white matter lesions deep within the brain. Exactly how the lacunes and tiny blood vessels relate (or which comes first, the clog or the lacune) we don't know. Regardless, they are there.

Perhaps at one site damage occurs and the victim doesn't notice. At another site, damage affects the use of the victim's left leg for walking. The muscles are fine, the bone is fine, the nerves are fine, but the leg no longer gets a message from the brain to move forward for the next step. The left leg still functions, but only when a different part of the brain, a part not affected, tells it to.

A bit of cognitive thinking goes—an association, memory, a speech function, use of a muscle group. A bit here, a bit there. Sometimes seizures occur.

Transient ischemic attacks happen commonly in the elderly. TIAs are generally temporary, their effects lasting a day or two before normal function returns. About one-third of persons experiencing TIAs will later develop an infarction, usually within a few weeks.

The onset of multi-infarct dementia is more rapid than Alzheimer's, and that's sometimes a fairly good way to tell them apart. It accounts for about 15 percent of dementias.

**Huntington's chorea.** One person in ten thousand, usually between the ages of thirty-five and fifty, will experience the dementia and movement problems of Huntington's chorea. We know why. The disease is caused by a dominant gene on the fourth chromosome of the victim. Fifty percent of the children of persons with Huntington's chorea will also carry the gene. About 25,000 people suffer from it now, with perhaps 125,000 children at risk.

Sometimes the dementia shows up first, and sometimes the irregular, jerky movements we call chorea appear first. The chorea's appearance usually clues us in to what's going on. But it's hard to diagnose the disorder when the dementia is presented first; the dementia could signal several disorders. However, we now have genetic screening to tell if the gene is present.

The sudden, jerky movements of Huntington's chorea usually start around the face, and as time passes the chorea proceeds outward and downward. Getting excited or upset increases the chorea. It disappears during sleep.

Memory and organizational skills slip. The personality may sour. Anxiety and psychosis appear. Death comes anywhere from fifteen to twenty years later. Often the immediate cause of death is pneumonia, when the patient's muscles deteriorate and the patient aspirates (draws into the lungs) food, drink, vomitus, or saliva.

**Normal pressure hydrocephalus.** People used to call this water on the brain. It occurs mostly in the elderly and causes shuffling, unstable walking, dementia, and loss of bladder control. We can sometimes spot hydrocephalus with resonance imaging; the brain cavities enlarge.

## Other Types and Causes

**Metabolic and disease dysfunctions.** A number of psychiatric symptoms and dementias arise when things go wrong with the body. When doctors can correct the physical problem, the dementias are corrected as well.

Endocrine imbalances frequently reduce brain functions. When this happens we work to restore the balance.

If the brain doesn't get enough oxygen (as, for instance, when the heart is weakened), memory loss, dementia, and sometimes anxiety result. Delivering oxygen eases the problem.

The wrong concentration of salts in the body, particularly sodium, causes fluids to move in the wrong direction—into cells instead of out of them, or vice versa. We control the salts with changes in diet and sometimes certain drugs.

Brain tumors and hematomas often produce dementia, perhaps days after the initial damage occurs—a blow to the head, for example. Slow-growing tumors can mimic Alzheimer's disease.

Kidney and liver ailments can cause intellectual impairment, particularly if the patient is on dialysis.

Vitamin deficiency, niacin in particular, can deteriorate into dementia. When the deficiencies are caused by or exacerbated by alcoholism, the dementia is worse because the effects tend to multiply. Pellagra, caused by niacin shortage, shows up in many alcoholics. Restoring an adequate source of niacin eases the problem.

**Drug reactions.** Any drug can induce at least temporary impairment, and particularly so if a person is taking more than one drug. It's one of the first things we look for in evaluating any disorder.

Elderly people tend to be more sensitive to drugs. A bit too high a dose or a few minor errors in following instructions can impair the patient. In some cases, a problem diagnosed as senile dementia would not exist at all were the patient not on medication. When the drug is withdrawn or altered, the dementia usually disappears.

**Metal and other poisonings.** Metal poisoning often causes brain dysfunction and dementia. This is why we monitor the mercury content of seafood so closely. Autopsy reveals that in Wilson's disease, which mimics other disorders, copper shows up in the brain and other organs. Heavy metals besides mercury that we know can cause problems are aluminum, arsenic, bismuth, lead (thus, no-lead paint and unleaded gasoline), and manganese.

People who work around and thus inhale fumes of substances such as toluene, methyl alcohol, and trichloroethylene, can suffer dementia, usually only after long exposure. Industrial workers and dry cleaning workers would be susceptible. At much higher risk are the folks who cook illegal drugs. They use dementia-inducing chemicals by the bucketful. Law enforcement officers claim that after a couple of batches of drugs have been cooked in a given house, apartment, or storage bay, you might as well tear the place down; the fumes have impregnated the walls, making the room, and often the whole building, too poisonous to use.

**Parkinson's disease.** People with Parkinson's disease walk with short, shuffling steps. Trembling is another characteristic of the disease. Although it primarily affects motor functions—moving, sitting, performing detailed movements—Parkinson's also brings on dementia in perhaps half of its victims.

Some people react to certain drugs with Parkinson's-like symptoms. We call that parkinsonism or pseudo-Parkinson's.

We're working hard at ways to cure these problems or at least alleviate their effects.

## Treating Dementias

Don Hannah shook his head sadly. "If ever we needed a miracle drug, now's the time."

How right he is.

We have not yet come close to a cure for Alzheimer's disease or the other dementias, but we can, to some extent, ameliorate the symptoms for a while. Researchers are tackling the problem from two sides: to reduce the symptoms, and to reduce the disorder itself.

It would seem that drugs that improve brain function, such as the stimulants that help persons with Attention Deficit Disorder, ought to sharpen deteriorating dementia victims. But that's not the case. Lithium is an amazing drug, but when it's tried on dementia patients, it's just another light metal. Other psychotropic drugs, such as antipsychotics, don't seem to produce much effect either. They sometimes show promise in experimental animals, only to fall flat when tried on human beings. It's one of the most frustrating aspects of dementia management.

One promising drug, Cognex (tacrine HCl), improves the cognitive functions—that is, the work that goes on in the cortex of the brain—of people with mild to moderate signs of Alzheimer's. It is not a cure; we emphasize that to patients and their caregivers. It does nothing but postpone the inevitable; however, most people gladly grasp at that straw. The downside is that Cognex, being powerful, can cause some powerful side effects—nausea and vomiting, diarrhea, jaundice, and other nasty surprises.

Once Alzheimer's and similar dementias become established, about the only thing we can do is treat the symptoms as best we can.

## The History of Treating Dementias

Senility has always been with us. Until the last hundred years, however, people usually died before senility had a chance to emerge. Hard-hearted as it sounds, conquering infection and disease has opened the door to dementia. Although life expectancy in the actuarial tables hasn't risen a whole lot, people who make it into old age live a longer old age. Some say that dementia is inevitable, that every person in the world who lives long enough will succumb to a senile dementia.

Loss of intellectual function sets a person up for errors of judgment and physical accident. You can count on a demented patient to pull feeding tubes and other lines. Given the opportunity, the person may stroll out onto the freeway, walk into a stairwell without remembering to use the steps, trip over furniture. Many and unavoidable are the traps into which a demented person may fall.

To prevent such accidents and errors, nursing homes and similar facilities in the past tied the persons down. This use of restraints was highly criticized, and rightly so, as being demeaning and harmful. Persons in restraints suffer more health problems and weakness than do persons allowed to move about.

On the other hand, what were nursing home and hospital staff to do? It's prohibitively expensive to employ a caretaker to sit at the person's elbow twenty-four hours a day, and impractical to constantly reinsert yanked IVs and feeding lines. Social and ethical considerations, therefore, weigh heavily in the management of these dementias.

Though not miracles, drugs were seen by some mental health caregivers as godsends in helping to manage the problems caused by dementia. Others saw them as totally unacceptable answers to complex questions.

In the long run, drugs so far can do very little to stem the tide of mental disintegration once it starts rolling.

Not that we aren't trying. The trick is to provide drugs that can halt or prevent either the deterioration itself or its effects without also causing intolerable side effects.

We aren't there yet.

## Drugs Used for Treating Alzheimer's and Other Dementias

### Levodopa

Parkinson's disease is associated with depleted dopamine (one of the neurotransmitters, remember) in the corpus striatum, a part of the cerebrum. Giving the person dopamine to jack the level doesn't work; dopamine can't cross from blood to brain well. But dopamine's precursor, levodopa, can filter through to an extent; the basal ganglia then convert it into the needed dopamine.

Unfortunately, a lot of the levodopa taken orally is sopped up by other nerves and converted before it gets into the brain, so you have to have a high levodopa level in order for the brain to get much. Also unfortunately, high levodopa levels cause severe side effects—nausea and mental imbalance, for example.

Adding another ingredient, carbidopa, slows down the conversion of levodopa into dopamine outside the brain and thus reduces the nasty side effects.

## Other Drugs

**Cognex** (tacrine HC1) improves the cognitive functions of people with mild to moderate signs of Alzheimer's. It is not a cure. A powerful drug, Cognex can cause nausea and vomiting, diarrhea, jaundice, and other side effects.

**Atamet** is a combination of carbidopa and levodopa designed to fight Parkinson's disease while being less irritating than either one used alone. The carbidopa eases the bad effects of the levodopa.

**Dopar** is straight levodopa. Patients taking MAOIs should not take Dopar. People with lung or heart problems should use it cautiously, if at all. Because side effects are common, we start very low and build the titer a bit at a time.

**Haldol** (haloperidol), and perhaps other antipsychotics as well; very occasionally, it may relieve some of the symptoms of Huntington's chorea.

**Inderal** (propranolol) may help with problems of violence. Be aware that it sometimes takes a month for the effects to become noticeable.

**Laradopa** is a different brand of levodopa, identical with Dopar.

**Parlodel** (bromocryptine mesylate) is usually given in conjunction with levodopa. Its purpose is to lower the long-term maintenance dosage of levodopa—still another ploy to lessen the side effects. If the patient does not respond well to levodopa, the patient is not going to get much use from Parlodel either.

**Sinemet** is a carbidopa-levodopa mix similar to Atamet.

**Symmetrel** (amantadine) alone or with L-Dopa seems to help Parkinson's sufferers by, in part, adjusting dopamine balances. This approach is called a "classic cure," meaning that it's what we've been using, but it doesn't do much good.

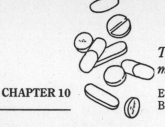

*Take two aspirin and call me in the morning.*

EVERY COMEDIAN IN THE BUSINESS

**CHAPTER 10**

# HEADACHE AND PAIN RELIEF

Lyddie Marks sat in her doctor's waiting area and thumbed through an outdated magazine. She paused to reflect on a full-page brand name aspirin ad. So what's to advertise? Like the rest of the world, Lyddie grew up with aspirin.

When she got her tonsils out in the 1940s, the doctors gave her aspergum to chew. It worked; her sore throat abated. The gum's candy coating wasn't bad. She disliked the taste of the gum itself, but not as much as she detested the taste of uncoated aspirin tablets. Aspergum was made for little kids like her.

When she sprained her ankle in high school gym class, she took aspirin. It worked. Right after she gave birth to her first child, the doctor told her to take aspirin. It worked. When she developed arthritis in the joints of her right hand, her doctor suggested aspirin. Again, it worked. When her husband graduated into the High Risk for Heart Attack ranks, several sources suggested he take one aspirin daily, so Lyddie did, too.

When she entered menopause, she tried aspirin for the monthly migraines that came as part of it. It didn't do a thing. This very minute, as she sat in the doctor's office leafing through the magazine, she felt like gnomes with blacksmiths' hammers were busily pounding on her skull just behind her right eye.

These days she was a bit plumper than she ought to be. Her lifestyle had certainly become more sedentary. Perhaps these changes contributed to the fact that aspirin no longer worked as well as it used to. She knew metabolism alters as one gets older. That didn't sit well with her; the constant little reminders of advancing years never did.

From the doorway, the nurse called Lyddie's name. Lyddie followed the nurse mechanically. She went through the routine of getting weighed, giving a urine sample, getting her blood pressure taken.

In the examination room she removed her clothes and slipped into the atrocious paper gown. She decided that mean-spirited people with a desire to embarrass and humiliate must have designed these gowns. Lyddie thought, *These are the ugliest, most undignified, most revealing, most insulting—*

"We look out of sorts today, Mrs. Marks. Is something troubling us?" Dr. Berrends said, stepping into the room and startling Lyddie.

"Why do you doctors always use the first person plural?" Lyddie asked, still fuming about the medical gown. With a hop, she perched on the edge of the examination table.

Dr. Berrends plunked down on the stool by the Formica counter and jotted something into Lyddie's folder. "Are you certain you're taking your hormone replacement pills faithfully, every single day?"

"I'm certain. And I'm still getting these migraines every month, on schedule. I have one right now," Lyddie replied.

"So I gathered," Dr. Berrends said.

Lyddie thought she detected a certain dry, ironic tinge in the doctor's voice.

"Nothing over the counter touches them," Lyddie explained. "I tried aspirin, buffered aspirin, ibuprofen, everything. I want you to increase the strength of the hormone medicine I'm taking."

"There are problems with that." Dr. Berrends turned on her stool to face Lyddie and leaned back against the wall. "Once the pills took effect, that is, about the time the hot flashes ended, they suppressed hormone production in your ovaries. If you're getting headaches now, it's something other than hormonal."

"Doctor, I made this appointment three weeks ago. Do you know why I made it for today? Because I knew I'd bring one of these headaches with me. They're that regular."

Dr. Berrends smiled with that familiar, cold, heartless smile Lyddie had grown to detest. "They must be due to something else, and we may never find out what it is. You may just have to live with a headache once a month."

Lyddie sat a moment as her reasoning mind quietly disconnected. "Of all the—"

She scooped up her clothes, marched out, and was halfway down the hall before she remembered how much the hideous paper gown fails to cover.

## The Giant Problem of Pain

Americans spend $90 billion annually on pain relief, and that cost does not factor in lost workdays—upwards of 600 million of them each year. Headaches (157 million workdays) lead the litany of woes.

There are several strong psychological aspects to pain and pain control. For one, pain can be disconcerting at the least, and chronic pain may be partly responsible for depression. It is a factor in suicide, particularly among the elderly.

Too, people fear strong pain relievers. "Will it change me

from my usual outgoing personality into a zombie?" How often we get that kind of question when we prescribe a narcotic or other powerful analgesic. Narcotics are viciously misused, being one of the most freely circulating of illicit street drugs. People fear not only possible addiction, but also the social stigma attached to such drugs. In some foreign countries you can be arrested and convicted of possessing certain drugs even when you have a valid American prescription.

Pain control, then, takes on important psychotropic aspects, even though the painkillers are not, properly speaking, psychotropic drugs.

## How Pain Happens

Some folks seem to go through life oblivious to pain. Lyddie was one of them. She seldom got a headache—except on schedule. She didn't have everyday aches and pains. People who put up with endless rounds of chronic pain would envy her.

We have learned some interesting things about why pain occurs in the first place, and why some people hurt more than others.

### The Mechanism of Pain

You're walking across your living room on your way to the comfortable overstuffed chair, when *wham!* you clunk your shin into the corner of the coffee table. Hurts like blue blazes! You may yell and clutch the offended shin. Over time, you will watch its pallid scuff mark swell and turn blue, green, charcoal, and yellow. The mark persists; the pain subsides. What went on in that first moment when shin met coffee table?

Struck by that solid, unyielding heavy force, your shin's living cells (skin and muscle, but especially the thin membrane covering your shinbone, the tibia) were compressed, momentarily misshapen. Some ruptured. Capillaries, the tiny vessels among the cells, popped open. The damaged cells instantly released certain chemicals that tell the rest of the body, "I've been insulted!"

The chemicals alerted nearby nerve endings (there are hardly any cells in the body, except in your brain, that aren't near pain-detecting nerve endings). They shot a teeny electrical impulse to the spinal cord. The spinal cord relayed the message immediately to the thalamus of the brain and on to the brain's convoluted surface, the cortex. Only when the signal reached there did you become aware, you clumsy oaf, that you just whanged into the coffee table.

Once cell deaths and insults ended, the alerting chemical dissipated and the pain abated. But it's not really all that simple. Other factors enter in.

## Factors Influencing Pain

**Threshold.** There is a great deal of variation in the way the pain notification system works in different people. Some people's cells don't produce much of the chemicals. They have to suffer greater insult to feel the same amount of pain other people do. They have a higher pain threshold.

This is a mixed blessing. Sure, they go through life with far fewer aches and pains than most of us. But pain is an important indicator that something is wrong. And if they don't feel it, they may not realize what is wrong early in the game, when they could correct the problem easily.

Other people seem extraordinarily sensitive to pain, usually because either their cells are easier to damage or the cells produce more alerting chemicals. Either way, when something goes wrong, however slight, they know it right away.

The pain threshold may be artificially raised in people on various illicit drugs. Says a law officer friend, "We got called on this guy at a sorority house, of all places. He was in love with one of the young women, he said, although she wasn't at the house at the time. He was high. He pounded on the door, but they wouldn't let him in."

"When we got there, he'd beaten his fists practically flat against the door, broken a window, sliced himself up like sashimi, and gotten a chair smashed over his head by some girl who was bound and determined he wasn't going to come in through the window.

"When we approached him, he turned on us—came at us with a knife—and we shot him. He didn't even know it. When an addict's so high he can look down at 747s, nothing hurts. Nothing."

Mental attitude plays an important role, also.

**Mental attitude.** "Now this won't hurt a bit," says the nurse coming at you with the hypodermic syringe. That's what they always say, and you're not going to believe it for a moment. More to the point, though, the nurse's statement is drawing your attention to the pain and the prospect of it. Some interesting studies have shown that when a person thinks about pain, whether anticipating that it won't hurt or expecting that it will, it hurts more. Thinking about it is apparently what makes the difference.

It's not just a fluke of the reasoning mind. After receiving a shot, babies who are held and comforted by Mommy cry more than babies who are not. Mommy's actions and words clearly convey the attitude that there is serious pain in this picture.

Conversely, if you think a product or method is going to relieve pain, it probably will. Of people given placebo—a sugar pill with no redeeming medical value—90 percent receive pain relief from it.

Does the pain represent a negative or positive situation? That also makes a difference. For example, a study revealed that persons injured in automobile accidents seemed to feel pain more so than did World War II soldiers wounded in combat. Most soldiers didn't even need pain relief. Questioning minds asked, "Why?"

We believe an expectation was involved. The soldiers knew they were walking into peril and more or less anticipated being killed or injured. The person driving to the gro-

cery store did not. The soldier was so happy to have sur-
vived, being wounded was the lesser of the evils—a positive
experience, all in all. The accident victim didn't have that
cheery vindication of the event.

Is the person inured to pain? Consider your average football player. For a solid hour on game day, he repeatedly flings
his two-hundred-pound body at other players weighing just as
much. They slam into each other at high speeds, trip each
other, pile on one another, and do their level best to take
each other out. They love to sack selected members of the
opposing team, over and over and over. This guy doesn't
think about pain anymore than he thinks about shoulder pads,
cleats, and other tools of his trade. It may not surprise you to
learn that in tests of pain tolerance in various groups of people, football players scored best.

Next best, though, came cross-country skiers, and here we
may be seeing another form of tolerance. In one particular
test, the pain was inflicted by immersing the subjects' feet
and calves in ice water, then measuring how long it took
them to feel so uncomfortable that they pulled their feet out.
Cold, wet feet? That's routine to your average cross-country
skier. The cells themselves, then, may build a certain tolerance. Or maybe the cortex chooses not to listen to those cold
cells complain anymore.

It seems then that when that pain message reaches the
cortex, it is combined with other cues, such as the attitudes
of other people, as well as the pain sufferer's own attitude
and the perceived circumstances.

So people who seem numb to pain or nearly so—that is,
who possess an innately high pain threshold—also possess a
mental expectation that it isn't going to hurt much, if at all.
People sensitive to pain naturally hold the mental expectation
that it is going to hurt. The mental attitudes of both types of
people magnify their natural tendencies.

So do age and stress.

**Age and stress.**   Joe retired two years ago. A bit rickety
with old age, he likes to amble down to Battery Park now and

then to feed the pigeons. He buys a bag of popcorn and heads down the street. Meanwhile, young Pete, who works for a stock brokerage firm, is about to lose an important client. He anticipates getting in financial hot water and is hastening up from the ferry terminal in Battery Park to make contact with the client and perhaps dissuade the man from transferring his considerable portfolio elsewhere.

Pete races around a corner and collides with Joe. They bonk heads. They both twist a wrist catching themselves as they fall on their derrieres. In short, they suffer essentially identical injuries. Who will suffer the most pain, old and infirm Joe or young and healthy Pete?

Pete. Poor guy, it's all against him.

Older people seem to have relatively more joint pain, a reflection of the various kinds of arthritis that come with advancing age. But the cards are stacked against young Pete. In just about any category of pain other than joint pain— headache, muscle, dental, stomach and other internal pains, menstrual and premenstrual pain—young people report more pain than do older people.

Too, people under heavy stress lose more days at work and experience more kinds of pain across the board than do persons who aren't stressed out. Pete qualifies in spades on that one. In a pain report issued by Nuprin, a brand name pain reliever, study subjects were grouped into high-stress and low-stress categories. In the high-stress grouping, 14 percent of the people experienced 101 or more days of headaches compared with 2 percent of people in the low-stress group.

It may be that Joe's cells, past their prime, do not put out as many alerting chemicals when injured as they used to. Joe is certainly under far less stress. Whatever the reason, there is a correlation between age and stress.

Regardless of all these mitigating factors, pain happens. Quelling it and restoring comfort rates as a miracle.

# Managing and Treating Pain

The term *pain relief* is an abstraction until you experience pain. Then you *need* it. Normal, sane people, when in pain, claw frantically through medicine cabinets and old dresser drawers, desperately seeking that bottle of pain-relieving medicine.

What you take, and whether that particular medicine will be effective, is determined by the cause and source of the pain. Whether the pain is acute (that is, immediate and temporary, as banging your shin or suffering appendicitis) or chronic (long-term pain, such as arthritis) also factors in. Too, understanding causes and sources of pain can be of great help when you discuss pain problems with your doctor.

## Handling Headaches

Understanding didn't help Lyddie much, though. Lyddie Deborah Goldberg Marks, unlike her mother, considered no doctor to be god. Dr. Emily Berrends did not appreciate lay-people, untrained in medicine, to question her wisdom and knowledge. Lyddie and Dr. Berrends fussed and fumed at each other a few minutes, ranted a bit with strident voices, then arrived at a cautious truce. The strength of Lyddie's hormone pills was not going to be increased or decreased—the doctor's victory. Lyddie would take a course of ibuprofen starting five days before her expected headache and extending five days beyond as a preventive measure. And Dr. Berrends would give Lyddie a prescription for a painkiller that would take care of the headaches if and when they came—Lyddie's victory.

Dr. Berrends, after delivering a lengthy lecture on the dangers of addiction, prescribed hydrocodone for the pain. She was not making a shot in the dark.

Nine out of ten people worldwide suffer headaches at some time or other. That's well over four billion miserable folks. Just by themselves, headaches send forty million Americans to the doctor every year. Let's look at why and when drugs are prescribed.

**Tension headaches.** By far, most headaches are tension headaches, the kind that feel tight all the way around the head. They result from stress, too much glaring sun, and other causes. When the cause abates, the headache abates. But we live in the real world, and most of the time there is no way to ease the conditions that bring on the tension headache. The stress still presses, the sun still shines. (Incidentally, if bright sun gives you a tension headache, the cause is not the light itself, but your face and eye muscles; they're pulling in so tightly they're getting tired.)

Generally speaking, tension headaches respond very well to nonprescription analgesics you buy at the drugstore (the major players are listed at the end of the chapter). Most major manufacturers and a host of minor ones turn out pain-relief products, and tension headaches are their bread and butter. If their products didn't work, they would be out of business in a hurry.

**Migraines.** Migraine headaches, characterized by intense, debilitating pain, seldom respond to the over-the-counter medications that banish tension headaches. Migraines tend to strike only one side of the head, usually in the temple area between eye and ear or above and behind one eye. They last from six hours to several days. You know exactly when they arrive and when they leave. Many migraine sufferers become so sensitive to light that they can do nothing except lie still in a dark room until the headache subsides.

Depression and malaise frequently accompany migraines. Lyddie discovered this with her migraines. Even when medication takes away the pain, it may not take away the depressed, sad feeling that comes with it. Lyddie's hydrocodone eased the discomfort; it did nothing for her temporary despondency. In fact, she could tell when the headache subsided even though the medicine had quelled the pain; her good spirits returned.

We attack migraines on three fronts. We try to abort headaches once they begin. We may use drugs temporarily to try to prevent them from recurring. And we go for the underlying causes of the migraines so that they are forever ended without recourse to drugs.

First, we try to abort the headache. Very few people can do it by sheer strength of will. Some find relief with nondrug treatment such as cold application (an ice bag cooling the head) or TENS—transcutaneous electrical nerve stimulation, wherein a weak electrical current enters the body through electrodes pressed against the skin. Most medical people voice serious doubts about the value of TENS beyond placebo effect.

Usually, we must resort to drugs to abort a migraine. Over-the-counter preparations rarely touch it. We'll often go to drugs developed just for migraines—ergotamine derivatives, Imitrex, and some others. Sometimes beta-blockers or antidepressants do a nice job. Now and then, nonsteroidal anti-inflammatory drugs (the acronym is NSAIDs) or minor tranquilizers help.

Toradol injectable works well, but it is also problematic, because when you get a migraine you are seldom in a position to reach a doctor for an abortive injection. Imitrex, designed specifically to abort migraines, works well, too. A prescription-only drug that you self-inject, it soothes nerve endings and probably also constricts blood vessels. It too can pose dangers. It has probably been used more than most other products.

Second, we look for a short-term fix to prevent headaches. Again, that's likely to be a drug. It may be as common as ibuprofen. Women whose headaches are linked to menstrual cycles, as Lyddie's was, might try taking ibuprofen for ten days surrounding the menstrual period. Other drugs include beta-blockers, MAOIs, and antidepressants.

Third, we go to the root causes that bring on tension and migraine headaches, which can include stress, food, and schedule upsets.

We teach the patient relaxation techniques to combat the stress. Next, we check the patient's diet. Certain nutrients can cause migraines in some people; among them monosodium glutamate (the MSG used to enhance flavor), nitrates, nitrites, phenylethylamine (found in some fruits and vegetables), and tyramine (used in many smoked and aged foods).

We inquire about the patient's routine. Does the patient eat and rest at regular times, or are sleeping and eating patterns erratic? If so, does this seem to bring on a migraine?

If an emotional or psychological problem (and that includes stress) lies at the root, and this is frequently the case, drug regimens are practically useless unless the patient undergoes psychotherapy to dig out the root causes for the headache.

**Cluster headaches.** Cluster headaches are the most intense headaches people experience, and the majority of cluster headache sufferers are men. The headaches strike briefly and cyclically, sometimes in clusters of stabbing pain every few minutes, sometimes each day at the same hour. Although migraines often immobilize the sufferer, cluster headaches torment their victims to such a degree they cannot even sit still. Months and even years of headache-free living can stretch between onsets of these headaches.

We're not certain what causes cluster headaches, although we note that they most frequently happen to men who live a fast-paced lifestyle, who smoke and drink, who suffer ulcers (one-fourth of cluster headache victims have ulcers; less than 7 percent of the general population ever gets them). One thing short of drugs to try is to maintain a regular sleeping and waking cycle—go to bed at the same time each night, wake up at the same time each morning. In some people, cluster headaches may follow an abrupt change in life rhythms, such as the switch to daylight saving time and back. Sufferers might be able to blunt its effect by making the change slowly over a couple of weeks instead of overnight.

Cluster headaches occur so suddenly that trying to abort them is almost impossible. However, we do try to prevent them with several drugs. Calan, Isoptin, Verelan (verapamil), and generic verapamil sometimes help prevent these miseries. Verapamil is a calcium channel blocker used to reduce blood pressure in hypertensive people.

We may not know what triggers cluster headaches, but we sure know what causes a hangover.

**Hangover.**   The body's metabolism of alcohol creates by-products that cause the headache. In addition, almost all alcoholic beverages contain chemicals to provide flavor or that simply result from the aging or brewing process. These chemicals work their own misery. They too metabolize and create unpleasant by-products. The sufferer gets a double whammy of noxious headache-producers.

Alcohol is absorbed by the linings of the mouth and digestive system and goes directly into the bloodstream. Although different people react to blood alcohol levels in different ways, the levels are remarkably the same. This uniformity is why law enforcement officials feel confident in using blood alcohol level to determine intoxication.

The liver metabolizes blood alcohol at a constant, plodding rate. You cannot speed up alcohol metabolism, nor can you slow it down (in severely diseased or damaged livers, however, the rate may become slower as the liver intrinsically loses efficiency). Only the removal of alcohol from the bloodstream by means of this steady metabolism will sober the person. Contrary to popular belief, coffee is not a sobering agent because it has no effect on liver function.

What cures a hangover? Precious little. Aspirin and some of the painkillers listed at the end of this chapter may help. It's obvious how to prevent a hangover: don't drink alcohol.

**Other types of head and facial pain.**   Other problems worth mentioning happen less frequently. A few people, usually older people, suffer from trigeminal neuralgia, in which a sudden searing pain rips across the side of the face. Sometimes the problem is triggered by touching the face, as when shaving (it's a dandy reason to grow a beard!), and sometimes it erupts spontaneously. The pain leaves just as suddenly.

When patients come to us with headaches, we do a complete medical workup. We don't want to miss something serious because the symptoms appear common.

Brain tumors may cause pain in the head, eye, or face. Depression seems to lower the pain threshold and generates more than its share of headaches. One young lad complaining of headache turned out to have a BB lodged behind his ear. Infection was starting to cause a real problem. We never could figure out how his barber missed it.

Many and varied as headaches are, they are but one of the possibilities for pain.

## Trauma and Illness

Pain comes with the territory when injury, surgery, or illness occurs. We approach the problem in any of three ways. Analgesics treat the pain problem systemically. They kill the pain. Certain barbiturates and opiates block the pain messages at the level of the central nervous system—the spinal cord and brain. Sometimes, though, the pain can be alleviated topically, at the site, as with ice packs or a topical spray.

Arthritis is a prime source of chronic pain in older people, and we attack it two ways. Anti-inflammatory drugs reduce the swelling and joint tenderness that contribute to pain, and analgesics bring the pain into abeyance.

The pain and itching of hemorrhoids respond to topical ointments. Several good ointments are on the market.

The pain that goes with recovery from surgery and illness in hospitals is not unexpected. However, independent studies have shown that frequently, doses of painkiller administered to hospital patients were, in some cases, one-fourth what physicians' orders allowed. If you are hospitalized, don't be shy about asking for sufficient medication to allay discomfort. Ask about a transdermal patch that delivers fentanyl through the skin.

## Pain and Terminal Illness

Like a horrific alien octopus, the tumor's multifarious tentacles probed into a hundred nooks and crevices of George Callan's brain. The day after the doctors declared his tumor inoperable, his tearful family moved him from the hospital to a nearby hospice. In a rocking chair by the window, he would spend his last days looking out across the Pacific toward the Santa Barbara Islands and fighting the demons of death closing in on him. Not the least of these demons was pain.

The brain has no pain cells and feels nothing, and any pain the head feels comes from pressure on other tissues or damage to them. George's pain, intense and constant, came from pressure the tumor exerted.

His doctor prescribed morphine. His daughter Althea did not want her father on morphine and sought a second opinion. "You'll make a drug addict out of him!"

"Addiction is long-term dependency," the doctor explained tenderly. "Your dad has three months, at most. There is no long-term."

When death draws nigh, physical and emotional comfort becomes the primary concern. Drug tolerance and dependency cease to be factors. Too often we forget that, and the patient suffers needlessly.

We usually recommend that treatment during final days be symptomatic. That is, if the patient is descending into a disturbing psychosis, we administer antipsychotic drugs. Likewise, if anxiety or depression comes on we administer antidepressants and/or anxiolytics. Appropriate counsel can greatly comfort a person facing death and the person's family.

So we work to alleviate the pain in the dying patient. If it requires heavy sedation with addictive drugs, so be it. Of all the times in a person's life, this is the time to pull all the stops and go for the most effective means of pain relief.

Although heavy-duty pain management may sedate a patient into a stupor, persons in the final stages of terminal illness often appear sedated when actually they are not. They space out, withdraw socially, appear numb. These are signs that appear in terminally ill persons, whether they are medicated or not.

## Managing Pain Without Drugs

We always look first for a way to abort pain without using medication. We mentioned several alternatives to medication for relieving headache pain. They may work for other pain locations as well.

People in chronic pain, such as cancer sufferers, may find help in support groups of people in similar circumstances. Relaxation training can lessen pain. Laughter can improve the body's natural pain-resisting chemistry.

In some cases of chronic pain we might block a nerve bundle or cut through a nerve connection. Extreme as they are, these techniques are occasionally superior to constant medication.

## The History of Painkillers

Egyptian hieroglyphics from seven thousand years ago describe headaches and head injury. For many centuries, some cultures have used acupuncture to control pain with success. 

Five thousand years ago, cultures in Asia and the Near East used poppy extract, raw opiate, for pain control. Some cultures found that chewing the leaves of certain plants relieved pain. Willow, for instance, provides salicylates—the ingredient in aspirin (the genus name of willow is *Salix*, from which we get the derivative *salicyl*). Foxglove, the ingredient in digitalis, allays the pain of angina pectoris.

Greeks and Romans prided themselves in their skill at setting broken bones to minimize pain and loss of function after healing. Archaeologists unearthed a Roman soldier who died during the great eruption of Vesuvius that buried Pompeii and Herculaneum. Researchers found evidence that the soldier had suffered and been treated for a broken leg. Ironically, he recovered from his wound only to suffocate in one of the world's worst catastrophes.

Both Old (Sumerian) and New World cultures (Aztec, Maya, Inca) practiced trephining, which is cutting holes in the skull. We tend to dismiss them as primitive, but they weren't. Using excellent metal surgical instruments, they operated successfully; the holes sported new bone growth, indicating healing through time.

During Europe's Middle Ages, pain control took a giant step backward. Pain was considered not only necessary to healing, but also beneficial to the process, and doctors actually encouraged it. They didn't know that extreme pain can actually kill a body already weakened by other problems. Pain intensifies the effects of traumatic shock. So they designed elaborate machines to torture the patient into wellness. Inscribed on one machine, "For every pleasure a thousand pains." They took their maxims literally.

It wasn't until the mid-1800s that doctors finally shook off the last vestiges of the idea that pain is a necessary component of healing and started using anesthesia and painkillers routinely. Ether served as anesthetic, opiates as analgesics.

And then, in 1893, came aspirin. The miracle drug.

The rest, as they say, is history.

## Pain-Relieving Medications

Every drug manufacturer knows that if you can come up with a product to conquer pain, your fortune is made. Of all the things humankind avoids, pain ranks at the top. Pain happens in and of itself, and it accompanies illness and injuries. Chronic pain can cause insomnia, and at times, even mental illness

When we prescribe a pain medication, we try to shoot for the simplest, gentlest drug that will do the job. We look first to products with the fewest possible side effects. If these first choices don't work, we move on to more powerful drugs.

The government's Food and Drug Administration occasionally makes an arbitrary decision that raises eyebrows, and it is certainly slow about accepting new drugs for sale and use in this country. But the FDA is certainly careful. In our nation, we can usually assume correctly that drugs sold over the counter, that is, purchased without a prescription, will be effective and safe *when used as directed.*

We cannot emphasize too much the importance of using a drug as directed. Just because a drug can be purchased over the counter does not mean the drug is "wimpy." Over-the-counter pain medications really do medicate. When seriously misused, they can pose dangers.

## Over-the-Counter and Prescription Analgesics

Lyddie had tried every pain reliever on the drugstore shelf. During her musings on aspirin, she thought about how thoroughly aspirin had permeated the painkiller market. There were so many brands. And look at how all the other analgesics managed to tie in the word: "Twice the pain relief of plain aspirin." "Aspirin-free pain relief." It would appear that aspirin was the yardstick by which the world measures its analgesics. And so it is.

There are three major classes of over-the-counter pain relievers: the salicylates (aspirin and its relatives), acetaminophen, and NSAIDs (nonsteroidal anti-inflammatory drugs), including ibuprofen.

**Salicylates, the multimiracle drug.** Aspirin, acetylsalicylic acid, is not a psychotropic drug. It does not alter mental states or attitudes. Nonetheless, it's a multimiracle drug.

Day in, day out, around the world, aspirin sales outstrip all other drug purchases. One dollar of every six spent on pain medicines buys aspirin, and it is the cheapest by far of pain medications. Few indeed are the medicine cabinets without a bottle of aspirin on the shelf. And that is one miracle: everyone can use it.

Another miracle: it's cheap. Everyone can afford it, even in its most specialized brand-name forms.

Still another miracle is that aspirin works for so many things. Although used primarily as an analgesic (that is, a painkiller), aspirin also binds blood platelets to retard clotting. This is why surgery patients are instructed not to take aspirin for some time before surgery. Blood donors—especially those in a phoresis program—should not take aspirin for a few days before giving blood. On the other hand, doctors may suggest a daily aspirin regimen for persons with a blood-clotting problem to keep things loose and flowing. Aspirin dropped into water vases can keep cut flowers from wilting so quickly. (It does not lengthen the life of cut flowers significantly. Might as well save your aspirin.)

Another miracle: although no one denies that aspirin can become a deadly foe under certain limited circumstances, by and large it produces few side effects. In an ad for a competing analgesic, an actor intones as a final comment, ". . . and [product name] doesn't upset my stomach." The implication, of course, is that plain old aspirin *does* cause stomach upset. And for a few people, that's true; it does. The vast majority of aspirin users (and we're talking millions and millions of people here) have no problem at all when using the drug as directed.

The one bugbear we've learned is the effect of aspirin on some children. Reye's syndrome, an all-too-often fatal reaction to aspirin in a few children, has just about ended aspirin use in kids. Now we give youngsters aspirin-free analgesics.

At the beginning of this section, we told you aspirin does not alter mental states or attitudes. That's not altogether true, however. Aspirin does change mental attitudes in an indirect way. When pharmaceutical companies test new drugs for efficacy and side effects, they give one control group the test drug and another control group a placebo. Placebos look exactly like the drug being tested but contain none of the drug. An interesting percentage of the group using a placebo will report the alleviation of symptoms the drug is supposed to alleviate. It is the mind functioning as healing agent, and the suggestion that a placebo might work is sufficient to trigger the mind into seeing improvement.

When someone takes aspirin, that person expects to improve, and that powerful expectation—an altered mental attitude—may be enough to work the desired improvement. Aspirin, of course, is not a placebo. It really does work. However, its reputation as an analgesic is so well ingrained, so accepted, that its effect can be significant, making it useful far beyond its actual ability to subdue pain.

Aspirin is available in a variety of forms. Plain aspirin is the chalky, white, nasty-tasting tablet. Buffered aspirin contains other ingredients to make the aspirin component gentler on the tummy. Unfortunately, the buffering ingredients rub some people's tummies the wrong way. Coated aspirin tastes better going down but is slower to be absorbed. The coating has to dissolve first. Aspirin also is available as a seltzer. Finally, aspirin can be part of a combination of ingredients designed to combat an illness or other problem.

Some of the best recognized names in our culture are aspirin brands: **Bayer** aspirin, **Alka-Seltzer, Anacin, APF** (arthritic pain formula), **Bufferin, Excedrin, Halfprin, Maprin, Norwich** aspirin, **Novasen, Presalin, Rhinocaps, Salocol, Synalgos, Triaphen,** or **Zorprin**. Equally effective is aspirin marketed generically as either aspirin or acetylsalicylic acid. In general, the salicylate-type pain relievers act by blocking messages at the tips of the nerve endings.

Aspirin is often used along with certain prescription drugs, particularly codeine. Talk to your doctor about combination products such as **Coricidin** with codeine, **Darvon, Empirin** and **Anacin** with codeine, **Lortab, Oxycodan, Percodan, Talwin,** and others.

**Acetaminophen.** Acetaminophen is usually the key ingredient in pain relievers advertised as aspirin-free. Over one hundred brand names and generics use acetaminophen for pain relief. Sometimes the drug is part of a larger remedy, such as **Thera-Flu,** which tackles flu, colds, and coughs.

Among the numerous brands: **Actamin, Allerest, Aminofen, Anacin-3, Apacet,** many children's pain relievers, **Comtrex, Contac, DayQuil** and **NyQuil, Pertussin PM,** many sinus remedies, **Tylenol,** and **Vicks Formula 44** multi-symptom cough mixture.

Acetaminophen and aspirin are combined for a one-two punch in products such as **Arthralgin, Excedrin, Tri-Pain, Trigesic,** and **Vanquish.**

**Ibuprofen and other NSAIDs.** Ibuprofen works differently in that it doesn't fight pain so much as it fights the swelling that causes pain. An NSAID, it was once a prescription drug. Sometimes it and its NSAID relatives still are, depending on the strength and what they're used with.

Ibuprofen is available generically and as a major ingredient of brand-name products such as **Advil** and **Nuprin.** Its anti-inflammatory property helps the bloating and discomfort of menstrual pain in products like **Midol, Motrin,** and **Medipren.**

Ibuprofen seems to work miracles apart from pain relief. As first reported in the *New England Journal of Medicine,* ibuprofen can slow down lung deterioration in cystic fibrosis patients. The younger the patient, statistically the longer and better ibuprofen retards the lung damage.

For long-term use, products such as **Feldene** (piroxicam) and **Orudis** or extended-release **Oruvail** (ketoprofen) provide relief from the pain of certain kinds of arthritis primarily by reducing inflammation in the joint. **Meclomen** (meclofenamate Na) has a tendency to cause diarrhea.

The first of a new wave of NSAIDs, **Relafen** (nabumatone), is good over the long haul for managing chronic pain, especially of osteoarthritis and rheumatoid arthritis.

**Toradol** (ketorolac tromethamine), an NSAID available as an oral or injectable medication by prescription only, offers pain relief as good as the narcotics, but it has none of the severe side effects, especially dependency and tolerance, that narcotics do.

**Topicals.** Little Jimmy's eardrum is as red as Santa

Claus's suit, and the pain of earache is making him miserable. While he lies on his side with his sore ear up, Daddy drops some medicine into it and then reads him a story. By the time Goldilocks runs away, the ear feels much better.

Topical antipruritics, analgesics, and anesthetics provide relief right at the site. They usually take effect immediately, or at least within ten minutes or so.

Jimmy's ear medicine, a prescription benzocaine product, **Americaine**, takes away the polarizing ability—that is, the ability to conduct tiny electrical charges—of the pain nerve endings. Result: they don't send any messages to the cortex.

Products such as **Nupercainal**, an anesthetic/analgesic ointment, can seem like miracles to people suffering from everything from hemorrhoids to sunburn. The medicines do their work on site (usually for a limited time) without disturbing any other body systems.

Some topicals actually cool the area they treat as they kill pain. Ethyl chloride products such as **Fluro-ethyl** and **Fluori-methane** are examples.

## Prescription Pain Relievers

Although aspirin and the host of other over-the-counter analgesics coming into use in the last few years are effective in many cases, obviously problems of pain and suffering exist that a quart of aspirin wouldn't cure. For stronger or differently directed pain relief, we turn to other prescription drugs.

**Antidepressants.** The **tricyclic antidepressants** act as analgesics, sometimes to a surprising extent. They can be used alone for pain relief. When prescribed together with narcotics, they also serve by rendering the narcotics more effective. Obviously, they are immensely helpful when depression is part of the picture. As a rule, tricyclics should be avoided if you have glaucoma or a problem with urination.

Most tricyclics work to some good effect. At the clinic we routinely prescribe **Elavil** (amitriptyline), **Sinequan** (doxepin HCl), and **Norpramin** (desipramine) as analgesics alone and in situations where pain relief is part of emotional healing.

We'll try MAOIs also.

**Imitrex (sumatriptan succinate).** This drug usually will not eliminate a migraine, but it may alleviate it to an extent. Sumatriptan is injected just beneath the skin with a do-it-yourself hypodermic device. The person who thinks he could never give himself a shot has never had a full-blown migraine. When the headache strikes, you would stick yourself with a garden rake if you thought it would help.

There is some cardiac risk here. Talk about that with your doctor.

**Ergotamines.** Prior to sumatriptan, ergotamine and ergotamine in combination with caffeine (**Cafergot**) were the headache sufferer's best hope. They don't work well unless you take them at the early onset of pain.

## Headache Preventatives

**Sansert** (methysergide), lithium carbonate, sodium valproate and, sometimes, prednisone (deltasone), an anti-inflammatory steroid, are worth a try. For short-haul prevention these usually work.

## Other Painkillers

**Midrin,** a combination of drugs, is usually less nauseating than the ergots. Sometimes **beta-blockers** such as propranolol (**Inderal**) help. **Calcium channel inhibitors**—Verapamil is an example—are tried now and then.

All these drugs were designed within the last ten to fifty years for perhaps some reason other than pain, but useful for pain as well. That doesn't mean that humankind has gone without painkillers until now. The hard hitters, the painkillers that don't mess around, have been with us for ages—the narcotics.

## The Narcotics

Narcotics are strictly and carefully regulated in this country because they are just plain dangerous. They may be addictive. Tolerance at times builds quickly, and it takes more and more of the drug of choice to achieve the same effect. The narcotics represent the worst that drugs can do.

And yet they also represent the best. Administered wisely, the narcotics are usually safe, and they also rank high as miracle drugs. When you need them, you really need them. And they deliver.

Whereas salicylates, by dulling responses at the tips of pain receptors, don't let pain messages get started, narcotics cut them off at the pass. The pain messages reach the central nervous system—that is, the brain and spinal cord—and go no farther. Because these two major sorts of painkillers work in such different ways, many products combine them in order to hit pain at both sides of the head at once, so to speak.

Codeine and certain other narcotics, incidentally, also suppress coughs, making them valuable as cold and flu remedies—they relieve the achy joints and other symptoms as well. Their greatest value, though, is in pain relief.

Let's pretend for the moment that the year is 1800 and you are riding down the street in the largest city in America, Philadelphia. Some kid with butter for brains comes barreling around the corner and spooks your horse. Your horse rears back and dumps you into a peddlar's cart. You break two ribs and boast some world-class bruises.

Your doctor is certain your extreme pain will speed healing. You point out, however, that you must go to work as a bricklayer and you can't afford to lose time with this pain. No work, no money to pay the doctor. Your supervisor certainly isn't going to pay you if you're not laying brick.

Reluctantly the doctor gives you laudanum, a strong morphine-type narcotic. The laudanum will quell the pain so that you can work your usual day. You will act and feel drugged because laudanum dulls all nerve responses, not just pain. You will not lay brick as well or as fast as usual. You will probably become constipated because laudanum slows *everything* down. Disgusted by the quantity and quality of your work, your boss will strongly recommend that if you can't stay in the saddle, trade for a more sedate horse.

Now let's fast-forward to 1889 and start over. Again you're navigating the bustling streets of Philadelphia. It's a considerable city, despite that in size it has been eclipsed by several others. The nation, one hundred years old, stretches coast to coast. You're riding the streetcar on your way to work, minding your own business, when the conductor abruptly stops the two horses drawing the streetcar to avoid colliding with a careless dray. The jolt throws you to the floor; you break two ribs and suffer some nasty bruises.

For one thing, you get your name in the paper as having been injured in the accident. Small comfort. You hurt terribly. The doctor gladly provides you with morphine. You could just as well get relief by purchasing from the apothecary any of several morphine, laudanum, or cocaine products. In the newspaper, on the same page where your name appears, you see ads for cough medicines containing powerful narcotics and ads for drug rehab clinics.

It is now 1996, and here you are in Philadelphia touring Independence Hall. A rowdy little kid who ought to be chained to a big anchor chases his sister across the polished floor. They veer and slam into you, tipping you into the Liberty Bell. For being cracked as it is, it sure rings loudly enough when you smash into it, hurting your head and breaking two ribs.

The pain relievers you receive could be relatives of laudanum and morphine, refined and tamed to minimize side effects. You will not act sluggish or appear drugged. You will be able to continue to perform your work well—even bricklaying. Because you hit your head, they will watch you carefully, because Demerol, the pain reliever they have given you, can raise intracranial pressure, magnifying problems of head injury.

Doctors know a lot about the effects of these drugs that were unknown twenty years ago—knowledge that works to your benefit. You rest in comfort and return to the mainstream shortly.

Will you become hooked on your narcotic? No, for several reasons. One, under a doctor's care, you can rest assured that the dosage will not be high enough to cause dependency anytime soon. Two, your doctor can recognize early signs of tolerance and dependency and will switch your medications if need be. Three, people in great pain who really need these medications rarely develop a dependency so long as the need is there. To a limited extent at least, the body differentiates between recreational use and necessary use. Four, the narcotics have been refined beyond those used even fifty years ago, let alone hundreds of years ago, and are tailored to do a specific job without creating a lot of side issues and effects.

There are many narcotic medications available today, and this listing is not complete by any means. These are the products commonly used. Remember there are others, specialized for special jobs, to which you can also turn. All are usually prescription drugs.

**Codeine** is popular as a cough suppressant and is found in a variety of cough and cold remedies. In industrial strengths, it requires a prescription.

**Darvon** (propoxyphene HCl) also comes as an aspirin-caffeine-propoxyphene combo, **Darvon compound 65.** If you are depressed or suicidal, stay away from this stuff. Also, if you use alcohol, you're better off with something else. Talk to your doctor.

**Demerol** (meperidine HCl) is what you'll get in the hospital post-op. Many hospitals now provide a self-medicating IV device, allowing the patient to medicate as needed for pain. Danger is minimal. They monitor delivery and can cut you off if you use too much too fast. Be aware that if your doctor prescribes oral Demerol, it does not absorb as quickly or as well as IV delivery.

**Dilaudid** (hydromorphone HCl), like other opiates, is dose-dependent. It will close down as much or as little pain as the dose dictates. The upper limit is drawn by the side effects of heavy dosage—nausea, vomiting, and respiratory depression. Overdose kills by numbing breathing and heart action.

**Dolophene** (methadone HCl), close kin to morphine, is also addictive like its relatives. It kills pain, just like its relatives. What makes it special is that its withdrawal symptoms are much less severe than are, for example, those of heroin. Too, it can replace heroin physiologically. The narcotics addict who switches to methadone can come off a severe addiction gently, using methadone as a stepping stone from the virulent substance through a more tolerable substance to complete absence.

We use methadone in the hospital all the time to allay withdrawal symptoms of addicts admitted for addiction or other reasons. Make no mistake, methadone is a tool with limitations, never a panacea.

**Duragesic** (fentanyl) is a recent innovation, a transdermal patch (an adhesive patch changed periodically), which you adhere onto your skin. It delivers the narcotic fentanyl for up to seventy-two hours continuously. When powerful narcotic medication is all that will work for severe, chronic pain, Duragesic may be the way to go. Fentanyl is as strongly addicting as any other opiates and causes much the same side effects.

**Hydrocodone** in assorted forms, such as **Vicodin** (hydrocodone plus acetaminophen), is a codeine variant. By itself, or intensified by additives, it kills moderate pain.

**Lorcet** combines hydrocodone with acetaminophen.

**Morphine** is a measure to which other painkillers are compared. For a long time, in a variety of forms, it has been handling the difficult jobs.

**Percodan** (oxycodone) is a moderately strong pain reliever with a low tendency to cause addiction or abuse. It comes with aspirin built right into it, so if you don't react well to aspirin, Percodan's not for you. **Percocet** substitutes acetaminophen for aspirin.

**Talwin** is representative of the many combinations of an essentially over-the-counter pain reliever such as aspirin with a prescription hard-hitter. In the case of Talwin, the other ingredient is pentazocine and the medicine takes effect within fifteen to thirty minutes. **Talwin Nx** adds naloxone to the mix to curb abuse because abuse is so easy to slip into. Some people can build tolerance to Talwin in ten days.

## CHAPTER 11

*My youngest of four sons is epileptic. He's also the most aggressive—the shortest fuse, the ugliest attitude. Believe me, he stretches the phrase "inability to control" to new dimensions.*

A FRUSTRATED MOTHER

# SEIZURES AND AGGRESSION

Alexis Shuler was three years old when she learned that she was different. She couldn't remember exactly what happened, except that all of a sudden Mommy was hugging her and rocking back and forth and sobbing. As she got older, she became aware of the seizures. They came on at unexpected times; they terrified everyone who saw it happen; and none of her friends experienced them. The many doctors who examined her talked about the seizures with her mother as if Alexis wasn't there. People would ask her sisters and brothers how they liked school, or how they felt about the upcoming holiday season. No one asked her how she felt about anything. Most adults avoided talking to Alexis at all. She was different.

The doctors gave Alexis drugs designed to control her seizures. The drugs worked pretty well. She entered kindergarten, and for the first time people didn't treat her like she was different. The teacher, Mrs. Preston, talked to her the way she talked to all the other children. The teacher helped Alexis mix her paints during art time and helped her lace her yarn through the perforated card during craft activities.

Alexis didn't run as fast as many of her schoolmates. She couldn't run for as long as they could, either. Sometimes at recess, when the other kids hooted and hollered out on the playground, Alexis would curl up with a book. If Mrs. Preston shooed her out the door to play, she would explore the long grass along the edge of the playground, seeking out ladybugs and tiger beetles. She liked insects, and she told her daddy she wanted to study them when she was grown up. Her daddy claimed that people who study bugs, entomologists, had to work for the government and didn't make much money, but Alexis didn't care.

Alexis liked school, too, that is until she suffered a seizure during class. It happened during story time just before lunch. The children clustered close around Mrs. Preston's feet. Alexis felt the funny feeling she so often felt before an episode. She tried so hard to keep it from happening! When her wits finally returned, she found out that the teacher had sent all the children out of the room. There lay their mats, all scrambled and empty. Aged, angular Mr. Cobb, the principal, towered over Alexis and glared at her.

A man and woman in dark blue jumpsuits came running into the room. The woman plunked a big red box down beside Alexis and whipped out a stethoscope. More doctors. More shots.

"No!" Alexis squirmed to her knees and swayed, too dizzy and weak to stand up. The man in the jumpsuit reached out to grab her.

"No!" Alexis twisted away.

"Alexis, you behave," roared Mr. Cobb.

She *was* behaving! She did everything Mrs. Preston asked,

but Mrs. Preston wasn't here now. "No doctor! No!" Alexis was barely strong enough to clamber to her feet.

The woman in the jumpsuit lunged forward, grabbed Alexis, and dragged her down into her lap. Arms too strong to resist wrapped around Alexis and held her close.

"You're safe, Sweetie. We won't hurt you. It's okay."

"No shots. Please no shots," Alexis cried.

"No shots. Relax. Good girl. We aren't going to hurt you. Know how your teacher says to call 911 in an emergency? Well, we're 911. We're here to make certain you're okay and that you stay okay. You can trust us."

Alexis struggled a little, but her heart wasn't in it. She wasn't strong enough to resist anyway, and her body was so tired and weak from the seizure. She let herself be encapsulated in the close, gentle arms as she listened to Mr. Cobb crabbing at the man.

"I'm calling her mother. They're pulling her out of here, right now. This sort of thing is never going to happen again!"

"I understand." The man's voice rumbled. "But you'd better talk it over with your school board first. There are guidelines about excluding children with disabilities. You could find yourself in a real legal tangle if you bar her."

"She's an epileptic, right?" Mr. Cobb's tone of voice clearly suggested that the problem was Alexis's fault. "Look at her! She'll never be able to lead a normal life."

Alexis felt the arms around her stiffen.

"Oh, really?" Strong and controlled, the woman asked, "You mean, like, be a teacher, or a paramedic?" She didn't wait for Mr. Cobb's answer. "I completed my paramedic training with honors, sir, at the top of my intake class. And I'm an epileptic."

## The Sources of Seizures

Epilepsy is one of the more common disorders in which seizures occur. And although many people equate seizures with epilepsy, the seizures can happen for any of several reasons. It is important to know about the different reasons, for they govern how the seizures will be quelled. Here are some possible causes. Many times, we simply do not know the cause.

## Physical Problems and Disease

A focal lesion in the brain or central nervous system can trigger seizures. We have to run elaborate tests to finger that particular cause. The symptoms mimic too many other problems.

HIV-related infections, and indeed the whole complex encephalopathy of HIV, can bring on seizures.

Small children are especially subject to febrile seizures. Febrile is fever. When body temperature rises above 103°F, convulsions may occur. The response is to cool the child, either with medications or by wrapping the child in cool, wet sheets.

## Alcohol

When the confirmed, severe alcoholic goes cold turkey, withdrawal can rip the person's life apart. Tremors usually show up first, accompanied by nausea and tension. The person wants to sleep, but cannot. The alcoholic suffers from DTs, delirium tremens, with its hallucinations, delusions, and disorientation. In severe situations, seizures follow. The person is afraid he will die, and pretty soon, he wishes he would die. Can the alcoholic die from DTs? Occasionally, yes. In fact, counting the persons who don't receive treatment, a significant percentage of alcoholics experiencing DTs die. The hallucinations may prompt an impulse to commit suicide. Infections can kill some alcoholics. Physiological problems, such as fluid and electrolyte imbalances or heart arrhythmias, also can be killers.

When seizures come in rapid, closely spaced outbursts, permanent neurological damage can result, so we seek to mute the withdrawal symptoms or prevent them entirely.

But alcohol is not the only drug that causes seizures.

## Drug-Induced Seizures

Occasionally, people respond to drugs in unexpected ways, what we call idiosyncratic reactions. Sometimes their bodies do just the opposite of what we think they ought to do, a paradoxical reaction. When people with a history of seizures receive antipsychotic drugs, particularly the low-potency drugs, their seizure threshold drops and seizures become more likely. Occasionally, an antipsychotic will induce seizures in people who never before experienced one.

We nip these problems by lowering the drug dosage, changing the prescription to a different antipsychotic, introducing an anticonvulsant, or increasing the dosage in a person who is already taking anticonvulsant medication.

Street drugs, particularly the hard stuff, can induce seizures without much provocation. People who overdose on cocaine and methamphetamines, to name two of many drugs on the street, show up routinely in emergency rooms.

In short, drug-induced seizures are managed by altering or adding drugs, fighting fire with fire.

## Epilepsy

About one in one hundred Americans suffers from epilepsy. Of that 1 percent, some will develop psychiatric problems arising directly from the cruelty and mistreatment that epileptics like Alexis endure daily. Anxiety, aggression and other personality problems, depression, and social withdrawal plague these people who suffer from an unpreventable brain malfunction.

Although the vivid convulsions such as Alexis experienced are the first thing people think of when the disorder is mentioned, different forms of epilepsy produce different types of seizures. Partial seizures focus on one limited area of the brain. Generalized seizures are more widespread.

**Simple partial seizures.** These seizures occur in about one-fifth of epileptics and bring no loss of consciousness. The person may "see" faint lights, spots or flashes, may "hear" humming, tapping, or voices, may "feel" electric tingling—the pins and needles your foot feels when it falls asleep. Without a careful analysis, these symptoms can be mistaken for psychosis.

**Complex partial seizures.** These seizures occur in another one-fifth of epileptics and feature a loss of consciousness to some degree. The person may slip into a dreamlike state or experience a feeling of déjà vu. Reality and time are distorted. Life takes on a surreal quality. In people with complex partial seizures, psychiatric symptoms show up with distressing frequency, and that includes the times between seizures.

We use the term *Temporal Lobe Epilepsy* to define the disorder of complex partial seizures.

**Generalized nonconvulsive seizures.** These seizures, also called petit mal seizures, impair consciousness without causing convulsions. The person's awareness checks out briefly as the body continues merrily along without instructions from the conscious mind. The inherent dangers are obvious, as when a person is driving a car when the seizure occurs.

**Generalized convulsive seizures.** These are the grand mal seizures, the ones people commonly associate with epilepsy. It's the type of seizure Alexis suffered.

What we call an aura, or strange, unidentifiable feelings, signal the onset of the seizure. The aura is similar to feelings of doom. When the epileptic senses an oncoming seizure, he or she can do nothing to stop it.

The person loses consciousness and feels drained and weary when consciousness returns. During the seizure the body goes rigid. Every muscle pulses and tightens simultaneously, slamming the victim to the ground. Teeth are clenched, eyes roll back, legs and arms jerk wildly, the head beats against the floor. It's not surprising Mrs. Preston made all the children leave the room when Alexis had her seizure. It's a sight that can give kindergartners nightmares.

# Treating Seizures

Perhaps because they startle and intimidate, perhaps because they are uncontrollable once they flare, seizures spread their effects far beyond the persons experiencing them to the persons observing them. Treating a victim of seizures, therefore, involves not just the medical problem itself, but also the psychological effects the victim suffers because of other people's reactions.

Mr. Cobb's disgust, were we to probe him a bit deeper, would turn out to be a cover for fear; he didn't know exactly what the seizure was, how to control it, or how to prevent it. Because of the behavior aspect of grand mal seizures, he might suspect, deep down, that Alexis was putting on a bit, just for attention. He would probably be convinced that were Alexis taking her medicine properly, this sort of thing wouldn't happen. He believed that somehow, to some degree, the seizure was the child's fault.

Mr. Cobb agreed completely with Mrs. Preston's decision to evacuate the other children, lest their tender eyes see so violent and degrading a display. But was this really the best way for Mr. Cobb and Mrs. Preston to handle the situation?

Children, even kindergarten children, can assimilate an amazing amount of information, as long as they understand what's going on. Mrs. Preston, with Mr. Cobb's backing, could explain what epilepsy is and that it is involuntary—it cannot be controlled the way we can control throwing a ball or jumping over a rock. She could illustrate the illness in story form. Were she teaching older children, she might ask the class to research the disease. She could emphasize that epilepsy, like other illnesses such as chicken pox, colds, or flu, can't be prevented. Most important, she could accept Alexis as just another classmate and insist (with oversight and supervision!) that the other children do the same.

The psychiatric problems that half of epileptics suffer could be thwarted in grade school by informed and caring teachers and principals. This understanding is crucial in helping Alexis and her classmates grow. The antidepressants, antipsychotics, and antianxiety drugs might not be necessary later if epileptics are treated consistently with understanding during these tender years.

Can epilepsy be cured? No. Can it be controlled? Usually.

## Controlling Epilepsy

If Alexis is typical, she will need two frequently monitored evaluations as she grows up. One will deal directly with her epilepsy. The other will keep track of her mental health.

Today we can usually control epilepsy well with Dilantin (phenytoin). It is not specifically a psychotropic drug; it does not alter the way the mind works. But what a miracle drug it is, all the same. It frees the mind from horrible chains.

Adults whose seizures are completely controlled with medication can safely drive cars. They function fully in our complex society. Like the paramedic who attended Alexis, they can soar as far as their wings will carry them.

In those cases where Dilantin does not work, we may sometimes resort to barbiturates. They may be addictive and may dull the person, releasing some chains only to impose others. On barbiturates, Alexis might not be able to connect thoughts well, to learn well, to respond well. Anyone who did not know Alexis was taking a drug might label her retarded. In her early years, when rapid growth is so important, Alexis could be severely set back for a lifetime. Still, barbiturates may help.

The other evaluation, mental health, requires periodic checks for depression, anxiety, or social dysfunction. We want to catch these problems quickly, before they become ingrained. Identified early, the problems can often be allayed without resorting to drugs. We remind you again that drugs, however miraculous they may be, are not the first line of treatment for many, many problems. We resort to them last.

Some seizure-related problems, however, we don't tiptoe around; we step on them immediately. Aggression and violence are examples. For reasons we are still debating, violence and epilepsy are linked, to a certain limited extent, particularly in the case of complex partial seizures. Epileptics, like some other groups, may lean toward aggressive tendencies, often fueled by rage. Rage and aggression, whether accompanying epileptic seizures or not, require attention in themselves.

## Treating Other Kinds of Seizures

When physical problems and disease trigger seizures, the obvious solution is to correct the problems if possible. The seizures then correct themselves. This is true also of drug-induced seizures, as we discussed earlier.

The treatment indicated for alcohol withdrawal takes several twists and turns. One of the major tools to ease alcohol withdrawal short of the DTs are Valium (diazepam) and Librium (chlordiazepoxide). Antipsychotics such as Haldol (haloperidol) can lower the seizure threshold.

For patients with a prior history of seizures, we administer the drug they are already taking for the condition, usually Dilantin (phenytoin). Nearly all patients who seize during withdrawal, whether given to seizures or not, can benefit from the generous use of Valium (diazepam), delivered intravenously if necessary. In fact, if the patient who is normally on Dilantin has been neglecting dosage, we will quell the seizures with Valium until we can build the Dilantin level back up to an effective level.

Some drugs do one major thing and do it well. Dilantin is one such drug. Often, though, we find that drugs effective in one situation are also effective in others; the hypnotics, lithium, and the major anticonvulsants are examples.

# How the Drugs Work

Imagine you are camped on the bank of a gurgling stream. A robin persistently chirps his serenade as shades of evening fall on the ground around you. Time to build the campfire. You could dump diesel oil on a log, torch it, and chant, "Burn, fire, burn," hoping that it will catch. Or you can arrange kindling in the middle of the fire pit, add some crumpled paper and maybe a few dry pinecones, lay shavings on that, then add sticks and larger branches. You light the paper to ignite the shavings, which ignites the sticks, which ignites the branches. Finally you place the log on the fire and prepare to toast marshmallows.

In the neurological context, kindling works somewhat the way it works in your campfire. Neural responses torch off other responses, which torch off still others. Although your log is too big to burn if lighted by itself, when it lies on a bed of burning kindling it will soon catch. Similarly, nerve impulses and responses that would not happen normally, or would not happen so intensely, are ignited off each other by kindling.

Unlike the campfire, wherein once wood burns it is gone, in the neurological context the same responses can light each other repeatedly, causing rapid cycling of thought or activity. Also, nerve responses can excite others in ever-widening circles to raise the person's level of anger or excitement or fear beyond reasonable levels.

In seizure, kindling runs amok. Large numbers of nerves—often the wrong nerves—"light" at almost the same time. You can see why the drugs that would retard kindling and curtail or prevent neurons from firing would be useful for mania and bipolar disorders, for sleep inducement, and also for control of seizures.

Basically, we use four drugs routinely to retard this kindling and quell seizures.

## Drugs Used for Treating Seizures and Aggression

### Drugs Used for Treating Seizures

**Dilantin** (phenytoin) has largely supplanted the use of barbiturates, and no wonder. Barbiturates close down the whole central nervous system. Too often, to control the seizures with barbiturates we had to drug the patient nearly to zombie status. That was occasionally preferable to life-threatening, violent grand mal seizures. Dilantin, which seems to act primarily by damping down kindling, allows the patient a normal lifestyle without looking and feeling doped up. Because it is metabolized in the liver, people with impaired liver function need careful monitoring.

**Klonopin** (clonazepam), formerly called Clonopin, is used to reduce anxiety as well as seizures. A benzodiazepine-like anticonvulsant, it inhibits kindling well, making it useful also in the management of obsession/compulsions, mania, and strange neural misfiring such as Tourette's syndrome.

**Valium** (diazepam) brings down the extreme agitation, violence, and seizures associated with alcohol withdrawal. It stops seizures immediately, but its effect doesn't last long. (In other words, it's not good for maintenance.)

**Valproic acid** comes also in its brand name versions, **Depakote** and **Depakene**. Depakene is the salt, sodium valproate. Depakote is a coated tablet containing sodium valproate plus valproic acid. These substances are absorbed quickly and act quickly. Because of its coating, Depakote's absorption is delayed a few hours, on purpose.

**Tegretol** (carbamazepine) works on epileptic symptoms within hours. (You'll recall it is also often useful for psychotic problems, mania, depression, and bipolar disorder.) It helps patients withdraw from the effects of alcohol or benzodiazepine dependency. It also can dampen aggressive behavior. When employing Tegretol, we keep a close watch on components of the patient's blood, such as platelets, which the drug can alter or damage.

Other drugs that may sometimes be used for seizures are phenobarbitol, Primidone, and ethosuximide.

## Drugs Used for Treating Aggression

**BuSpar** (buspirone) can occasionally handle chronic aggression, but it takes a month to six weeks to really kick in and become effective.

**Corgard** (nadolol) may help in aggression. A beta-blocker, it essentially slows down heart rate. It does not affect liver function, being excreted pretty much as is by the kidneys. Other neuroleptics can also serve when the aggression and violence are tied to psychosis.

**Haldol** (haloperidol) can be quite helpful for acute aggression—when the problem is *now* and therefore the solution must be also. Used to quell tics and psychoses, it's one of those drugs that can encourage the potentially irreversible problem called tardive dyskinesia.

**Inderal** (propranolol), also a beta-blocker that reduces heart action, has a good record for easing antisocial phobias and disorders of that nature. Aggression, of course, certainly qualifies. Inderal is often used when Alzheimer's patients, who have little understanding or control of what they do, develop violent behavior.

**Ativan** (lorazepam) can reduce inhibitions, so it must be used cautiously, if at all. Neither Inderal nor Ativan should be taken for longer than six weeks, and adjusting dosage can be touchy.

Most benzodiazepines are fairly limited in managing aggression, and they can trigger paradoxical reactions. Instead of reducing rage, they occasionally multiply it.

## Friends or Foes?

Nowhere does the friend and foe tug-of-war show up more clearly than in the antiseizure and antiaggression medications. In bridling uncontrollable rage and easing frightening seizures the drugs are certainly friends. They are especially welcome when the rage they control is that of an elderly person who no longer has the mental capacity to act responsibly. That person can be just plain dangerous to the self and to others.

So what are the foe aspects? Any drug can produce minor or major side effects. Drugs can cure and drugs can kill. Drugs are friend and drugs are foe. The important question is whether potential side effects outweigh potential benefits.

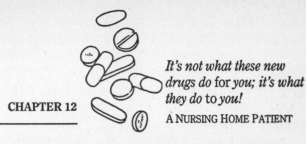

*It's not what these new drugs do* for *you; it's what they do* to *you!*

A NURSING HOME PATIENT

**CHAPTER 12**

## COMBATTING SIDE EFFECTS:
# THE ANTICHOLINERGIC DRUGS

Ralph Cammer sat on the hospital's sunporch and reflected on days gone by. Suddenly his head dipped aside so violently that his neck hurt afterward. An awful lot had happened to Ralph's body over the last forty-five years, but this was a new one. Sure, his old body was starting to show signs of wear and tear, but didn't he do a barrel full of hard living in that near-half-century! He had plenty of memories—except for what the alcohol-induced amnesia blotted out . . . and the psychosis.

He didn't really belong in here, but it was either submit to this mental hospital or go to jail, and he knew what the inside of a jail was like. Much as he hated this place, he'd put up with it since he had the choice. The cuckoos here were preferable to the young toughs who were always trying to prove something to you in the jail. Most of the yahoos in the hospital were harmless.

A couple of hours later, it happened again, that dipping movement. Ralph didn't like getting shots, and every blinking nurse in this outfit seemed determined to stick him with one, so he kept his mouth shut. He got through dinner and made it back to his room before it happened again. If he mentioned this to anyone, they'd inject him with something sure as blazes. He could tell when the world was out to get him.

The world's pogrom against him didn't seem quite as pressing anymore. For several days now he had been taking the antipsychotic Haldol, and just as the doctor promised, Ralph didn't feel as persecuted as he did a week ago. He didn't mind taking the Haldol. It was oral.

Twice more before bedtime, that crazy dip happened. His head would tilt suddenly aside, way aside, and his chin would wrench around. He'd bring it back into line. Before long, it happened again. Now that he thought about it, he remembered the doctor mentioning something like this might happen, but he didn't recall exactly.

During the night he got up to use the bathroom. His head had tilted aside at that weird angle and wouldn't come back into line right. He banged his head on the bathroom door jamb. He slammed into a wall when his head dipped while he was walking.

Nurse Jane, a humorless old woman with a square build and gray, Brillo-pad hair, stood in his doorway, arms akimbo. "You were supposed to tell us if your muscles started contracting involuntarily, Mr. Cammer."

"I'll do it in the morning," he muttered, as he crawled back into his bed.

Sure as God made little green apples, here came Nurse Jane two minutes later with a hypodermic syringe. There was no way out. Grumpy as a mule, Ralph turned over so she could stick still another horse-sized needle into him. "There ain't no justice, I tell ya. What's that stuff?"

"Benadryl. Look on the bright side, Mr. Cammer. It brings relief in a few minutes."

"Rather have the neck going funny than the needle. That's

why there ain't no justice. You people see the least little thing, the least bit wrong, and you gotta inject me. Don't sweat the small stuff, I always say."

"That's not what you said last week when you swore Saddam Hussein's militia was after you. I'll be back in five to see how your neck is."

## The Extrapyramidal Side Effects

The problem that suddenly came upon Ralph isn't small stuff. Of patients given antipsychotic drugs, a significant percentage will experience extrapyramidal side effects or extrapyramidal symptoms (commonly abbreviated EPSs), and Ralph's sudden onset of wryneck is one of them. EPSs are serious problems.

Incidentally, if you see the word *neuroleptic* in your reading, know that it's a classification encompassing most antipsychotics.

Once in a while Haldol, the drug Ralph Cammer was taking, or some other drug will cause one or more EPSs. As you've learned, the psychotropic drugs work their magic by altering body chemistry. That alteration can cause untoward problems, artificially created imbalances that we then must correct with additional drugs.

## How the Drugs Work

A ten-year-old child being prescribed seizure medication thoughtfully studied the full-color chart of the human nervous system spread before him. "This is the brain, right?"

"Right," the doctor said.

"What is this glob of pink with the nerve running out in all directions?"

"That's a basal ganglion—a big glob of nerves. Basal ganglia are clearing centers for involuntary movements."

"Like my seizures, right?" the boy said.

"Not exactly. They are movements you make without having to think about. Like breathing, and your heartbeat, and the way your gut works to pass food through it. That's involuntary. Some ganglia take care of other things, too."

The child studied the chart another moment. "Looks to me more like a spider somebody stepped on."

That's what they look like, all right. Those squashed spiders, the basal ganglia, handle a lot of what goes on in the body. Through them and from them pass the nerve messages that control most bodily functions. When something goes wrong in them, things go wrong all over.

Normal basal ganglia keep a supply of different kinds of neurotransmitters at hand to use as needed. They also maintain a carefully balanced ratio between the neurotransmitters—dopamine and acetylcholine, especially.

When certain drugs alter the quantity of dopamine or block its receptors, that careful ratio is thrown off balance. Antipsychotics are especially notorious in this regard, but other neuroleptic drugs also cause EPSs. We changed the quantity of dopamine on purpose, to achieve some desired effect. So now we must change the amount of acetylcholine as well to bring the relative quantities back into balance.

We call the chemicals used to restore this balance the anticholinergic drugs.

## Exactly What Goes Wrong?

Several different signs (called extrapyramidal symptoms or simply EPSs) indicate that the dopamine-acetylcholine balance is dangerously off. The patient may display only one symptom or a couple at once.

### Dystonia

Two-fifths of all EPSs include dystonia to some degree. The suite of symptoms called dystonia are basically unintended muscle contractions. Those basal ganglia are acting up because their chemistry is out of balance. The contractions can be intermittent, the way Ralph's started out, or continual.

Nearly all the time, if the problem is going to appear it will show up somewhere during the first week of treatment.

Ralph Cammer's manifestation was *torticollis* (*torti*, twisted, and *collis*, neck). We call it wryneck in common terms. His head not only dipped but rotated. *Retrocollis* tilts the head back rather than to the side, and with *opisthotonos*, not only does the head draw back, but the spine arches so that the body forms an uncomfortable, grotesque C.

Ralph might also have experienced an *oculogyric crisis*, wherein the eyes move involuntarily. Usually the eyeballs sweep upward.

Haldol (haloperidol) and forms of Prolixin (fluphenazine) are the agents that most commonly cause dystonia.

## Akathisia

Akathisia can be described as agitation. Unlike dystonia, it develops slowly over a spread of weeks, usually within the first three months of treatment with antipsychotics. It starts with an uncomfortable feeling that the muscles ought to be doing something they're not. It's hard to explain. Before long, the patient feels a powerful urge to be in constant motion, a restlessness. A foot starts bobbing incessantly. The person can't sit still and starts pacing. The restlessness may extend to feelings of fear or anxiety, even psychotic manifestations.

Akathisia is the problem least likely to respond to anticholinergic drugs. Unfortunately, it also accounts for half of all extrapyramidal symptoms. In fact, a significant percentage of all patients taking neuroleptic drugs, such as the antipsychotics, will display symptoms of akathisia within three months or so. If their medication is being delivered by a slow-release means, the symptoms could start showing up within four days. Women are twice as likely to develop the symptoms as are men. We tackle it with Inderal (propranolol) as a first try.

## Parkinsonism

If parkinsonism appears at all, its symptoms show up two or three weeks into treatment with neuroleptics. Antipsychotics tend to be the worst offenders. Note that parkinsonism induced by drugs is not the same as the problem called Parkinson's disease. They appear similar on the surface; that's the only connection.

Elderly females are most vulnerable to this particular suite of side effects. The tremors are a telling sign, as is a slow, deliberate, retarded movement called bradykinesia. The body becomes rigid in a manner we call cogwheel; when you attempt to flex the person's limb (an arm, for example) it bends in jerky increments, as if the joint were a ratchet. These three signs, tremors, bradykinesia, and cogwheel movement, seem to fit together. Other signs are drooling, difficulty swallowing, a problem walking normally (the person takes little steps, as if the ankles were roped closely together), and a problem starting a desired movement or stopping it once it begins. Akinesic people may develop a profound apathy.

## Rabbit Syndrome

You know how a rabbit's split upper lip and little pink nose are constantly wiggling? The upper lip of a person displaying rabbit syndrome acts like that. It's a rapidly cycling movement that may occur by itself or become part of the suite we call parkinsonism.

We group together all the extrapyramidal symptoms because all, to a greater or lesser extent, respond to the anticholinergic drugs we prescribe specifically to alleviate them.

Note that the syndrome called tardive dyskinesia is not an extrapyramidal side effect. Not only do anticholinergic drugs not affect tardive dyskinesia in a positive way, they can exacerbate it or bring it on when it otherwise would not have developed.

## Treatment with Anticholinergic Drugs

Ralph Cammer hated like the dickens to admit it, but Nurse Jane's shot did take care of his head-dipping problem. Sure, his muscles ached for a day or two afterward, but the problem itself was resolved. To his good fortune, dystonia responds very nicely to medication. To his further good fortune, that initial shot was the only injection he needed. He continued the Benadryl course from then on with oral administration.

Akathisia frequently does not respond well to anticholinergic drugs. However, the drugs do manage parkinsonism well. When we use anticholinergics to quell Parkinson-like side effects, we try to taper them off after a few months. Once a patient is weaned off them, she usually does all right from then on.

Just about any anticholinergic clears up rabbit syndrome.

Different anticholinergic drugs tend to work best at different times, depending on whether the side effects to be managed appear rapidly (acute), as did Ralph's, or emerge gradually over time. Benadryl and Cogentin hit hard and fast when time is important. Once the extrapyramidal side effects are reversed, we can use any of several agents.

In addition, if we can we will switch the patient's primary medication to a lower-potency drug.

The following drugs produce the anticholinergic effects we need to readjust chemical imbalances caused by neuroleptics.

## Drugs Used for Treating Side Effects

**Akineton** (biperiden) is considered a fairly weak-acting drug, but it does a good job on parkinsonism. It also helps most other EPS problems.

**Artane** (trihexyphenidyl) relaxes muscles and works well on all forms of parkinsonism. We often use this drug when the cause of EPSs is Compazine, Mellaril, Thorazine, thioxanthenes, or butyphenones.

**Ativan** (lorazepam) serves primarily as an antianxiety medication, but it also counteracts EPSs.

**Benadryl** (diphenhydramine), often used as an antihistamine, also works very well on EPSs. Administered intramuscularly or intravenously, it usually stops dystonia immediately. Administered orally over time, it keeps the extrapyramidal symptoms at bay. We generally begin anticholinergic treatment with either Benadryl or Cogentin.

**Cogentin** (benztropine), an antihistamine as well as an anticholinergic, also hits dystonia fast and well. We find it especially useful for parkinson–like side effects of neuroleptics.

**Dantrium** (dantrolene) is hard on the liver, so we try for a minimal dosage and monitor blood chemistry frequently in people using it. Caught early, its deleterious effect on the liver can be reversed. Dantrium's major use is as an antispastic, particularly in cases of stroke, multiple sclerosis, and spinal injury.

**Inderal** (propranolol) (used also for anxiety and seizures) is the drug of choice when dealing with akathisia. Valium and Ativan are second choices if Inderal fails to alleviate symptoms.

**Kemadrin** (procyclidine) is used for EPSs in general and has a special gift for ending drooling in parkinsonism patients. It has only a limited effect on tremors but aids coordination.

**Parlodel** (bromocriptine) is a group of drugs used for Parkinson's disease as well as the parkinsonism reactions. (The other drugs listed at the end of Chapter 9 also are used.)

**Protopam** (pralidoxime Cl) is tried very occasionally in persons not responding to other drugs. Its main use is in counteracting the effects of pesticide poisoning. It may be used along with a belladonna derivative, e.g., atropine.

**Symmetrel** (amantadine) is usually used for extended treatment, as when a person subject to neuroleptic side effects will be on an antipsychotic for an extended period.

**Valium** (diazepam), an antianxiety medicine, may help with akathisia, but to a lesser extent on other EPSs.

## When to Commence Drug Treatment

Two schools of thought address the question of when to begin a course of anticholinergics, if at all.

First, do we begin them at the same time we begin the psychotropic course? There are advantages in this. More than half the people who begin taking drugs to correct a condition, people who really need the chemical correction, will quit before the course is completed. A major reason they quit taking the drugs is the side effects. Anticholinergics, by blocking the development of serious side effects, prevent the problem.

The extrapyramidal symptoms are bad stuff. At the very least, they are uncomfortable. In one opinion, the high-potency neuroleptic drugs cause the EPSs often enough that a person is justified in using the anticholinergics as preventive medicine. This is particularly true for younger patients who have less patience with such things.

On the other hand, people who object to the automatic prescription of anticholinergics voice sound arguments, also. "Never give anticholinergics with low-potency drugs," they urge. "Those drugs rarely produce extrapyramidal side effects anyway. You're complicating the patient's chemistry trying to prevent something that probably won't happen."

Worse, the anticholinergics have side effects of their own and can intensify nonextrapyramidal things like dry mouth and confusion that the original neuroleptic causes. Ample evidence shows that anticholinergics can produce or intensify tardive dyskinesia.

Opponents of using anticholinergic drugs as a preventive measure recommend using them only if and when the side effects develop.

At any rate, after a half year or so of long-term therapy, we can generally withdraw the anticholinergic drugs carefully and safely. Even if Ralph Cammer needs Benadryl, he won't need it for long. Anticholinergics are not indicated for the life of the maintenance therapy.

When we withdraw them we do so slowly, gradually tapering the dose. Cutting them off abruptly can cause nausea, drooling, headaches, insomnia, and nightmares.

## CHAPTER 13

*Drugs, alcohol; ain't no difference. They're both deck chairs on the Titanic.*

A FORMER USER

# ALCOHOL, DRUGS, AND ABUSE

Everybody loved Melodie. All her neighbors commented on how friendly and energetic she was. Each morning she cheerily waved to the mail carrier, and whenever the UPS driver dropped off a parcel she greeted him brightly.

Melodie's doctor husband appreciated the understanding way she supported his long hours and his struggle to establish his practice. Melodie's mother, who lived in the next state, boasted to all her friends that Melodie called her every Sunday without fail.

But cheerful, perky Melodie looked pretty dragged out the Wednesday she met her friend Chris for lunch at their favorite restaurant.

Chris had a reputation of having been around the block. Local gossip claimed she had been kicked out of three private schools and jailed on at least one occasion. On the other hand, no one could prove it. She was a rarity—a single mother of three receiving adequate child support. Gossipmongers speculated that she somehow had blackmailed her ex into supporting his family.

When Melodie met Chris at the restaurant, Chris tactlessly blurted out, "You look terrible."

"Bad hair day," Melodie replied, not bothering to sit down. "Order the club sandwich for me, will you?" With that, she headed off toward the ladies' room.

Three minutes later she returned, perky and cheerful, and slid into the seat. "There! That's better. What I really needed was a potty stop. How're the boys?"

Melodie and Chris chatted through two tall tumblers of iced tea and the restaurant's specialty club sandwiches. Halfway through lunch, Melodie made another trip to the ladies' room.

Moments after the waiter brought them a third round of tea, Melodie rose for yet another trip to the rest room.

Chris raised a hand. "You got a bladder infection? I've seen dogs pay less attention to fire hydrants."

"No, it's all the tea." Melodie smiled fetchingly.

"It's not the tea. Sit down, Mel."

Melodie sat down and cautiously watched her friend's face. "Chris . . ."

"Your husband's a doctor. Okay, he just finished his residency, so he's a new doctor. But he's a doctor all the same. How do you keep it from him?"

"Keep what?"

"The coke, Mel. You're doing lines in the bathroom. Using the handicapped stall, right? It has that convenient steel shelf to put your purse on. Or your snow."

"Chris, how can you say that?"

Chris shrugged. "Just out of curiosity, how much are you into?"

Melodie studied her friend's face a long moment. She settled back in her chair. "Not much. Five, ten dollars a day at most. I didn't think it showed."

"It probably doesn't to most people. You forget, this is Chris, the woman with the shady past."

Melodie snickered mirthlessly. "You asked how I keep it from Jerry. Chris, he isn't home long enough to look at me, let alone ask questions. I could run around with a paper bag over my head and he wouldn't notice. So what are you going to do?"

"Nothing. What would do any good? Turn you in? Spank you?" Chris shook her head sadly. "You'll get caught soon enough. Buying your next load, loaning someone a snort, Jerry walks in on you in the bathroom. You'll get caught." She grimaced. "And ten dollars is nonsense. You're doing fifty a day, at least."

## Abuse

One of the most powerful foe aspects of drugs is abuse, and it is also one of the hardest to combat. We can almost always manage drug side effects. And one way or another, we can usually get around noncompliance (that is, patients taking medication improperly or not at all, either inadvertently or on purpose). But abuse? The patient doggedly determined to misuse drugs is going to, at least until we catch on.

Our patient might escalate dosage for a more pronounced effect—to get a bigger buzz or bang. With many drugs, escalation invites further escalation.

Moreover, abuse of one substance frequently opens the door to abuse of others. All too frequently, an abuser keeps using one drug and adds on others, thereby becoming mired in simultaneous, multiple addictions.

When Melodie's insomnia failed to respond to the usual hypnotics, her doctor prescribed the barbiturate Seconal. Melodie got hooked on the Seconal and kept hitting the coke as well. She found that a glass of beer or wine in the evening helped her relax. Within months she was using drinks to relax at any hour of the day or night.

Psychotropic drugs in particular may invite abuse *when they are employed outside of prescribed use* for several reasons. For one, they alter mental states, and the person using them is usually a person whose present mental or emotional state cries out to be altered. That's why the drugs are prescribed for that sort of thing in the first place. Furthermore, these people are not as stable as most. Too, psychotropic drugs kill pain of various sorts, as we've noted all along, and the people to whom they appeal are hurting deeply.

Inside a medical setting, with prescription use monitored by a doctor, they are safe. Popped indescriminately, they are not.

And here's the hooker: alcohol is the oldest and most common nonprescription psychotropic drug in the world. Alcohol a foe? Absolutely. Drug? Yes, in every sense of the word. Ingested alcohol alters body chemistry, mood, and consciousness, and damages organs when used extensively. In overdose, alcohol can cause death.

Although what we've just said about alcohol can be applied to narcotics as well, there are differences, especially when we consider the overreaching harmful effects of alcohol and drug use on society.

Alcohol-related crime, accidents, and fatalities are immediate. By that we mean they most frequently occur while a person is intoxicated. The person loses physical and emotional control, good judgment, coordination and normal reflexes, and in this state the person breaches the law or causes the accident.

Drug-related crime, accidents, and fatalities also happen while a person is under the influence. But the danger expands far beyond the immediate as distributors and dealers wage battles over disputed territories, fight each other and law enforcement, and extract vengeance for wrongs, both fancied and real. Many of these crimes are carefully calculated, but battles can erupt on the spur of the moment, as well. In all this chaos, the damage, body count, and costs are inflicted not just on the people involved in the drug trade, but on innocent people as well.

## Who Is Affected?

In a city in Washington, a carload of teens inadvertently throw eggs at a gang's crack house. The armed residents pursue the unarmed teens and kill two of them. Not one of the participants in the incident is old enough to vote.

In Arizona, a child thought to be the son of a drug overlord is kidnapped, tortured, and killed. The overlord laughs in his enemies' faces; in error they had snatched not his child, but the son of visitors from Missouri. Meanwhile in Missouri, a turf war unrelated to the tragedy in Arizona breaks out, leaving four people dead.

"Yes," you say, "but that doesn't happen to Us. It only happens to Them." Alcohol and drug problems are perceived as only happening to a certain infraclass of people, none of whom go to church. That could not be farther from the truth. The problems run amok even in the "best" circles. Indeed, they affect all sectors of society.

The kids who died in the egg incident came from a "nice" neighborhood, went to a "good" school, and had no criminal records. They did not themselves use drugs or alcohol. Nearly half the persons killed in alcohol-related traffic accidents had not consumed any alcohol at all—zero blood alcohol readings.

Probably every person reading this book can relate personal stories of loved ones, neighbors, and friends who have suffered grievously and quite possibly died due to the direct effect of alcohol and drug abuse. How many people do you know who have benefited from alcohol and drug misuse?

Every person is affected.

Let's examine separately the two great classes of abused drugs: alcohol and the other psychotropics, including opiates.

# Alcohol

## The Oldest Psychotropic

Almost every culture has learned the art of fermenting foods to produce alcoholic beverages, North American aboriginals being an exception. Egyptians made wine and Babylonians brewed beer thousands of years before Christ. So did the Chinese and the European Celts. Romans floated their orgies in a vat of wine. The woes of drunkenness turn up repeatedly in the Bible from Genesis to Revelation. South American Indians have long made a heady hooch by chewing up vegetables and spitting them into a tub to ferment. In A.D. 800, a Viking's wife was known by the quality of the beer she brewed; no matter how good her stuff, though, the truly wealthy Viking served imported wine to his most favored guests.

Wine for the cultured, beer for the masses, whisky for the serious drinker; a wild and extensive lore has grown up around alcoholic beverages through the centuries. Folk beliefs have given alcohol a far more attractive mystique than it deserves.

Certainly it alters mood, for better or worse. Of course it numbs pain, on occasion. Is it therefore a friend? Hardly. For the benefits it bestows, many of them dubious, it exacts a very high price.

Forty percent of all arrests and 50 percent of all traffic fatalities are alcohol related. Alcohol is involved in half the cases of child abuse, more than half of boating accidents and drownings, and more than four-fifths of deaths caused by fire. The death rate of alcoholics is two and one-half times higher than that of the general population. Need we go on?

How does a mere beverage wreak this kind of havoc? Let's look at the effects and how they happen.

## The Effects of Alcohol

Melodie was incensed. She ordered a glass of port after dinner in a restaurant, and look at what they brought her!

"This glass is half the size of a wine glass!" she fumed. "Port is wine. When I ask for a glass of wine, I want a full-sized glass of wine!"

There is a reason for the serving size. A stein of beer, a glass of regular wine, a glass of fortified wine (port, sherry), and a shot of whisky all deliver about the same alcoholic bang per serving. Because fortified wines have about twice the alcohol of regularly prepared wines (20 percent as opposed to about 10 percent), they are traditionally served in a smaller glass. Volume is less, but gross alcohol content is similar. They are meant to be sipped.

Sipping, as any whisky drinker can tell you, delivers the alcohol to the bloodstream most efficiently. The alcohol need not make it clear down to the stomach and intestine in order to be felt; at least part of it is absorbed immediately by the lining of the mouth and esophagus. Absorption is slower in persons who simultaneously sip an alcoholic beverage and eat fatty foods.

As disgruntled Melodie sips her itty-bitty glass of port, the alcohol is passing into her bloodstream rapidly. As the alcohol and its congeners (the chemicals in the drink additional to the ethyl alcohol) enter the blood, they are carried to every cell in the body. Alcohol numbs, or depresses, the central nervous system. This will slow down Melodie's reflexes and dull her speech, perceptions, and thoughts. Her inhibitions and sense of caution will be impaired. The net effect of alcohol as a drug is that of a depressant. Although Melodie might feel a happy buzz at first, that will pass as the full effect kicks in.

Meanwhile, the alcohol is coursing through Melodie's liver as well as her other organs. Her liver will recognize the alcohol as an energy source and begin converting it into sugars, glycogen, and fat, along with some other things. The liver also goes to work on the congeners, changing them into a variety of compounds.

About two-thirds of the calories in a glass of beer come from the alcohol. (Molson's, at 5.1 percent alcohol, delivers

154 calories. This is why lite beers generally have a lower percentage of alcohol by volume; that's where the calorie cut is made.) The alcohol provides no other nutrients.

Although 95 percent of the alcohol will be processed via the bloodstream to Melodie's liver (alcohol is not excreted from the body by sweat or feces, though a little is lost through the kidneys and lungs), her intestinal system will digest some of the ingredients that accompany the alcohol. Depending on the kind of drink imbibed, the breakdown products of digestion and liver metabolism will probably be useless or even toxic. Some people, for example, are born with a body chemistry that metabolizes alcohol to acetaldehyde, which is poisonous to brain cells.

If Melodie puts more alcohol into her system than her liver can take out, and the liver is rather slow at the task, her blood alcohol level will climb. Her body is now so infused with alcohol that it and its congeners will invade her lungs, giving her mouth a particular aroma. You can indeed smell booze on someone's breath, more or less, depending on the beverage and its congeners.

Eventually, for one reason or another, Melodie will have to quit putting alcohol into her system (that is, she will voluntarily quit drinking or she will become sick or pass out). Her liver will continue metabolizing; her blood alcohol level will drop slowly and steadily. When the alcohol finally leaves her system, she may suffer a ringing, howling, debilitating hangover. Even though her blood alcohol reading is now zero, she will not regain adequate function until the hangover dissipates. Running at maybe 80 percent of par, if that, she still will pose a menace in traffic or other tight, stressful situations.

If Melodie persists in drinking to excess, even if her habit is sporadic or limited to certain hours of the day, her body is going to suffer.

## Physical Damage

As alcohol and congeners are processed in the liver, damaging chemicals form as by-products in the liver. So the liver is first to receive the brunt of chemical abuse. A healthy liver looks about the color and texture of the beef liver in the butcher shop window. Cirrhosis, the common disease of the alcoholic, burns and shrivels the liver so that it looks like a chunk of scorched cork. The liver is no longer able to perform its other functions, such as providing bile for fat digestion, processing energy sources, and filtering bacteria and foul wastes, so the alcoholic will experience a sharp decline in health and, eventually, death.

By numbing nerve cells, alcohol throws blood pressure out of kilter. Increased blood pressure, with its attendant dangers of stroke and cardiac problems, awaits the alcoholic. The alcohol also irritates nerve cells in the brain, which often disturbs sleep.

Diabetes is extremely common in alcoholics. Because the liver treats alcohol as an energy source and converts it into sugars, among other things, the pancreas has trouble keeping a good blood sugar balance. Too much sugar sometimes pours into the bloodstream. If the alcoholic doesn't eat a proper diet, which is often the case, the body is devoid of sugar when it ought to be getting some. Too much, too little; the pancreas faces the sort of chaotic production problems that a short-handed fast-food crew feels when a bus pulls up out front.

Gout, usually hereditary, can have a medical/alcohol connection. The body retains uric acid, a by-product of metabolism. The acid collects at the joints, causing pain and swelling. By interfering with metabolism, alcohol can greatly aggravate a natural tendency to gout.

Should Melodie become pregnant while abusing alcohol or drugs, her chances are one in three that her baby will be retarded and deformed. In fact, Fetal Alcohol Syndrome has a specific suite of signs—slowing of mental and physical growth and peculiar, characteristic deformity in the face, head, arms, legs, and heart.

If Melodie were to pursue a course of alcoholism through years, she might display what we call Wernicke's syndrome, or alcoholic encephalopathy. The sixth cranial nerve, serving eye muscles, would be affected so that she would be unable to control her eyes properly. She would be unable to control other supposedly voluntary muscles also, and might act confused. At times, a bout with Wernicke's leads to short-term memory loss. We call this Alcohol Amnesic Disorder, or Korsakoff's syndrome. In fact, we often tie the two together as Wernicke-Korsakoff's syndrome. The effects are permanent or nearly so, and if the syndrome strikes hard enough, institutionalization may be necessary.

In the examination room, psychiatrists and other doctors look also for a history of seizures, evidence of endocarditis, hepatitis, cellulitis, and chronic sinus problems. Depression very often accompanies abuse. So do mood swings.

This is the kind of relentless, vicious foe we are talking about.

Do all these symptoms, not to mention Melodie's predictable, unerring response to drinking, signify that alcoholism is a disease in itself?

## Alcoholism as a Disease

In 1956, the American Medical Association ruled that alcoholism is a disease, and the philosophy of Alcoholics Anonymous agrees. The AMA offered several reasons for the determination (a major factor was to enable the treatment of alcoholism to be covered by insurance according to rules and allowances then in place). Compare alcoholism with some classic disease—for example, diabetes. Alcoholics display a specific suite of symptoms in sequential order; so do diabetics. Diseases have an identifiable causative factor; in alcoholism, it's alcohol, and in diabetes it's an insulin imbalance. Hospitals and drug regimens can go far in controlling alcoholism just as they go far to control other diseases.

We are finding that there can be a genetic predisposition to alcoholism, just as there is to diabetes. Too, alcoholics and diabetics both experience permanent physiological changes as their condition advances.

But.

Big but.

We cannot overlook a serious factor that distinguishes alcoholism from classic diseases: one does not voluntarily develop diabetes or cancer or appendicitis or glaucoma; but drinking, as well as drug abuse, is deliberate and voluntary.

Furthermore, the diseased persons identify a number of background factors as causes for alcoholism, and this is not true of classic diseases. Marriage issues; job fears or dissatisfaction; an unhealthy family situation; ethnic and cultural values; stress, anger, and denial; personal preference; peer pressure—people place the blame for their drinking problems on an astonishing array of outside factors.

Alcoholism is indeed multifactorial. We see strong medical and genetic components. Psychological factors do indeed exist. They may influence choices but they do not control choices.

To give alcoholism disease status allows the alcoholic a way out he or she should not be permitted. "Oh, well, since it's a disease, I'm not the cause; I'm a victim." "Diseases are hopeless. Why try to quit?" Efforts to regain health then become merely symbolic or spasmodic or cease entirely, and personal responsibility flies out the window.

Genetic disposition also sometimes becomes a scapegoat. "I'm doomed to it; it's in my genes. I can't fight it."

Hardly. Diabetics who know about their genetic predisposition take steps to prevent or retard the disease, using diet, careful habits and scheduling, and exercise to counteract the genetic tendency. These steps work to some extent and often to a great extent. Persons with a genetic predisposition to diabetes may not be able to hold off fate forever, but they can soften the blow through sensible and circumspect living.

Similarly, the person who suspects predisposition to alcoholism can take deliberate steps to thwart the onset. The easiest and most obvious: stay off alcohol.

Can alcoholism be classified as a disease when a person persists in escalating his drinking in the face of opposition from loved ones, not to mention the law? The alcoholic goes to great lengths and considerable expense to feed the habit, knowingly altering it from a matter of choice into a fatal compulsion.

Many of the same ethical and philosophical questions face persons who abuse drugs.

## Abuse of Drugs Other Than Alcohol

Balance is crucial. A tendency to go overboard in limiting the use of narcotics is footed in the prevalent tendency of people to go overboard in misusing the drugs. The reaction is extreme because the problem is extreme. And drugs are so easy to come by.

### Drugs Are Not Difficult to Obtain

Melodie had no trouble purchasing cocaine. And when the doctor prescribed Seconal, Melodie had no trouble getting three times a sensible allowance of it; she simply went to three different doctors with the same ailment and patronized three different pharmacies.

And alcohol? You can't get away from the stuff. It's in grocery stores in most states and available to any adult over twenty-one. Says a recovering alcoholic about her tour through the western states, "I'd never been west of Chicago, so I took along a whole suitcase of booze; I was afraid that out there in the wilderness, I'd be cut off. You know, forest primeval and all that. Hey, I could buy the stuff anywhere I went—in the parks, outside them. There's a single gas station at a crossroads in the middle of hundreds of miles of nothing, and there's a liquor shelf in the gas station. Supply was never a problem."

As a rule, the most misused drugs are also the most addictive or damaging.

*Opiates,* of which heroin and morphine are representative, are among the most dangerous and abused of drugs. They jump right in and bind to specific sites on brain neurons that normally receive naturally produced endorphins. Tolerance and dependence develop quickly, and withdrawal is fierce. Overdose can kill.

Opium has been around for six thousand years. Originally used for medicinal purposes—to allay pain, cough, and diarrhea—it spread from the Mediterranean into eastern Asia, probably with Arabian traders. The Europeans taught the Chinese how to smoke it, then used it as an exchange medium. In 1729, the emperor outlawed it, but to no avail. By 1800, opium addiction ran rampant in China. In the mid-1800s, the Chinese tried to block its import, and the Europeans sent gunboats to keep their trade routes open—the infamous Opium Wars.

Opium derivatives are still by far our best medicine for severe pain and are used legitimately every second of the day in hospitals, clinics, and sickrooms all over the world. A friend and a foe, opiates have alleviated pain and misery and caused pain and misery as no other drug group has.

*Cocaine* was first developed during the Civil War era for use as a local anesthetic. It still is used in that capacity today.

In the 1960s and 1970s, people started snorting or smoking cocaine to experience the temporary euphoria. Many people thought cocaine was nonaddictive. Not so, by any means. Addiction can develop quickly, sneaking up on you, and even in occasional or small doses, cocaine possesses the potential to kill. The treatment of cocaine dependence has become a major practice in psychiatric clinics and hospitals.

The high the coke provides is followed by a crash, an immediate low—so low, persons may have thoughts of suicide. Seizures, strokes, death by cardiac or respiratory arrest, and impotence are some of the problems a coke dealer won't mention.

*Amphetamines* and their ilk stimulate. They can make you feel faster, sharper, happier. They can also make you twitch uncontrollably, suffer restlessness and sleeplessness, lose control of your thoughts and actions to the extent that you embarrass yourself or others, and at the extreme, suffer paranoia and delusions. A form of methamphetamine called ice has been sending increasing numbers of people into emergency rooms.

*Barbiturates* are not as popular now as they once were, either for legitimate medical use or on the street. Heavy users may shoot barbiturates as an adjunct to other drugs or alcohol to increase the zing, an act that is exceedingly dangerous.

*Quaalude* (methaqualone) used to be hot stuff. Now it's not even made in this country. Some people claim it heightens sexual excitement, which is doubtful because quaalude is a sedative and sleep aid, two effects that are unlikely to enhance one's lovemaking. Using quaaludes with alcohol can be fatal.

The *benzodiazepines*—Librium, Valium, Dalmane, and the like—are mild enough that they are not often seriously abused. They don't produce much of a high.

*Marijuana*, extracted from the hemp plant, is the second-largest agricultural crop in the U.S. as measured in dollars generated. Most evidence indicates that persons cannot become physiologically addicted to marijuana, but it is possible to become psychologically dependent on it.

Some people get high off the fumes of acetone, gasoline, toluene, and other paint solvents; the truly dedicated abusers sniff glue or solvent for a buzz. High school kids and other athletes may abuse anabolic steroids, not knowing that a third of the abusers will go psychotic, or that aggressive tendencies will multiply. Withdrawal of steroids generates miserable depression. Nicotine, usually delivered in cigarettes, chewing tobacco, or snuff, is highly addictive. A person who quits smoking can suffer nicotine cravings for two decades. Caffeine, a stimulant similar to amphetamines, is a psychotropic because it can increase alertness, promote a feeling of well-being, and even improve some skills. Ubiquitous, it turns up in many medicines, soft drinks, chocolate, and of course, coffee. Tolerance builds with heavy use, and caffeine withdrawal can produce migraines of epic proportions.

These substances all alter mood and mind. Misused and abused, these drugs really can alter personality, and always for the worse.

## Drug Abuse in the Workplace

Drugs in the workplace is another problem. Someone estimated the financial cost of on-the-job drug abuse at $85 billion annually. That's a tremendous drain on our economy. It comes in decreased production, absenteeism, accidents, faulty work and products, and theft.

As Melodie demonstrated, it's easy to do a line or two of coke in a bathroom stall. It's just as easy to pop a methamphetamine pill while getting a drink of water.

But although some addicts can hide their problem for years, in almost all cases, signs eventually point to the obvious. Drug abuse can't be hidden forever.

## Signs and Symptoms of Abuse

In most situations when you donate blood, you must let the attending nurses see the insides of your wrists and arms. What are they looking for? Needle marks. In the doctor's office and on the street, they are called tracks. Drug abusers using injectables are at high risk for HIV infection, and the blood-donation workers are trying to keep HIV/AIDS out of our blood supply.

If you're involved in an auto accident, what s the first thing the police will check? Okay, your driver's license. What's the second thing? Blood alcohol level. Whether or not you were responsible for the accident, if your blood alcohol level is up, you're in big trouble.

Continued heavy use of alcohol usually causes a W. C. Fields nose—bulbous and red because minor blood vessels are breaking down within it. Continued snorting of cocaine causes "frozen" cells in the nose to slough off. In common lay terms, the nose erodes. Police officers and medical workers often can determine if a person is abusing drugs by asking the person to hold his hands out flat, palms down, fingers extended. The practiced substance abuser won't be able to keep his fingers still and stationary, no matter how hard he tries.

Another way to tell if a person is high on alcohol or drugs is by looking at the pupils of the eyes. The pupils dilate or contract unnaturally when a person is under the influence. These signs and many others reveal the drug abuser's secrets to the careful observer.

If you are examining the possibility of alcohol or drug abuse in someone you care about—perhaps even yourself—here are some signs to look for.

## The Person Is Frequently Impaired by the Drug

When a person uses a substance of choice four times a week or more to the point that it alters her feelings or consciousness, that is drug abuse. Whether it's getting drunk, getting high, or numbing out, the individual is frequently impaired by the effects of drugs.

## The Person Frequently Gets into Trouble

Persons who abuse alcohol or drugs may get into trouble frequently. Driving under the influence, getting into arguments or brawls, and being late for or slacking off at work, are just a few examples.

With kids, the trouble may be sagging grades and lack of interest in school activities. Substance abuse can wipe out youthful enthusiasm.

Another form of trouble is health problems. Cardiac or digestive problems, insomnia, irritability or nervousness, depression, and constant anger are warning signs.

Frequent accidents or injuries are other kinds of trouble abusers can get into. People under the influence account for far more than their share of mishaps.

## The Person Has Little or No Control Over Drug Use

A person who abuses drugs will have to have that drink, snort, or pick-me-up to feel normal and get through the day. He can't seem to stop or slow down his use of the substance, and if he does stop taking the drug he may feel physically ill or irritable and nervous.

If a person you care about is exhibiting any of these signs, that person could have a problem with alcohol or drug abuse. If so, you may wonder why and how it happened.

## Why It Happens

Adults who become addicted to substances seek a wildly diverse variety of places to lay blame and maintain a solid wall of denial about their addiction:

- "I can handle it."
- "It's not that bad."
- "This stuff can't hurt you."
- "I can't deal with life without a little snort now and then. That's not addiction. That's coping."
- "I'm not hooked. I can stop any time I want."

The adult comes up with long lists for why the addiction happened. These lists are excuses, covers for truth. Some abusers maintain that the addiction just snuck up on them. But it wouldn't have had a chance to sneak up without denial on the abuser's part from the beginning.

The only true source of blame lies with the person. An adult knows the costs of substance addiction. Information on drug and alcohol abuse is so pervasive in our society, no one can be in the dark about it.

The bottom line always remains with the self. The adult is responsible for his or her behavior.

Drug abuse in children, on the other hand, is another story. A child does not have the knowledge about life that an adult has accumulated; the child genuinely does not know the costs and consequences of misuse. Teaching about drugs and alcohol in a school setting is abstract. Such teaching does almost nothing toward keeping a kid clean in later years. As the child enters the turbulent teens, this abstract intellectual knowledge never triumphs over the needs of the heart. And yet, the essential knowledge about life that would help the child take intelligent responsibility still has not accumulated.

Also, a child does not have sufficient self-awareness to pick up signs of addiction. Kids don't have a clear understanding of dependency issues, let alone the skills to evaluate them in themselves or others. Kids' medical knowledge is close to zip. They don't know what normal body function is and what it is not.

How then does a child become addicted?

Kids are imitators. They try what they see the adults doing. But this does not account for the many cases of addicted kids in clean families—families where drugs and alcohol are not misused.

Kids are experimenters. They have to be; how else do you accumulate the life knowledge you need? They try stuff, whether that stuff is licit and approved or not. In fact, as separation and individuation take powerful hold, they're more likely to try what is not approved. Many children (by which we mean kids under age thirteen) experiment. With almost all of them, it ends there. They catch on that the behavior isn't good, and they drop it.

But this is not the case with kids in pain. If children's pain and problems are not dealt with some other way, the kids will self-medicate, and they cannot understand or control the substances they try.

In our practice, we talk to many distraught parents whose kids are abusing alcohol or drugs, and punishment isn't doing a thing to help. Very seldom do we find we need to deal only with the addiction problem. Almost always, the real problem is underlying family dynamics. Kids are reactors rather than actors. They play out the unspoken family problems and dysfunctions, and addiction is one of the major ways they do it.

Consider the case of twelve-year-old Ryan. Ryan and his parents came to Dr. Minirth for counseling after the parents found out Ryan was using drugs. Ryan came from a model family. Just ask his parents.

"I made certain I stayed at home until the kids were well into school," said Ruth, Ryan's mother. "Even when I went back to work, I kept it part-time so I could be home when they got home."

"I'm not like these dads who don't have time for their kids," claimed Pete, Ryan's father. "I spend a lot of time with the kids, mostly on weekends. I supported Ryan's Little League career all the way. We go out to the ballpark when the Astros are in town. I even go to PTA meetings. Ryan doesn't have a reason in the world to go bad like this."

Dr. Minirth asked a few other questions, mostly filling in blanks and verifying what he already suspected.

Ryan certainly looked the picture of a boy any parent would be proud of. He wore jeans and a polo shirt. His hair was neatly styled. He sported a healthy tan, probably from playing ball. In short, Ryan looked like a kid right out of the fifties.

And that was a problem.

"Most of the guys in Ryan's age group wear baggy pants, oversized T-shirts that cover the knees, and ball caps turned backward," I ventured. "Does Ryan always dress this well?"

Pete snorted. "My son isn't going to look ludicrous, and he knows it."

Ryan's peer group certainly did look ludicrous—on purpose. As children enter their teens they have to somehow separate themselves from the family and become independent individuals. Costume is an easy way to begin that separation without a major commitment. It's a surface change; it's adjustable. When children Ryan's age do not dress like their peers, we ask why.

Pete not only carefully monitored and controlled Ryan's

dress, he also chose Ryan's friends for him. Pete showed up at PTA meetings not so much to help the education process as to control every detail of Ryan's schooling—or attempt to. The teachers hated to see him coming. Pete not only supported Ryan's Little League career, he also tried his best to direct it. In private consultation later, Ryan admitted he was embarrassed and ashamed by his father's domineering attitude toward coaches and umpires. Pete took the kids places to make sure they didn't have time on their own to go places or do things of which he didn't heartily approve.

Control. Pete exerted more and more of it as Ryan approached adolescence, and Ryan was bucking it harder and harder.

Understand that none of this was conscious on either person's part. Pete was a naturally controlling person who dominated his wife and employees. Ryan needed space to grow and Pete wasn't allowing it, but neither Ryan nor Pete realized that. Ryan only knew that he felt overwhelmed by painful forces beyond his control. He was restless, but he didn't know why. He felt rebellious, but he couldn't describe his feelings. Ryan yearned for something he could not articulate. His inner, innate need was to soar, to break away, but his father's iron grip, applied ever harder, dragged him down.

And yet the more Pete attempted to control his son's growth and destiny, the less he succeeded. He was trying to control things over which he had no control—Ryan's choice of friends, his habits, even his dress. In desperation Ryan kept a separate wardrobe at school and changed clothes before the first bell. And he and his buddies used drugs.

It was a lark at first, buying an upper from a kid in the eleventh grade. Just the act of buying an illicit drug gave Ryan a scary thrill. A can of beer cost a dollar; he could get one from Harry's cousin's friend. Sometimes Harry's dad gave him one. Ryan's father didn't approve of Harry, but that didn't stop Ryan from being best friends with him.

Neither Ryan nor his parents could see these dynamics

and sort through them. It usually takes an outsider to sift through the rubble and find the truth. And this is a key to effective treatment, finding and easing the source of pain, and showing the participants where the problem lies and what changes will help—and which ones won't.

But insight is only one of two keys. The addiction itself must be addressed. Sometimes, a temporary alternative drug regimen is necessary to counteract the effects of the addictive substance long enough for force of will to grab hold.

## Treating Alcohol and Drug Abuse

Treatment follows two parallel tracks—break the chemical hold of addiction and ease or eliminate underlying causes that would encourage relapse or new addictions. Breaking a chemical hold usually requires chemicals—fighting drugs with drugs. Remember that alcohol, too, is a drug.

Ryan did not require any drug intervention. Certainly he was misusing a drug, alcohol, and sometimes other substances as well, but his body chemistry had not altered to the extent that it had to be forced back nearer normalcy. Although psychiatrists are often accused of being drug-happy, of wanting to cure every ill with a pill, we avoid medication if we can, particularly in a child like Ryan.

Rather, in counsel, I sat down with Ryan's parents to show them how children must develop as individuals. We set some priorities about what's important enough to warrant confrontation and what is not. (Being repairable with time, dress and hairstyle usually are not, but Pete had a hard time accepting that.) We discussed support groups and control issues. We talked about exerting reasonable control as opposed to ineffectually trying to maintain absolute control.

Ryan and I talked about growing up, what he needed, how and what he felt, and how most kids separate themselves and build an identity. We discussed making choices and exercising personal responsibility. Not once did I lecture Ryan on the dangers of drug or alcohol use. That never works. Ryan's dad had already done enough of that, and to no avail. Instead I led Ryan into insights about his own needs as a maturing adult, and how he could make intelligent choices.

For Ryan's sake, the parents had to change their attitudes and tactics enough to let Ryan (and their other kids) develop his own paths. That would ease the family pain and tension. At the same time, Ryan had to take better responsibility for his choices.

If Ryan really wanted to persist with his self-medication, he would do so. You can't stop a determined kid. The trick was to bring Ryan to an understanding of himself and how he was changing, as well as an enthusiasm for himself—confidence—and alternative ways to ease the conflict. The right choices would follow.

Melodie's addictions present a much thornier problem. She was enured to abuse; that is, she'd been doing it so long, it had become a well-established lifestyle. One of the major reasons alcoholics and other addicts fall back into their old habits so easily is that they are accustomed to them and, in a deep, dark way, prefer them. At a psychological level, the addict is ever vulnerable to re-addiction. To the addict, getting through life without chemical backup is scary.

The other major reason addicts fall back is biochemical. The body's whole chemistry has changed to accommodate the addictive substances. Melodie's physiology was used to the addiction and had adjusted as much as possible to the drugs. Now it was going to have to adjust again, and sometimes that's not even possible. Some changes such as brain cell damage are permanent.

Melodie, therefore, was an excellent candidate for a drug intervention. Her addictions had such a firm grip on her that she would not be able to break free and return to normal without help. Often in cases of chronic or strong abuse, drug intervention is, in the long run, the quickest, cheapest, and least uncomfortable route to wellness.

## The First Step in Treatment: Get Started

The first step toward recovery is beginning, always much harder than it sounds, and to do that well, one must want to recover. Melodie didn't. Oh sure, she gave lip service to recovery; addicts do that. But that was her head speaking, not her heart.

Her life probably would have continued its downward spiral, as her drug costs escalated and her health deteriorated, had her husband, Jerry, not found out about her drug use and intervened. It all happened when he was preparing to go mountain biking one day.

Jerry and a buddy went to the garage to get the two mountain bikes. They were gone. Both bikes had disappeared. Melodie insisted they must have been stolen, yet the garage's locks and windows were not disturbed, and other items of equal value were still there. Wait. Some of Jerry's power tools were missing, and where was the lovely Queen Anne dresser Melodie's aunt gave them? A sneak thief doesn't pick up a dresser and cart it away.

Jerry confronted Melodie, but Melodie denied any involvement with the missing valuables. Jerry wasn't buying it. Moments later the phone rang, and Jerry answered it.

"Jerry, this is Chris, is Melodie there, please?"

"You! You're the one who got my wife into this!"

Reputation so often fosters assumptions like that. Jerry's tone of voice told Chris what was happening at the other end of the phone line, and his accusation infuriated her. For Melodie's sake, though, she stifled what she wanted to say and instead snapped, "Put her on the phone!"

He did so, albeit hesitantly.

Chris could barely hear Melodie's querulous, "Chris, later. I can't talk now."

"Yes, you can. Spill it all, Mel. Let him know. If he guesses, he'll imagine the problem to be even worse than it is. Take it from one who knows."

"You'll tell him—"

"No, I won't, Mel. But you have to. He's half of you. That's what marriage is about. Then call me to tell me how I can help. Whatever you need. God bless you, Mel."

Click.

Whether she wanted it or not, Melodie was on her way to recovery.

## The Second Step in Treatment: Identify Problems

The second step is identifying the problem and the substances. We must know that, because different substances require different treatments.

In our counseling situations, we can't always trust what the patients tell us. Denial and just plain lying combine to whitewash the situation, to minimize the bad things the patient fears will happen. Shame is a powerful motivation in most cases of addiction.

Jerry asked a friend to run some tests as a professional courtesy. These tests would tell him and his friend what kinds of substances were in Melodie's system. The tests would reveal how much tolerance she had built up when the doctors compared the actual quantities of substances in her blood and urine against her behavior. Were a few milligrams altering her behavior significantly, or had tolerance built to the point that she needed a big dose to get a little effect?

Let's assume for a moment that Jerry was not a doctor and had no medical training or laboratory resources easily at hand. How might he assess what he saw?

**Observe behavior.** Serious alcohol or drug use may mimic the symptoms of other disorders we've covered in this book—psychoses, bipolar disorder, anxiety. Depression almost always accompanies problem use. Melodie's depression was masked by the temporary highs her substances provided. When she was denied her drugs, her mood dropped like a rock.

Does the person seem drugged at times? Lethargic and

out-of-it? Sleepy or insomniac? Manic? People on drugs or who drink alcohol heavily often have difficulty speaking well; words come out slurred or wrong, the speech stumbling. While under the influence, Melodie might have trouble controlling muscles and eye movement. She might break out in chills or sweats, or show other signs that her body is too messed up to maintain itself comfortably anymore.

The careful observer can pick up on these fairly subtle signs. The external environment also provides clues.

**Observe financial circumstances.**   Jerry noticed missing items of value. Had he been more observant, he would have picked up on it much earlier.

Alcohol and drug habits cost money. Sooner or later, money becomes an ogre, a looming, threatening, overriding issue in the addict's life. The addict has to have money to buy the next dose, the next bottle.

Melodie went through their meager savings account within a few months. Her birthday money lasted three days. The sale of the heirloom Queen Anne dresser and the mountain bikes set her up for a few more months. She fully intended to replace the savings account with some of the money she got from the sales, but she never did.

Remember, the user has to pay for the habit somehow, and such habits are seldom cheap. Take a close look at where that money might be coming from. A serious drain in finances can tell you a lot.

**Never assume anything.**   Jerry forbade Melodie to leave the house, assuming that if she stayed home she would be cut off from supplies and have to dry out. Most of all, he forbade any contact with Chris. He was still assuming that wayward woman had misled his sweet Melodie.

At first, Melodie recognized that she ought to end her dependence and cooperated willingly. The cooperation didn't last long. Her addiction was stronger than her will to cooperate.

When it got tough, Melodie phoned in prescription refills to two different pharmacists. For an extra few bucks, she could have the prescriptions delivered to her home. Unfortunately, it took two Seconal doses to give her the same relief one used to. The Seconal supply dwindled rapidly, so she called a neighbor and asked her to drop a bottle of port or sherry by. Melodie claimed she was having guests for dinner and didn't have any after-dinner wine to serve with dessert. Unaware of Melodie's circumstances, the neighbor gladly agreed.

Jerry's false assumption played right into Melodie's hands.

## The Third Step in Treatment—Consider Hospitalization

We call for hospitalization whenever these signs prevail:

**The patient won't quit.** Melodie couldn't stop using drugs on her own. Her good intentions melted like snow in Phoenix. No amount of resolve was strong enough to master the body's altered needs. Melodie needed constant monitoring; Jerry's naive assumptions served nothing.

Melodie's denial sat firmly enthroned in her conscious mind, while a lack of desire to quit ruled her subconscious. That in itself is reason for hospitalization. But there are more compelling reasons to hospitalize.

**Severe symptoms plague the patient.** Severe psychiatric symptoms and signs call for severe measures. The person who is morbidly depressed or suffers psychosis, delirium, or serious physical problems (for example, extreme nervousness or high blood pressure) needs a hospital setting in which to stabilize. Cessation of symptoms is not going to happen at home or on the street.

**Withdrawal might result in illness or death.** Withdrawal from some substances, especially if they are seriously abused, can lead to death. A small percentage of people facing delirium tremens without treatment will die. This is one reason doctors have to know which substances, specifically, the patient is using abusively. Some threaten life when withdrawn, some don't. If there is any question at all, we hospitalize.

Death is not the only nasty response to withdrawal. Persons going off heroin or other opiates cold turkey are afraid they won't die. Nothing is so unremittingly excruciating for so long a time as precipitate opiate withdrawal. Sudden withdrawal from Seconal, a barbiturate, would not kill Melodie, but she would suffer severe sleep disturbances, among them frightening nightmares.

Finally, we hospitalize patients who would not otherwise receive any means of support.

**The patient has no support.** Melodie had Jerry and Chris backing her up all the way, right? Not really. Jerry was putting in a fourteen-hour day trying to get his practice started. Chris worked a ten-hour shift four days a week. That was a lot of time for Melodie to be on her own and get into trouble. Melodie could expect a general outpouring of enthusiasm for clean living, but no actual support.

If Melodie lived with people who actively contributed to her problems, we would hospitalize her until her strength built back up. Negative support, which is contact with people who permit or even encourage abuse, comes in many forms. The dealer on the corner makes it easy to go back to using drugs. Friends and relatives who continue substance abuse will draw the patient back in by example. Even television programs or films may, in the viewer's mind, make drug use seem okay. Whether or not that is the actual message of the story, it's how the viewer interprets it that counts.

For persons who have no recourse beyond the hospital, many cities have established halfway houses. The houses, often a rooming-house or dorm arrangement, provide supportive surroundings for people who need a wholesome, drug- and alcohol-free environment in which to grow in strength and resolve.

Not one of the recovery steps is exclusive of others. We tailor treatment to individuals by choosing combinations of steps. The fourth step, for example, is often employed in conjunction with others.

## The Fourth Step in Treatment: Consider Drug Intervention

Some people foster an opinion that drug and alcohol addicts might as well suffer awhile getting free of their addictions. They had their fun; let them sweat this one out. A related opinion suggests that if the addicts suffer enough breaking free, they'll assiduously avoid relapse in order to avoid a repeat of the suffering.

Apparently, it doesn't work that way. The severity of withdrawal symptoms bears absolutely no relationship to the frequency of relapse and re-addiction. Compassion dictates that the way be smoothed if possible. And certainly we must avoid the chance of mishaps and death.

The drugs used in treating addictions serve one of two purposes: they prevent misuse of the addictive drug, or they make the recovering patient feel a little better during recovery.

Some of these drugs perform miracles, but never are they panaceas. Too, they may cause problems of their own, particularly if carelessly prescribed. Still, their benefits far outweigh their dangers and shortcomings.

## Drugs Used in Treating Alcohol and Drug Addictions

### Drug Intervention for Alcoholism

**Antabuse** (disulfiram) is a drug many people have heard about, but few people ever see the effects of it. That's because the drug does absolutely nothing, unless the person who takes the drug also takes a drink of alcohol.

If a person on Antabuse takes one little drink of alcohol, he becomes flushed and hyperventilates. Nausea strikes, accompanied by vomiting, sweat, and thirst. The heart races and the chest aches; it's like a heart attack with low blood pressure. The person becomes dizzy and faints easily. And the headache! Throbbing! The whole episode lasts one-half hour to an hour—the longest, most horrible hour of the person's life.

Should the person really load up on alcohol, causing a severe Antabuse reaction, actual heart problems, convulsions, and possibly death may occur. Persons on an Antabuse regimen do well to avoid even innocent external contact with alcohol; inhaling vapor from products such as aftershave and certain astringents can touch off a reaction. Too, the alcohol in vanilla extract and some cough syrups can start the reaction. Antabuse can make dilantin toxic; epileptics must use it with care.

Antabuse is neither a permanent nor a long-range answer. It is a temporary measure.

**Ativan** (lorazepam), an antianxiety agent, is useful for helping the recovering alcoholic get past the jitters and fears. Persons who have never dealt with alcoholism may not realize that fear looms as an immense ogre in the alcoholic's life. We try to help these people make fear manageable. Ativan, Valium, and other benzodiazepines offer help for acute withdrawal symptoms.

**Librium** (chlordiazepoxide) is occasionally employed.

**Naltrexone** in many people takes away the craving for alcohol. It's a new application.

**Revia** (naltrexone) can reduce cravings temporarily. It is not a magic cure by any means. But for the person whose body chemistry is so messed up that cravings are intense, Revia seems like a miracle. Unfortunately, too few doctors know about it. Revia, of course, is always used as an aid and stopgap in conjunction with other therapies. By itself it is next to useless.

**Thiamine and vitamin supplements** are always a good idea during alcohol treatment. Not only do alcoholics usually fail to eat right, the alcohol affects food metabolism. We provide thiamine by injection at first, then switch to oral dosage. Thiamine seems to prevent or ameliorate the alcoholic encephalopathy and amnesic disorders—Wernicke-Korsakoff syndrome. Persons suffering Wernicke-Korsakoff may benefit from massive daily doses of thiamine. Thiamine won't reverse anything, but it sometimes mitigates the problem.

**Valium** (diazepam) alleviates alcohol withdrawal symptoms. We use it frequently in hospital and clinical situations for that purpose, when the inebriate poses a danger to self or others.

## Drug Intervention for Abuse of Other Substances

How does one handle Melodie's Seconal dependence? In his fledgling practice, her doctor husband, Jerry, had watched too many addicts give up hope. During his internship, he had witnessed two overdoses and one death caused by a barbiturate withdrawal. He would never forget the victim's seizures and convulsions, or the way the kid's skin turned blue as his heart struggled and finally gave out. Sad and frightened, Jerry turned Melodie's care over to his mentor at the teaching hospital.

Melodie was hospitalized and given phenobarbital. This is one of the major methods we use in bringing people safely through withdrawal, and we do it with drugs other than just barbiturates. Phenobarbital is longer-acting than Seconal and is not so toxic. Melodie's doctor kept her a little bit intoxicated with the slower, safer medicine. Then he tapered it carefully, a small increment at a time over a period of some days, easing her out of her dependency.

To drop barbiturates when the patient is a heavy user abruptly invites seizures, the equivalent of delirium tremens, insomnia, sweating, weakness, heart problems, fever, and sometimes psychosis—a complete break with reality.

Opiate addicts—heroin users, for example—may receive methadone for much the same reason. Methadone is a stepping-stone between heroin and abstinence. Although methadone is addicting, it is easier to get off of than heroin, it doesn't cripple the person's ability to hold down a job or otherwise function normally, and one oral dose lasts a full day. Methadone blocks the same neuron receptors that other opiates do, but it doesn't do as much damage, so to speak. When the time comes to detoxify the patient from the methadone, the patient may receive clonidine to ease the withdrawal effects.

Opioid antagonists such as naloxone and naltrexone (Narcan, Talwin) preferentially block the opioid receptors so the opiates can't reach them. The result: the user goes into withdrawal within a minute or so.

Persons in opium withdrawal suffer intense aches, cramps, diarrhea, runny nose and eyes, and goose bumps (these poultry-like bumps are what give us the phrase "going cold turkey").

## The Bottom Line

Psychiatric diseases and psychological problems are not stigmas any more than are chicken pox or a broken leg. They are bathed in ignorance. They are misunderstood. Ignorance and misunderstanding hurt the victims of the illnesses, but they hurt the people who practice them just as much.

The ordinary person with a loved one who has descended into psychosis does not know what to do or how to respond. "Why do I not feel more compassion? Why can't I look past the obvious and love the person trapped within?" The result: shame, guilt, anger, withdrawal—the last things this old world needs more of.

Psychotropic drugs can help the people for whom they were developed. But these drugs help us all by making many mental problems manageable and understandable. They certainly have their dark side, their down side, their foe aspect. But as friends, they contribute to peace within families and neighborhoods.

Peacemakers. Blessed are they.

# APPENDIX:
# Side Effects

No two drugs do exactly the same things; moreover, each person taking a given drug will respond uniquely to that substance. Please remember:

- These side effects are possibilities, not probabilities; many people never experience any of them.
- Just because they've been noted in some people does not mean they'll happen that way in you. You may not experience the most common ones, and yet some rare little effect may result from your drug regimen. It's not predictable.
- Almost always, the side effect is a small price to pay for the benefits accrued. *However:*
- Some can be dangerous. Side effects marked with an asterisk should be attended to immediately.

## Side Effects of Antidepressants

**Nausea.** This usually goes away in a few weeks. Some people quit taking medicine when they get queasy; we recommend you hang in with it. This too shall pass.

**\* Eye problems.** Nothing to mess around with! Usually, it's nothing. Blurred vision produced as a side effect passes. Rarely it might signal a problem such as narrow-angle glaucoma. Glaucoma is excessive pressure within the eyeball, pressure that can damage the receptor nerves. A symptom you can't miss: seeing a ring, a halo, around outside lights such as parking-lot lights or street lamps. Other symptoms include eye discomfort and blurred vision.

**Low blood pressure.** Some antidepressants temporarily lower blood pressure, which sometimes causes dizziness. You can minimize it by standing up slowly or pausing to lean on something solid for a few moments after you stand. The problem should abate as your body becomes accustomed to the new pressure.

**Other cardiac abnormalities.** Cardiac changes don't happen often, but they can happen and you should watch for them. Look for increased heart rate, maybe even a spate of what you'd call a racing pulse. Sometimes the heart rhythm goes a little wacky; nothing serious, just frightening. Your feet may swell, indicating reduced circulation. Notice this item has no asterisk, but talk about it with your doctor anyway.

Very, very rarely does sudden death occur. When it does, it is almost always in people whose hearts are already damaged. Usually, a drug overdose is involved.

**Constipation.** Don't take laxatives during the whole course of treatment. Occasional use of mild laxatives is all right until the next medical appointment, when you can talk to your doctor about a better solution. There are several, such as stool softeners or a change of diet. Sometimes the problem works backward and you have:

**Diarrhea.** This too should be a topic of conversation the next time you see your doctor.

**Dry mouth.** Technically, this is a minor problem, but it can be so incredibly annoying that patients cease medicating. The discomfort can be eased, so hang in with it.

Some patients report a peculiar taste in their mouth, a hard-to-describe metallic sort of taste, or simply altered flavors. Foods don't taste the same.

**Urinary hesitance or retention.** Holding back urine

whether intentional or not. Inability to void comfortably or normally.

**Dry eyes.** The eyes may burn or feel scratchy, even gritty, especially when you're reading or doing close work. The problem is often exacerbated by contact lenses. Try artificial tears, available over the counter, or the moistening agent used with the contact lenses.

**Photophobia.** The vampire effect. Sunlight bothers you, sometimes extremely so, and you sunburn easily even if you never did before.

**Nasal congestion.** This happens especially with people who already suffer bronchial or asthmatic problems.

**Weight loss or gain.** Whichever way you want to go, you may assume your medication will send you off in the other direction. Actually, some varieties of medication tend to help you lose weight, others help you gain it. You may pick and choose somewhat if you are really unhappy with your weight maintenance.

**\* Skin rash or irritation.** Cease medication immediately, even before reading the next sentence.

A rash often indicates a strong and therefore dangerous allergy to something in the medication. This is nothing to fool with. Notify your doctor right away and let him or her take it from there.

**\* Priapism.** If you are a male on trazodone and you experience an unintended, uncomfortable erection, *get help immediately.* You must have medical intervention within four to six hours or the condition can cause permanent, irreversible damage. If your doctor or clinic attendant is uncertain what to do, call this number for Bristol Myers: (800) 321-1335.

Having scared the willies out of you, we rush on to reassure you that priapism rarely ever occurs, and when it does, the drug concerned is almost always trazodone.

**Changes in sexual responses.** Some people also report changes in sexual functions—either more or less interest in sex, delayed or altered orgasm, impotence. A simple alteration of dosage might solve the problem, but let your doctor do it; don't try to adjust dosages yourself.

# Side Effects of Antianxiety Drugs

**Low blood pressure.** Heart rate slows (or, with clonidine, speeds up), you feel dizzy or light-headed.

**Nausea.** If you're on benzodiazepines, you usually won't throw up.

**Dry mouth.** Technically, not a serious condition, but it can be terribly annoying. The mouth feels pasty; not enough saliva. Or sometimes the mouth may react by creating too much saliva.

**Elimination problems.** Constipation, occasional diarrhea, and urine retention may occur.

**Decreased sexual interest.**

**Eye problems.** Blurred or double vision, dry or burning eyes may occur.

**Weakness, occasional tremors, spasms, cramps.**

**Nightmares.**

Other side effects to look for are depression, headaches, insomnia, hallucinations, confusion, and agitation. If the drugs cause a paradoxical effect (it happens very occasionally), you may feel even more anxious.

# Side Effects of Sleeping Aids

Remember that barbiturates are highly addictive.

**Sleep apnea.** Sleeping aids can aggravate this condition. Breathing stops for a few seconds during sleep (and is usually accompanied by snoring). People with known sleep apnea should not take hypnotics.

**Amnesia.** Short-term loss of memory in some cases begins when the medicine (usually Halcion) begins and ends nearly twelve hours later. The sleep lasts only seven or eight hours, which leaves several hours in which the patient cannot remember important information—like why he is on this airplane and where he's supposed to be going. Amnesic effects are spotty and unpredictable and transitory. Our air traveler should be able to take Halcion the next night with no effect.

**Drowsiness.**  Certainly you want to be drowsy; that's why you took a sleeping aid. But not *excessively* drowsy.

Other side effects to look for include dizziness, light-headedness, weakness, lethargy, upset stomach, and perhaps a change in taste bud responses (foods don't taste the same or taste metallic).

## Side Effects of Antipsychotics

**Delirium.**  Loss of awareness and disorientation should not last more than two or three days. Haldol (haloperidol) can help.

**Dementia.**  Refers to a loss of intellectual capacity and abstract thinking—reduced control of language, loss of simple math skills, lousy judgment, but not loss of awareness or consciousness. Once dementia gets a grip it usually stays and medication doesn't affect it.

**Anticholinergic side effects.**  These include dry eyes and mouth, constipation and urinary hesitancy, glaucoma and blurred vision, and runny nose.

**\* Extrapyramidal symptoms.**  EPSs include dystonia, parkinsonism, neuroleptic malignant syndrome, and tardive dyskinesia. All these symptoms require immediate attention; drugs to combat the symptoms are available.

**Sexual problems.**  Problems include difficulties with erection, menstruation, and orgasm.

**Weight gain or loss.**  Most antipsychotics contribute to weight gain; a few, such as Loxitane (loxapine) and Moban (molindone), may encourage weight loss.

**\* Blood problems.**  Agranulocytosis is the loss of certain needed white blood cells called granulocytes. Related bone marrow problems may accompany it. The white blood cell count can drop or spike. It's best to keep a count periodically.

**Parkinsonism.**  Characterized by a suite of symptoms resembling Parkinson's disease: a cogwheel rigidity when you try to move limbs, stiffness, slow or absent movement, shuffling, drooling, trembling, apathy, or anger.

**Rabbit syndrome.** The lips move rapidly, like a rabbit nibbling lettuce.

**Seizures.** Seizures occur in 3.5 to 5 percent of patients—that's one in twenty—so we advise people not to drive, operate heavy machinery, or engage in any activities where spasms or a sudden loss of consciousness would cause a disaster.

**\* Tardive dyskinesia.** Characterized by jerking, twisting, sudden grimaces—in other words, groups of muscles suddenly run amok. The effect can be so slight not even the patient notices, or quite drastic. It's reversible if caught early.

**\* Neuroleptic malignant syndrome.** This can be fatal in 15 to 25 percent of the people it strikes. A violent reaction to neuroleptic drugs, its symptoms include high fever (to 107°F), muscle rigidity or agitation, sweating, increased blood pressure and heart rate, and incontinence.

**Motor restlessness and dystonia.** Agitation, the jitters, insomnia may appear or disappear spontaneously. Dystonias are spasms, which may include difficulty swallowing or tightening tongue muscles that cause a thick or stiff tongue. Barbiturates or just plain reassurance usually bring them under control.

**Bronchial pneumonia.** This has occurred in some patients using Haldol.

**Elimination problems.** May include constipation, urine retention (which may encourage urinary tract and bladder infections), and urinary hesitation.

## Side Effects of Anticholinergic Agents

ACAs can trigger much the same kinds of reactions as the ones just mentioned, namely, dry mouth, confusion, constipation, nausea, rapid heartbeat, some reduced sexual interest, urinary hesitancy, fever, and rashes. Very occasionally they produce tingling or numb extremities, over-stimulation and, in rare instances, psychosis.

# Side Effects of Lithium

If the lithium level rises rapidly in the blood, you can expect stomach upset, lethargy, an increase in bathroom trips, and possibly even some delicate tremors. In the long term, you may experience diarrhea, weight gain and bloating, dizziness, and again, increased urination, thyroid problems, skin conditions such as acne, rashes, or psoriasis, hair loss, and occasionally skin sores.

We often see a strange sort of tremor develop in patients in which primarily the fingers are affected. They tremble and shake or jerk about. The tremors normally subside in a few weeks. Very rarely do seizures develop; when they do, the patient usually is susceptible or subject to them before lithium was commenced.

# Side Effects of Anticonvulsants

## Drugs for Seizures or Aggression

By and large, the side effects produced by lithium can also show up during courses of other anticonvulsants. In addition, look for leukopenia, which is a diminution of white blood cells; appetite shifts (too much, too little); vision problems.

If you feel "weird" or your body acts in ways it had not before, consult your doctor. Anticonvulsants also produce some very rare side effects not listed.

Tegretol (carbamazepine) is used to block aggression as well as convulsions and seizures.

Agranulocytosis is described above under *Blood problems.

# Side Effects of Stimulants

Stimulant side effects include insomnia, nausea, appetite changes, constipation, and possibly dizziness. Weight loss often occurs. Watch also for heart rhythm changes, palpitations, and blood pressure changes. You may be too alert or irritable.

# NOTES

---

**Chapter 1**
1.   Sherrye Henry, "America's Hidden Disease," *Parade,* February 12, 1995, p. 4.

**Chapter 2**
1.   Nora Lopez, "Two Charged in Death of Son's Wife," *Dallas Morning News,* February 11, 1995.

**Chapter 3**
1.   Warren, Paul and Jody Capehart, *You and Your ADD Child* (Nashville, TN: Thomas Nelson, 1995).

**Chapter 8**
1.   See Daniel 4:28–36; and Daniel's prophecy in 4:24–25.

# GLOSSARY

**Agranulocytosis**  A loss or lack of the white blood cells called granulocytes.

**Anhedonia**  (*An* = lack of, *hedon* = pleasure.) A lack of interest or pleasure in life.

**Anticholinergic side effects**  These include dry eyes and mouth, constipation and urinary hesitancy, glaucoma and blurred vision, runny nose (hay fever with a vengeance).

**Arrhythmia, Cardiac Dysrhythmia**  Alterations or hiccups in the heart's normal rhythm of beating. The heart may skip a beat, send one hard on the heels of the one before, or speed up and slow down inexplicably.

**Ataxia**  A lack of coordination or muscle control. Actions aren't as smooth and effective as usual. The ataxic person falls, fails to negotiate steps, can't thread a needle.

**Attention Deficit Disorder and Attention Deficit with Hyperactivity Disorder ADD/ADHD**  An inability to concentrate, to stay with a project to its completion, to pay attention. The mind wanders. A bit over half of ADD people are also hyperactive—unable to sit still, stop wiggling, get to sleep early or sleep late. Slowest gear is third, and it goes up from there.

**Bipolar**  What we used to call manic-depressive. Heady enthusiasm alternates with depression in the course of a year.

**Blood pressure**  When your beating heart squeezes itself together, it squirts blood out into your arteries. The pressure this exerts on your arteries' walls is your blood pressure. We measure it in millimeters of mercury (i.e., the distance the blood would push a column of mercury up a vacuum tube) during the height of the squirt (systolic pressure) and between squirts when pressure is minimal (diastolic). Systolic of 125 is average and is recorded over the diastolic, which averages around 90.

Low blood pressure, **hypotension,** anything around 100 systolic or less, shows as dizziness under certain conditions. Blood pressure in your brain drops slightly whenever you stand up. That is normal and is governed by laws of hydraulics. If your blood pressure happens to be temporarily lower than your body is accustomed to, and you then stand up, the double whammy of drug effect plus standing up—the overkill, so to speak—can make you light-headed or tipsy for a few moments, and perhaps even cause you to faint. You can minimize it by standing up slowly or pausing to lean on something solid for a few moments after you stand.

High blood pressure, **hypertension,** usually gives no hints that it's there. It causes excess wear on the cardiovascular system. If it blows out a weakened vessel in the brain, it's a stroke. If it balloons a weakened vessel, it's an aneurysm.

**Bradycardia**  A slower-than-normal heartbeat (less than 60 or so. In a few people, slow is normal. We're talking averages).

**Cardiac**  Anything having to do with the heart or even peripherally involving the heart.

**Cataplexy**  A condition, often in conjunction with narcolepsy, in which the person loses all muscle control and sort of melts at inappropriate times. Strong emotion or sudden spates of activity can trigger it. The cataplectic laughing uproariously may take a header off the chair she's seated in.

**Central nervous system (CNS)**  This is the brain and spinal column, which are intimately connected. As the body's nerve system goes, when the CNS ain't happy, ain't nobody happy.

**Cirrhosis**  Progressive damage to the liver, almost always caused by excessive use of alcohol.

**Constipation**  Fewer bowel movements than normal—usually, less than one a day. Typically, the feces will be stiffer than expected and perhaps larger.

**Delirium**  Disorientation, a partial loss of awareness or consciousness, sometimes temporary memory loss. "Deliriously happy" is a misnomer if ever there was one.

**Delusion**  A thought or conviction, usually pretty off the wall, that no amount of reason or common sense will shake.

**Dementia**  A condition characterized by diminishing intellect and abstract thinking, crippling judgment and language skills, and increasing impulsivity.

**Depression** Lack of interest in life, indefinite malaise, constant feelings of lethargy. We think its immediate cause is a lack of available neurotransmitters in the brain.

**Diarrhea** Bowel movements several times a day, the stool typically loose or fluid.

**Diplopia** Double vision.

**Dopamine** One of the brain's neurotransmitters, bridging the gap between brain cells to form a thought connection. Many antipsychotic drugs work by manipulating dopamine.

**Dry eyes** Eyes burn or feel scratchy, even gritty, especially when you're reading or doing close work. The problem is often exacerbated by contact lenses. Try artificial tears, available over the counter, or the moistening agent used with the contact lenses.

**Dry mouth** Lack of saliva. Although it is certainly not life-threatening, dry mouth can be terribly annoying as teeth stick to inner lips and the tongue feels pasty.

**Dysthymia** What used to be called a low-grade depression. The blahs occurring repeatedly over several years, or just hanging on. Sadness, lack of pleasure, and insomnia are some of its signs.

**Dystonia** Involuntary movement, usually exhibited as muscle spasms. Uncontrollable spasms in throat muscles may interfere with swallowing.

**Enuresis** Bed-wetting. Release of urine during sleep. The psychotropic imipramine often helps.

**Epilepsy** A disorder characterized by seizures of varying degrees. The disease has many causes and many kinds of seizures.

**Euthymia** Feeling normal. Not up, not down.

**Extrapyramidal symptoms** EPSs include dystonia, parkinsonism, neuroleptic malignant syndrome, and tardive dyskinesia.

**Febrile** Referring to fever.

**GABA—gamma-amino butyric acid** One of the neurotransmitters governing brain activity (dopamine, noradrenaline, norepinephrine, and serotonin are others). We believe GABA calms brain activity. The benzodiazepines, antianxiety drugs, help GABA do that.

**Gastrointestinal** The route food takes; the system starting with the mouth through the esophagus, stomach, intestines, and anus.

**Glaucoma** Increased fluid pressure within the eyeball. Pressure kills nerve cells, and the inner lining of the eye is packed full of nerve cells. Increased pressure can destroy them, causing blindness.

**Hallucination** Experiencing something that isn't actually there. You can hear things, see things, feel things, even smell things that seem real, and yet they don't exist.

**Hepatitis** Liver infection.

**Hypnotic** An agent inducing or promoting sleep.

**Impotence** Inability to maintain erection or complete the sexual act.

**Insomnia** An inability to fall asleep or stay asleep. Awakening too early is also a form of insomnia.

**Kindling** The phenomenon of some nerves torching off others in a rapidly cycling, rapidly growing circle of excitement. Kindling causes seizures by "lighting" many nerves at once.

**Kinesia** Anything having to do with action or movement. Hypokinesia, for example, is less movement than usual.

**Lethargy** Lack of get-up-and-go. Tiredness, lack of interest in doing anything.

**Leucopenia** Low white blood cell count (your blood has both red and white cells; red vastly outnumber the white, but white are critical for fighting infection and other jobs). Some drugs, such as certain antipsychotics, may destroy white blood cells.

**Libido** Sexual interest, sex drive.

**Mania** The person and personality running in overdrive. Hyperactive, hyper-talkative, hyper-enthusiastic. Essentially, nerve cells are firing easier and more often than they should.

**Monoamine oxidase** The suffix *-ase* indicates an enzyme; this one oxidizes, which is adding an oxygen atom or two. It breaks down neurotransmitters; a paucity of neurotransmitters induces depression. Monoamine oxidase inhibitors—MAOIs—keep MAO from doing that, raise the level of available neurotransmitters, and thereby relieve depression.

**Monopolar** Monopolar is one state, usually depression. (Compare to *bipolar*, which is two states, mania and depression.)

**Narcolepsy** An apparently inherited disorder in which the person involuntarily falls asleep (not a seizure) at inappropriate times.

**Narcotic** Medically speaking, a sleep-inducing agent. We usually limit meaning to opium and opium-like drugs, as well as barbiturates and cocaine at times.

**Nasal congestion** Fluid in the nose, requiring constant snuffling and blowing. The irritation can persist consistently or come and go.

**Nausea** Queasy stomach; feeling that you have to vomit. In medical lingo, nausea refers only to the queasy feeling. If vomiting accompanies nausea we refer to that separately.

**Neuroleptic** Another term for antipsychotic.

**Neuroleptic malignant syndrome** A group of symptoms occurring as side effects to certain drugs, especially antipsychotics. They include high fever, muscle rigidity or jitters, sweating, increased blood pressure and heart rate, and incontinence—loss of elimination control. NMS must be caught quickly. It can be fatal in some cases (statistically, about one-fourth of the people it strikes).

**Neurotransmitter** A bit of chemical, usually GABA, dopamine, norepinephrine, or serotonin, that connects synapses. When synapses, the gaps between brain cells, are filled in, the tiny electrical impulse in one brain cell continues to the next, completing or advancing a thought. The neuron (brain cell) tip makes the transmitter, uses it, then blots it up again. Too much neurotransmitter makes for hyperactivity and wild, uncontrolled, rapidly cycling thoughts. Too little creates depression.

**Norepinephrine (noradrenaline)** One of the brain's neurotransmitters that connects brain cells to form pathways for thoughts and actions.

**Obsessive-compulsive disorder (OCD)** Rapidly cycling nerve impulses cause the person to perform ritual, cyclic, usually nonsensical behaviors. Obsession is intrusive, repetitive thought. Compulsion is intrusive, repetitive action.

**Palpitations** Thumping heartbeat that you can feel in your chest. It may be fast or slow.

**Panic attack, panic disorder** An intense surge of fear disproportionate to events or surroundings. Characterized by racing heartbeat, sweating, light-headed feeling. Antianxiety agents and some antidepressants can control panic disorders.

**Paranoia, paranoid delusion, paranoid schizophrenia** The conviction that someone or something is after you. The conviction has no basis in reality.

**Parkinsonism (pseudo-Parkinson's)** A side effect of antipsychotics and a few other drugs. The syndrome resembles Parkinson's disease. Characterized by a cogwheel rigidity when you try to move limbs, stiffness, slow or absent movement, shuffling, drooling, trembling, apathy, or anger.

**Perfusion** The exchange of gases, wastes, and other products between cells and the blood. Also the circulation of fluids in an organ. Our major concern is brain perfusion. Brain cells need a constant, rich supply of oxygen. If your breathing and pulse are too weak, oxygen cannot perfuse adequately and brain cells suffer or die.

**Phobia** Intense, exaggerated, uncontrollable fear, usually of something that does not pose a realistic threat, and that most other people do not fear as much as you do.

**Photophobia** Literally, fear of light. More specifically, a feeling that you want to get away from light. It hurts your eyes and may even irritate exposed skin.

**Priapism** Involuntary erection that lasts longer than customary. A male on trazodone experiencing priapism should call a doctor or 1-800-321-1335 (Bristol Myers) *immediately*. Priapism, which also can be caused by some other problems, such as a broken back, can create permanent damage. It must be treated quickly.

**Psychosis** A break with reality. An imagined world is mistaken for the actual one.

**Rabbit syndrome** This extrapyramidal side effect is characterized by the lips moving rapidly (like a rabbit nibbling lettuce).

**Rapid eye movement (REM)** A stage of sleep in which the closed eyes dart back and forth. In normal sleep, this stage alternates with others.

**Renal** Anything having to do with the kidneys.

**Seizures** Sudden changes in consciousness and muscle tone. They occur for a variety of reasons. They may be slight with only a pause or cessation of mental awareness. They may be pronounced to the point that all muscles spasm simultaneously and the patient slams about uncontrollably. They are caused when a number of nerve cells fire simultaneously. Drug use can cause seizures and prevent seizures. Withdrawal from drugs may trigger seizures, particularly in susceptible people.

**Serotonin** One of the brain's neurotransmitters, connecting cell tips to provide pathways for thoughts. In depressed people, the serotonin is blotted back into the cells too quickly, forming a lack where it is needed. SSRIs, Specific Serotonin Reuptake Inhibitors, keep the cells from blotting it back up, making more serotonin available for use.

**Side effects** The effects drugs create that are separate and different (and usually unwanted) from what they're designed to do.

**Somnolence** Sleepiness.

**Spasm** Muscular contraction. In general terms, involuntary or overdone muscle movement. Often violent and jerky, sometimes so slight they are unnoticeable.

**Specific serotonin reuptake inhibitor (SSRI)** An antidepressant such as Prozac that prevents nerve cells from taking up serotonin, a neurotransmitter, once they've made it.

**Synapse** A tiny space between brain cell tips. The space prevents thoughts from forming by blocking electric impulses that nerves use. Neurotransmitters momentarily form a switch or bridge across the synapse, allowing the impulse to cross and making a pathway for thought or action.

**Syncope** Fainting.

**Tachycardia** Rapid heartbeat, usually faster than 120 beats per minute. Tachycardia is expected in marathon runners and high schoolers in the closing moments of a crucial sporting event; in patients, it's a warning sign.

**Tardive dyskinesia** Involuntary spasms of whole groups of muscles. The victim cannot control twitches, grimaces, jerking movements. Effects may be slight or pronounced. Deal with it quickly, while it is reversible.

**Trigeminal** A nerve from the brain to the face. It's a source of excruciating pain called trigeminal neuralgia.

**Urinary hesitance** Difficulty urinating; unable to maintain a strong stream of urine.

**Urinary retention** Holding back urine whether intentional or not. Inability to void comfortably or normally.

# INDEX

Imipramine, 30-31, 33, 145
imipramine HCl. *See* tofranil
Imitrex, 212
Inderal, 189, 212, 229, 238
insomnia, 134-36, 145, 147
    chronic, 135
    short-term, 134-35, 145
    transient, 134
Isoptin, 202
isocarboxazid. *See* Marplan

## J

janimine, 33

## K

Kemadrin, 238
ketoprofen. *See* Oruvail
ketorolac tromethmine. *See* Toradol
Klonopin, 78, 105, 124, 149-50, 228

## L

Laradopa, 189
laudanum, 214
levodopa, 188-89
Libritabs, 78
Librium, 75, 77, 78, 226, 268
limbitrol, 33
Lithane, 123
Lithium, 117-24, 186
lithium carbonate, 122, 124, 212. *See also*
    Eskalith; Lithane; Lithobid
Lithobid, 124
Lithonate, 124
Lithotabs, 124
lorazepam, 147. *See also* Ativan
Lorcet, 216
Lortab, 209
low-grade depression. *See* dysthymic dis-
    order
loxapine succinate. *See* Loxitane
Loxitane, 172
Ludiomil, 33, 79
Luminal, 150
Luvox, 32, 93, 105

## M

magical thinking, 95-96, 160-61
magnetic resonance imaging (MRI), 93
major depression, 20-21. *See also* depres-
    sion
malaise, 199
mania, 106-24, 139
    signs and symptoms of, 112-15
    treatment of, 117-24
manic-depression, 22, 111, 115-24. *See
    also* bipolar disorders
Maprin, 209
maprotiline HCl. *See* Ludiomil
marijuana, 253
Marplan, 105
Mebaral, 150
meclofenamate Na. *See* Meclomen
Meclomen, 210
Medipren, 210
Mellaril, 171
Mepergan, 151
meperidine HCl. *See* Demerol; Mepergan
mephobarbital. *See* Mebaral
mesoridazine besylate. *See* Serentil
methadone, 269-70
methadone HCl. *See* Dolophene
methamphetamines, 52
methylphenidate HCl. *See* Ritalin
methysergide. *See* Sansert
midazolam HCl. *See* Versed
Midol, 210
Midrin, 212
migraine headache, 199-201
Minimal Brain Dysfunction, 53
Minirth, Frank, (*Sweet Dreams*), 143
Moban, 169, 171
molindone HCl. *See* Moban
Monoamine Oxidase Inhibitors (MAOI),
    25, 31, 33, 34, 79, 105, 120, 147, 189,
    200, 212
mood swings, 106-24
morphine, 204, 214, 216
Motrin, 210
multi-infarct dementia, 182-83
multiple personality disorder, 161
multiple sclerosis, 167

# About the Authors

**Frank Minirth, M.D,** is cofounder of the Minirth Meier New Life Clinics, one of the largest mental health care providers in the United States, with headquarters in Dallas, Texas, and more than seventy branch clinics in cities across the nation.

A diplomate of the American Board of Psychiatry and Neurology, Dr. Minirth received his M.D. from the University of Arkansas College of Medicine. He also holds a graduate degree from Dallas Theological Seminary. He is the author or coauthor of more than thirty books, including *The Headache Book, Love Is a Choice, You Can!, The Father Book, The Power of Memories,* and *The Anger Workbook.*

**Paul Meier, M.D.,** is cofounder of the Minirth Meier New Life Clinics. He received his M.S. in cardiovascular physiology from Michigan State University and his M.D. from the University of Arkansas College of Medicine. He completed his psychiatric residency at Duke University. He also holds an M.A. degree from Dallas Theological Seminary.

Dr. Meier is the author or coauthor of more than forty books, including *Windows of the Soul, Don't Let Jerks Get the Best of You, The Third Millennium,* and *Love Hunger.*

**Stephen Arterburn, M.Ed.,** is cofounder of the Minirth Meier New Life Clinics and cohost of the clinic's national radio program with a listening audience of over one million.

Arterburn holds degrees from Baylor University and the University of North Texas. In 1993 he was named Socially Responsible Entrepreneur of the Year by *Inc. Magazine,* Ernst and Young, and Merrill Lynch.

Arterburn is the author of seventeen books, including *Winning at Work Without Losing at Love, Gentle Eating, The Angry Man, Addicted to "Love,"* and *Faith That Hurts, Faith That Heals.*